THE MODERN CHURCH

THE MODERN CHURCH

*From the Dawn of the Reformation
to the
Eve of the Third Millennium*

GLENN T. MILLER

ABINGDON PRESS
Nashville

THE MODERN CHURCH:
FROM THE DAWN OF THE REFORMATION TO THE EVE OF THE
THIRD MILLENNIUM

Copyright © 1997 by Abingdon Press

All Rights Reserved.

Library of Congress Cataloging-in-Publication Data

Miller, Glenn T., 1942–.
    The modern church: from the dawn of the reformation to the eve of the third millennium / Glenn T. Miller
        p. cm.
    Includes bibliographical references and index.
    ISBN 0-687-00605-8 (alk. paper)
    1. Church History—Modern period, 1500– I. Title.
BR290.M55   1997
270—dc21   97-7866
                                                                      CIP

This book is printed on acid-free, recycled, elemental-chlorine–free paper.

97 98 99 00 01 02 03 04 05 06 — 10 9 8 7 6 5 4 3 2 1

MANUFACTURED IN THE UNITED STATES OF AMERICA

For My Parents:
Elmer and Gwen Miller

ACKNOWLEDGMENTS

With Thanks

No book is ever the product of one person, and many people should be thanked for this volume. The Library at Southeastern Baptist Theological Seminary provided invaluable service as did the Library at Duke University. The Bangor Theological Seminary Library has been both helpful and very patient with me and my constant demands for this or that book. Both Cliff Davis and Paul Schroeder have gone far beyond the call of duty. I also want to thank the Board of Trustees of both Southeastern Theological Seminary and Bangor Theological Seminary for their generous support of this work. To Southeastern for the half-sabbatical during which much of the writing was done and to Bangor for granting me the summer of 1995, free from administrative duties, thank-you. I appreciate all of the colleagues and fellow staff people who picked up extra work in the classroom and in the office so that I could write. To all others who have helped, a special thanks for all that you have done, especially, to Frankie, my wife, who has put up with the creative process and its by-products. A special word of thanks to Robert T. Handy, teacher and friend, who read several early versions of the text.

Glenn T. Miller

CONTENTS

Contents

CHAPTER ONE

RENEWAL AND REFORMATION

In 1492 Christopher Columbus (1451–1506) stepped ashore in the Americas. An adventurer testing an ancient hypothesis about the circumference of the earth, Columbus believed the world was significantly smaller than most geographers had calculated. In this he was magnificently wrong. The distance around the earth was almost twice what Columbus had anticipated, and the Americas separated the western ocean into the Atlantic and the Pacific.

Columbus's voyages were part of Europe's recovery from the Great Plague that struck the continent from 1350 onwards. Approximately one-third of the population died. Whenever the numbers inched up, new onslaughts would reduce them again. By 1450, the plague had begun to recede, with the last major outbreaks coming in the 1700s.

While the plague persisted it influenced the military struggle between East and West. After 1350, the Ottoman Turks relentlessly advanced into a weakened Europe. In 1453 they conquered Constantinople, transforming the great church of Saint Sophia into a mosque, and entered the Balkans. The Turks reached Vienna in 1529, only to be forced back. As a result Western explorers found it safer to brave the Cape of Good Hope, than to trade in Constantinople or Cairo.

Faith in the Shadow of the Plague

The fall of Constantinople and the Balkans transformed Eastern Orthodoxy, shifting its center of gravity to Moscow. Later, the Turkish threat to Vienna made the military conquest of the Lutheran princes by Roman Catholic forces all but impossible. The Holy Roman Emperor Charles V (1500–1558) had to commit too many of his resources against the infidels to have enough left to crusade against heresy.

Subtle changes also occurred in the life of the Western church. The captivity of the papacy by France in 1309 led to a disastrous papal schism in 1378 that continued until the Council of Constance reunited the Western church under a single head, Martin V, in 1417. Unfortunately, the new popes were no better than the old. Extravagance, decadence, political machinations, and sexual immorality marked the fifteenth-century papal court. When the Reformation threatened the church, Rome had no leader equal to the challenge.

Petty ecclesiastical abuses abounded, often rooted in the church's need for money. Clerical concubinage was common with the priest paying a yearly fine for his mistress. Since the church bureaucracy drained off many educated priests, rural and small parishes often had a nonresident rector who hired a vicar to say mass and hear confessions. Many vicars, badly paid and even more badly educated, were little more than mumblers whose ministrations skirted paganism. The economic gap between the wealthy higher clergy and the ordinary priest widened.

By 1500 healing shrines made important contributions to the church's purse. Usually staffed by effective preachers, the shrines collected funds through donations, endowed masses, and hospitality (rooms and meals). As in many ancient temples, priests displayed the relics of past cures, including crutches, on the walls as earnest for future miracles.

The continued popularity of pilgrimages and relics appear to have been more prominent than in earlier times. Almost everywhere relics of the Savior, the Apostles, and the Saints were displayed. Those who viewed them were promised blessings in this world and the next. Skilled traders sold models of popular statues as talismens.

Some abuses arose simply from outdated practices. The various begging or mendicant orders originated when popular opinion equated poverty and sanctity. The friars were to renounce all earthly possessions and wander the earth as preachers and evangelists. Small and not-so-small adjustments eroded the mendicant life-style, and the mendicants became prosperous monks whose principal task was university teaching. Missionary service in the Americas, however, encouraged some Franciscans and Dominicans to recover some of their older traditions.

Throughout the fifteenth century, successive German Diets issued lists of these abuses. Elsewhere in Europe, the Kings of the strongest monarchies—England, France, and Spain—brought the churches in their kingdoms under government control. However, since ecclesiastical corruption was just below the level where popular opinion would demand legal action, abuses continued for some time.

In the shadow of the plague, the church became obsessed with heresy, and the list of heretics expanded to include Jews, Spanish Muslims, witches, and other foes. Often dissent was demonized, and theological experts asserted that Satan inspired all heresies. Inquisitors claimed that witches made a pact with the devil in which they exchanged their souls for earthly benefits.

The inquisition's power grew, especially in such areas as Spain. Significantly, the inquisition's more memorable punishment, the *auto de fé*, involved the burning alive of the victim, an earthly preview of the hell that awaited the unrepentant.

The world was seen as a place of struggle between God and Satan, and the distinction between hellish intervention and ordinary mishap was not always made. The strange figure of the Antichrist, who was both natural and supernatural, dominated much popular thinking. Was this terrible ruler the Sultan or even someone closer to home, perhaps the emperor or an evil pope?

Individual believers were caught between fear that salvation might be lost and the church's repeated promises of deliverance. The church warned sinners constantly of the danger of damnation and hung an apocalyptic cloud over daily life. One might die suddenly, without warning, and without the sacraments. Simultaneously the church multiplied the means of grace, making indulgences and other forms of assurance easier to obtain. For a fee, the fearful might be buried in a monastic habit to help avoid punishment. Of course, church leaders urged the rich to endow churches, masses, universities, or other good works for the salvation of their souls.

The scholastic theology of William of Ockham (c. 1285–1347) and his successors such as Gabriel Biel (1420–95) supported this oscillation between comfort and terror. Ockham's message was that Christians should do their best and trust God to remedy any deficiency. Yet God was not bound to save anyone, and only Ockham's God knew the names of the elect. Ockham's theology—known as nominalism—also pointed to other, more fruitful, avenues. With its emphasis on experience, nominalism was an important antecedent for the development of modern science. Further, the nominalists stressed the careful study of texts, particularly the Scriptures and the writings of early church bishops, as part of theology.

Signs of Recovery

The Swiss historian Jacob Burckhardt popularized the term "renaissance" or rebirth to describe European culture in the fifteenth and sixteenth centuries. Partly because many teachers fled west after the fall of Constantinople, Greek became part of the intellectual equipment of European scholars. The more adventuresome also learned Hebrew. Throughout Europe writers created a new Latin prose. The medieval scholastic style gave way to an exuberant rhetoric, rooted in Caesar, Cicero, and Cato the Censor. Simultaneously, vernacular literature mushroomed with popular and sophisticated books appearing in English, French, German, Italian, and Spanish. The visual arts also prospered with Michelangelo and da Vinci, among others, producing masterpieces. Even music, the most ephemeral of the arts, flourished as musical notation became more sophisticated, and written music was increasingly circulated.

The cultural contrast between the Medici's Florence or Sixtus VI's Rome and an intellectually limited medieval monastery appears to be one between light and dark. Yet the Renaissance was no miracle. Despite the barbarian invasions and the demise of Roman rule in western Europe, Europeans had retained most of the technical expertise of antiquity, including the ability to build in concrete. The workshops of the middle ages developed this technical base, and Europeans also imitated and modified other people's technology. For example, the flat Chinese waterwheel was turned on its side to power large mills, and Chinese fireworks were transformed into rifles and cannons.

Printing was perhaps the most ingenious European transposition. The Chinese made block prints on hand-manufactured paper as a decorative art. In contrast, the Europeans took the three components of printing—ink, paper, and press—and put them to practical use. New forms of ink were developed that did not fade, and ways were devised to manufacture large quantities of paper. Instead of highly stylized letters, Europeans put a single character on each block so that the blocks could be used repeatedly and cast their type in metal. In 1450 Johann Gutenberg printed the *Constance Mass Book*, and almost overnight print replaced the handwritten manuscript.

The publishing industry grew rapidly. By 1510 every major city and most small towns had their own presses. University teachers printed texts for students in order to reduce the time spent taking notes. Humanists used the press to produce critical editions of classics, comparing several manuscripts and printing the preferred readings with variations noted in the margins. Governments used the press to standardize various laws and regulations. Authors found the new form of publication a useful way to transmit ideas.

The new industry was voracious. Once craftspeople had invested in the needed press and type, they had to keep busy to avoid bankruptcy. Many printed whatever was available. Between commissions, printers might produce an edition of a Latin or Greek classic or reprint a popular work. Printers also benefited from academic or religious controversy.

Further, printing subtly changed the meaning of texts. Scholars scattered over great distances could now examine the same text and share comments and references. Printing enabled texts to circulate rapidly as an item in trade. Many of Luther's Latin works, for example, were available in England within months of their publication in Germany.

Although some founders of the humanist movement such as Francisco Petrarch (1304–74) antedated printing, the new technology greatly aided and expanded the humanities. At its heart, humanism was both a current literary ideal and a critical approach to the past. Consequently, humanism encouraged textual and historical study. Lorenzo Valla (1406–57) proved that the Donation of Constantine—a document which purported to record the Emperor Constantine's "donation" of authority over western Europe to Pope Sylvester I—was a forgery and that the Apostle's Creed could not have been composed in the first century.

At the same time, humanism was often profoundly religious. Desiderius Erasmus (1469?–1536) produced a critical edition of the Greek New Testament with a new Latin translation of the text. As a religious reformer, Erasmus was offended by hypocrisy and poor morals and believed that the authorities should eliminate current ecclesiastical abuses. Erasmus had no taste for the theological and metaphysical riddles of scholasticism or, later, of Lutheranism. In his 1504 *Enchiridion Militis Christiani*, Erasmus argued that the church should adopt the imitation of Christ as its theological and ethical model.

Was humanism a secular or secularizing movement? Skepticism did not affect many people in the sixteenth century. But humanism did shift its adherents' perspective. Classical Christianity was theocentric; humanism, anthropocentric. The humanists measured all things, including God, with a human reed.

Martin Luther: Reluctant Reformer

Martin Luther (1483–1546) was born in Eisleben to Hans and Margarethe Luther. The family was middle class, and Hans moved to Mansfeld shortly after Luther's birth to improve his economic condition. Like many children of newly prosperous parents, Luther received a thorough education. In 1501, he entered the University of Erfurt Faculty of Arts; four years later, he enrolled in the Faculty of Law.

A strong religious experience altered Luther's course. Returning from a friend's funeral, a sudden storm caught him off-guard. In the midst of wind, rain, and lightening, Luther promised St. Anne, Mary's mother and the patron of miners, that if God spared his life he would become a monk. Although this vow was not binding under medieval canon law, Luther fulfilled his word, entering the Erfurt chapter of the Augustinian Hermits, a mendicant order. Like the Franciscans and the Dominicans, the Augustinians had by this time exchanged their begging ministry for university teaching.

Luther had chosen his monastery well, perhaps evidence that he had considered the decision earlier. Once admitted, Luther followed his order's dictates carefully and initially received some of the peace monasticism promised. After his first year, however, he experienced deep spiritual anxieties, *Anfectungen*. Luther followed the entire monastic regiment, yet whatever he did—whether it be fasting, frequent confession, or flagellation—he received no satisfaction. At his first mass in 1507, he was unable without help to say the words of consecration to transform the bread and wine into the body and blood of Christ. His embarrassment increased when his father questioned his vocation at the celebratory meal.

Although Luther's superiors worried about his inner state, they insisted that he continue his education. In relatively short order, Luther passed through the theological degrees and received his doctorate from the new University of Wittenberg in 1512. Appointed to succeed his counselor and friend, Johann Staupitz, as Wittenberg's Professor of Bible, Luther began a career of lecturing and, as was now expected, preparing materials for the press.

Luther was an excellent Bible teacher. Although he retained some medieval exegetical traditions, he used many newer humanistic methods, especially grammatical and word studies from the original languages. Luther's early university lectures have survived, and historians have used them to trace his theological development. At some point during his lectures on the Psalms, Luther made his "evangelical discovery;" that is, he realized that God was the primary actor in salvation and that all human beings had to do was accept God's promised deliverance. Although the doctrine is often referred to as justification by faith, the heart of the new theology was *grace*. At Christ's cross, God redeemed humankind once and for all.

The medieval university tested truth-claims through disputations, lectures, and discussions. Luther used these methods to spread his interpretation, and he convinced many of his Wittenberg colleagues of the truth of his approach. He also began to prepare serious studies for the press, such as an edition of the *German Theology*.

At this point, however, events changed Luther's career. Archbishop (and later Cardinal) Albrecht of Brandenberg asked Pope Leo X to grant him a dispensation which would allow Albrecht to hold several bishoprics simultaneously, a violation of canon law. Albrecht's need and the pope's greed met, and after long negotiations, the archbishop and the pope agreed on the desired favor's price. But one problem remained: Albrecht did not have the money. After further diplomacy, Albrecht allowed an indulgence to be preached in his territories, part of the money from which would be used to fund the construction of St. Peter's in Rome. Since Albrecht would receive half of the funds generated by the indulgence, the Fuggers, a noted banking firm, advanced him the money to pay the pope.

Dating back to the Crusades, indulgences were technically releases from the temporal punishments that the church imposed in penance. Since the time that an individual owed in purgatory was proportional to the suffering he or she was due as a result of sin in this life (temporal satisfaction), the church extended indulgences to that realm as well. The scholastics maintained that the church possessed a "treasury of merits," the surplus merits of Christ and the saints. In effect, indulgence were withdrawals from this heavenly account. The church attached indulgences to viewing certain relics, praying in certain places, and performing selected good works, especially financial contributions.

The ancient church required those who committed mortal sins to pass through a humiliating public penance before the church readmitted them to the Eucharist. Some remnants of this ancient rigor remained, particularly in the practice of requiring unmarried mothers to stand in a white sheet with a candle before the congregation. But for most people, private confession and absolution had replaced public humiliation. Although the priest was not to grant absolution without imposing satisfaction or punishment, the sentences tended to be routine acts of piety, such as several prayers, a visit to a shrine, or the like. These acts

21

were similar to those for which the church granted indulgences. For example one might visit religious relics, either because a priest had imposed the visit *as a form of penance*, or in order to acquire an indulgence *as a replacement for penances*.

The selling of indulgences was not theological business. A preacher, often a member of a mendicant order, would come to town and erect a cross in the marketplace. He would then preach on sin and repentance. At its best, such preaching might encourage real soul searching. The climax came, however, when the preacher offered the indulgences. Technically, indulgences were not sold and no specific contribution was assessed. What the church freely received, the church freely gave. But the indulgence preacher did list recommended contributions, often on broadsides displayed before the congregation. In keeping with the intense medieval class consciousness, indulgence preachers encouraged people to give in proportion to their rank.

The pope's and Albrecht's indulgence was less rigorous than most, and the instructions were hastily and carelessly drawn. Whatever the two might have intended, their words implied that the indulgence granted salvation. Further, to secure the maximum revenue, Albrecht engaged the Dominican Johann Tetzel to preach the indulgence. Tetzel was an experienced indulgence seller, a skilled orator, and a master of persuasion. His sermons found the soft spots in his audience's hearts when he stressed children's duties toward their deceased parents and the need to secure the salvation of dead children. Why should one's parent or child suffer in purgatory when a contribution to the church would liberate them? Tetzel's little ditty, "when the coin in the coffer rings, another soul from purgatory springs," reinforced the message for those who had not followed his discourses.

This particular indulgence offended many, and Frederick of Saxony, Luther's prince, prohibited its proclamation in his territory. Luther's temper arose when some in his congregation nonetheless purchased indulgences and presented them in the confessional, claiming that they could be substituted for the penance Luther required of them. Luther put his objections to indulgences into Ninety-Five Theses designed to spark academic debate, and, according to tradition, posted them on the door of the Castle Church on October 31, 1517. Copies were sent to Archbishop Albrecht and Bishop Jerome of Brandenberg. Whether Luther also provided copies to the printers is not known, but within a fortnight, they had been translated, printed, and distributed widely.

As intended, the Theses provoked controversy and debate. In one sense, the academic exchange worked as intended. Luther's opponents forced him to admit that his questions had radical implications for church authority. Johann Eck, a leading theologian, even forced Luther to admit similarities between his position and that of John Hus, a heretic condemned and executed by the Council of Constance. Unfortunately, the debate was not only academic. In 1518 the pope asked his censor, Sylvester Prierias, to examine Luther's writings. Prierias hastily concluded that Luther was a heretic and cited him to Rome.

The papal action raised legal questions, including the question of where Luther would be tried. A long-standing grievance of the German princes was that the church denied their subjects the benefit of a trial in their homeland. Another issue was whether the church had defined indulgences formally. Luther used both to gain time. His prince, Frederick, refused to have Luther tried outside Germany. When Cardinal Cajetan ordered Luther to recant at Augsburg in 1518, Luther and his prince maintained that the process was not in accord with German law.

Political events provided Luther some protection. Emperor Maximilian died in 1519, and Frederick, as an elector (those nobles who elected the new emperor), was in a politically advantageous position, since both the supporters of Charles of Spain and Francis of France needed his vote. Once the election was decided, events moved rapidly. In 1520 the pope issued the document *Exsurge domine* legally declaring Luther a heretic and outlaw. But the new emperor still owed Frederick for his support, and Frederick managed to secure Luther a place on the agenda of the Diet of Worms in 1521.

In 1520 Luther clarified his position. The reformer published a series of brilliant pamphlets—*On Good Works*; *The Babylonian Captivity of the Church*; *An Appeal to the Christian Nobility of the German Nation*; and *The Freedom of a Christian*—all of which forthrightly proclaimed his theological convictions. Luther stated three positions clearly. First, he maintained that salvation came only by faith through grace. This meant that the whole system of penances, days of obligation, and obligatory pious practices was unnecessary. While Luther believed that many practices were "things indifferent," none could be commanded. Second, Luther set aside the rigid medieval distinction between laity and clergy. All believers are priests, including the princes. Those in authority could and should move to correct abuses without waiting for a general council. Further, Christian authority was located in Scripture, a book available to anyone who could read. Third, Luther reduced the number of sacraments from seven to two and located the effectiveness of the sacraments in the faith of those who believed the biblical words of institution.

Luther's appearance before the Diet of Worms in 1521 was brief. The Emperor refused any discussion of the merits of Luther's case and asked him to acknowledge and recant his books. After a night of agonizing reflection, Luther refused. The emperor honored his safe conduct, and Luther left town. Once outside the limits, an armed band seized the professor and carried him to the Wartburg, a castle owned by Frederick, where he lived in disguise. Meanwhile, the Emperor declared him an outlaw, meaning that anyone could take his life with impunity. Tortured in mind and spirit, Luther translated the New Testament into German and waited.

Although Luther's theology was the backbone of the Reformation, he did not reform the church. The princes carried out the actual reformation by adopting new liturgies, new church orders, and new regulations for the ministry. In Luther's own Saxony, the process was slow. While Luther was at the Wartburg, his colleague Andreas Karlstadt led the city council to mandate some radical changes that included a German service, the end of vestments, communion in two kinds, and iconoclasm. Luther was so appalled by the disorder that he returned from exile in 1522 and preached a series of sermons on the subject of waiting for the weaker neighbor, and encouraged the authorities to roll back the reforms. Although Wittenberg adopted an edited mass without any reference to sacrifice, the city retained the traditional Latin for several years.

At Luther's insistence, Saxony appointed ecclesiastical visitors in 1526 who would travel throughout the region, taking stock of the spiritual state of its people. When the visitors reported wide-spread religious ignorance, Luther responded by composing two catechisms in 1529, one for clergy and one for children, that summarized the new faith. The catechisms, the new hymns (most of which were chorales), and the German Bible were the spiritual foundations of the new church.

Luther was not a systematic theologian. While his writings inspired the Reformation in Germany, his thought was too disconnected to present it effectively. His colleague and friend, Philip Melanchthon (1497–1560), Professor of Greek at Wittenberg, made the new theology clear and concise. His *Loci Communes* or *Commonplaces* (first edition, 1521) gathered Luther's insights under the traditional scholastic headings.

Melanchthon also wrote the Augsburg Confession, arguably the single most important Lutheran doctrinal standard. Since Luther was still an outlaw and prohibited from attending the 1530 Diet of Augsburg,

Melanchthon represented the Protestant cause there. When the Lutheran princes were asked to present the Emperor a confession of faith, they asked Melanchthon to compose that document. The Confession, irenic in tone and carefully stated, gave Lutheranism much of its later theological shape. In addition, Melanchthon, often called the "Teacher of Germany," reformed the curriculum of many universities. Primary and secondary education also received his attention, and Melanchthon composed textbooks that remained in use throughout his century and, in some areas, well beyond it.

Once one accepted Luther's doctrine of salvation by faith through grace, monasticism lost its legitimacy. What could monastic vows add to the all-sufficient work of Christ on the cross? The reformers extended the same argument to the secular clergy's vow of celibacy. But these longstanding institutions were not only the victims of a syllogism. Luther rejected the medieval interpretation of marriage as principally a means of begetting children and satisfying lust. Marriage was part of God's work of creation, a good gift from a good God, that humans should receive thankfully. Luther's own marriage to Catherine von Bora in 1525 was a potent example. Despite the usual ups and downs of married life, Luther's home was happy and prosperous.

The Politics of Reformation

Wherever Lutheranism triumphed, a city council or (more often) a prince, acting as the *summus episcopus* (highest bishop) passed concrete legislation to establish the new faith. The actual shape that Lutheran reform took in any particular area followed from these laws. Since married ministers cost more than celibate priests, many of the new laws were financial. In most Lutheran lands the governments offset the increased expense through the secularization of church property, particularly that of the monasteries. To replace bishops most Lutheran rulers appointed superintendents and consistories to discipline the clergy.

The Peasants' Revolt of 1524–25 severely tested the Reformation's link between church and state. Although Luther had carefully avoided any interference with the political order, some of those whom he inspired did not distinguish between ecclesiastical and political reform. For instance, Thomas Müntzer (c. 1490–1525) followed Luther's advice to search the Scriptures, but instead of St. Paul, he turned to Daniel and Revelation. These texts seemed to promise that Christ would establish an earthly kingdom in which God would make the rich poor and the poor rich.

In 1524 the South German peasants revolted and demanded concrete economic and religious reforms. Such revolts had occurred periodically before. In times of prosperity the peasants won new privileges and set aside obligations. In more depressed times the nobility imposed new financial and personal burdens. On this occasion the peasants presented their demands in Twelve Articles which sparkled with religious and scriptural references.

At first Luther gave the peasants moral support. In his *Admonition to Peace* (1524) Luther conceded that many of their requests were well founded. Yet even in this treatise Luther was uneasy. He believed that the peasants had confused God's reign with earthly government. While Luther knew that a good prince was a rare bird, he believed that Christians owed rulers obedience and respect. As the revolt continued, Luther worried that the princes had not done enough to preserve order. To encourage them, the reformer issued his *Against the Thieving and Murdering Horde of Peasants* (1525), which demanded that the rulers put the rebels down with sword and fire. The rulers did so, massacring the peasants at Frankenhausen after the rebels refused to hand over Thomas Müntzer—who was nonetheless captured and executed.

Both friends and enemies criticized Luther's writings on the peasants, and the criticisms stung Luther. The reformer had overstepped his bounds, and Luther almost apologized for these writings in later years. Yet Luther's writings against the peasants reflected Luther's dark side. Luther was a polemicist who rarely missed a chance to goad his enemies or to attack their character. Regrettably, after attempting to convert the Jews, Luther turned his considerable literary talent against them in a similar vein. In addition to repeating many traditional stereotypes, Luther urged the burning of the Talmud and the expulsion of the Jews from Germany.

The survival of Lutheranism depended upon the ability of the Lutheran princes to defend themselves and their position in the empire. Much depended on the military situation. Thus in 1526 the Diet of Speyer did not act against the Protestants, because the Turkish advance into Hungary mandated military unity. In contrast, when the Catholics were stronger in 1529, the Diet passed laws permitting Catholic worship everywhere. The Lutheran protest of this action, the *Protestatio*, led to their nickname of Protestants. Yet another change in the international situation led the emperor to be more conciliatory at the 1530 Diet of Augsburg.

In the 1540s, Charles V, temporarily freed from the dangers of the Turks and the Mediterranean pirates, consolidated his power in Germany. The Protestant Schmalkaldic League had suffered a blow when its leading prince, Philip of Hesse, was caught in bigamy. In 1541, Charles required Philip to end his negotiations with all foreign powers, including France, in exchange for his life. Five years later, Charles invaded and defeated the Protestant forces. The resulting Augsburg Interim of 1548 allowed the Protestants to teach justification by faith but restored most Catholic practices.

Ironically, Maurice of Saxony, whose earlier defection from the Protestant cause had helped defeat his coreligionists, changed sides again. Allying the Protestants with Henry II of France, Maurice marched south and defeated the emperor. The 1552 Treaty of Passau ended the military struggle, and the 1555 Peace of Augsburg granted each ruler the right to determine the faith of his own realm (a principle known as *cuius regio, eius religio*).

Although the Peace of Augsburg established a principle that permitted Protestant and Catholic coexistence, it did not end military conflict between representatives of the two Christian confessions. Religious warfare continued sporadically until 1648, when the Peace of Westphalia marked a more lasting religious peace. As many as one third of Germany's people may have died in these conflicts, and Germany, one of the centers of medieval civilization, was the last of the Western European states to achieve political unity.

CHAPTER TWO

THE SWISS REFORMATIONS

Zwingli

Ulrich Zwingli (1484–1531) was the first noted Swiss reformer. Unlike Luther, who was trained in the theological faculty, Zwingli devoted his university studies to the classics. After graduating from the University of Basel, Zwingli entered the priesthood and became a skilled careerist. He began his ministry in Glarus, served there for ten years, and then moved to the pilgrimage center of Einsiedeln. In 1516 he purchased a copy of Erasmus' Greek New Testament, and his preaching increasingly reflected his biblical studies. In 1518 Zwingli got his big chance. The Zürich city council owned the right to name the preacher of the Great Minster Church. After some bickering (partially because Zwingli had an illegitimate child), the Zürich burghers awarded him the position. In January 1519 he announced that he would expound the Gospel of Matthew verse by verse as part of his new responsibilities.

About this time, Zwingli began to read Luther's writings. While the Saxon's teachings impressed Zwingli, he did not become a Lutheran. If Luther's spiritual experience informed his theology, the same was true of Zwingli's. Zwingli's decisive religious moment came early in his Zürich ministry. In 1519 the plague hit the city. Rather than desert his parishioners, Zwingli stayed. As one might have expected, he contracted the disease. Although Zwingli was near death, he recovered from his illness; his subsequent model for faith was trust in the sovereign God to deliver his people.

The Reformation in Zürich began with small matters. In 1522 printers preparing for a large book fair broke the Lenten fast by eating meat. The resultant debate in the city council was the first of many test cases. The city council would announce a disputation, invite representatives of all sides to speak, and then decide the issue. Thus in 1523 the council debated the question of whether they should allow Zwingli to preach on the need for reform. The council voted that he should be encouraged to continue in his course, and the process of reform proceeded item by disputed item.

Zwingli passionately wanted corporate worship to reflect biblical patterns. He led a crusade, for instance, to remove the images from the Zürich churches and, despite his own skills as a musician, prohibited organ music. In 1525 Zwingli's liturgical reforms were completed when the Lord's Supper was celebrated according to Zwingli's order of service. After prayer and Bible reading the ministers read the words of institution, prayed, and distributed the elements to a seated congregation.

The difference between Zwingli and Luther emerged in their debate over the Lord's Supper. Early in his study of the New Testament, Zwingli became convinced that the service was merely symbolic. Christ was present with the congregation through prayer, but the flesh and blood of Christ were not in the elements. This conviction was reinforced by the Dutch humanist Cornelius von Hoen, who taught that Jesus' statement in the Gospels "this is my body" meant that the elements signify his body. But Zwingli's position did not depend on exegesis. To him, the salvation offered by Christ was spiritual and, therefore, the means by which Christ offered salvation must also be spiritual.

In contrast, Luther maintained that when a believer heard in faith Christ's words "this is my body; this is my blood," Christ was substantially present in, with, and under the bread and wine. Luther did not believe that this required any change in the elements themselves. Christ did not become the bread; rather, Christ was present "in" it. Pressed to explain, Luther appealed to the ubiquity of Christ. Since God is present everywhere and Christ has all the idioms or characteristics of God, then Christ's body and blood are also everywhere.

Philip of Hesse, the most politically able of the German princes, called for a Colloquy between Luther and Zwingli at his castle of Marburg in October 1529, the purpose of which was to unify the proponents of the nascent Reformation movement. Luther was accompanied by Melanchthon, and Zwingli had the able counsel of Oecolampadius (1482–1531) of Basel and Martin Bucer (1491–1551) of Strassburg. The discussions were frank, honest, and inconclusive. As a result the Reformation divided into two wings: the Lutherans (or Evangelicals) and the Zwinglians (or Reformed).

Since Zwingli assumed that the Reformation was God's cause, he discussed Swiss politics from the pulpit. As tensions grew between the Protestant and Catholic Swiss cantons, he advocated military action.

When the second Cappel War broke out between Zürich and the forest cantons in 1531, Zürich's army was defeated and Zwingli was killed.

The Anabaptists

Felix Manz (1500–1527) and Conrad Grebel (1498–1526), close friends and supporters of Zwingli, came to believe that Zwingli had failed to reform the church quickly or thoroughly enough. Both believed that it was immoral to wait until the secular authorities concluded whether a practice of the church was biblical. They also concluded that New Testament baptism was only for adults who made a public profession of personal faith. The theologian Balthasar Hübmaier (1485?–1528) shared this belief. In 1524 Zwingli discussed the issue of baptism with these critics, without finding common ground.

The city council held a formal disputation on infant baptism and, after hearing the arguments, required everyone to present their unbaptized children for that sacrament. Further, the council ordered unauthorized preaching and teaching to cease immediately. The radicals were not cowed. On January 21, 1525, they administered "believer's baptism" to each other. Persecution of the dissenters began almost immediately, with the Zürich city council favoring drowning as a means of punishment.

This group called themselves the Brethren. Their baptismal practice was related to their doctrine of Scripture. Their conviction was that "believer's baptism" was the only true baptism, since is was the only baptism found in the New Testament. Their opponents, however, called them "Anabaptists" or rebaptizers. Although the charge placed the sect under the Roman law imposing the death penalty for rebaptizing a Catholic, the term did not influence most persecutors, who executed them under the laws prohibiting heresy.

Persecution spread the Anabaptist movement throughout Europe. Michael Sattler was particularly effective in the Southwest parts of Germany. He and his followers were responsible for a 1527 meeting of Brethren at Schleitheim that issued a confession of faith. The confession taught that Christians should avoid the oath and the sword and that true believers should withdraw, as far as possible, from the world. Since the message of the Bible was clear, the confession explained that pastors were to be chosen by lot. The only church discipline permitted was the ban, a form of exclusion from the fellowship of the congregation.

Anabaptist theologians were often forced to live in hiding. The death of Michael Sattler convinced Pilgrim Marpeck (c.1495–1556) of the truth of Anabaptism. For a season, Marpeck led the Anabaptist movement in Strassburg, one of the more tolerant European cities. However, after Martin Bucer defeated Marpeck in a series of disputations, he fled the city and lived underground in Augsburg. Marpeck led the South German Anabaptists until his death.

The persecution of the Anabaptists encouraged a vibrant apocalypticism. Melchior Hoffmann, an eccentric preacher who asked Strassburg to imprison him, taught that Christ would return to that city to begin his millennial reign. Hoffmann's teachings influenced Anabaptists in the city of Münster. Seizing power, these believers hoped to construct an ideal community, but a large army, composed of both Lutheran and Catholic soldiers, surrounded the city and put it under siege. As the siege tightened, order in Münster broke down. The leaders proclaimed the common ownership of wealth and introduced polygamy. Hunger, disease, and madness defeated the defenders, and the city fell. Menno Simons (1496–1561) helped the movement to recover from the Münster debacle by insisting on a return to the movement's original teachings, especially the prohibitions against military service and the oath. Menno also strengthened the Anabaptists' use of the ban.

John Calvin and the City of Geneva

John Calvin (1509–64) led the Reformation in Geneva. His father Gérald Cauvin (the French spelling of the Calvin family name), a lay church official in Noyon, France, destined his son for the priesthood. But when the elder Cauvin found himself in trouble with the church authorities, he switched his talented son to law. Although Calvin obediently completed his legal studies at Orléans and Bourges, his deepest commitment was to humanistic scholarship. After his father's death in 1531, Calvin moved to Paris to pursue his studies, and in 1532 published his *Commentary on Seneca's Treatise on Clemency.*

The facts about Calvin's conversion to Protestantism are not available. Since many young humanists in Paris had taken that step, friends may have convinced Calvin that theological and religious reform was necessary. Yet Calvin may have embraced his new faith as a result of his private biblical studies. In any event, between 1528 and 1532 Calvin had an experience of God that convinced him that the Bible's affirmations about God and humankind contradicted the official teachings of the church. In his *Institutes of the Christian Religion*, first published in 1536, Calvin defined faith as that knowledge of God that enabled people to understand themselves. Significantly, he contrasted this knowledge with that of the philosophers who, despite their wisdom about the natural order, were religiously as blind as moles.

Calvin's friend, Nicholas Cop, the rector of the University of Paris, delivered a passionate appeal for reform in November 1533. Calvin's name was on the list of those suspected of supporting the appeal, and he wisely fled the city. In 1536 he came to Geneva where Guillaume Farel (1489–1565) was preaching the Reformation.

Geneva was a conflicted city, involved in a complicated political struggle. Originally ruled by its bishop, the house of Savoy had largely replaced him. In the early 1530s the city renounced its obedience to bishop and prince and became an independent oligarchy. Religion was a major weapon in this bid for independence. Although Catholic Freiburg offered an alliance, continued adherence to the traditional church might invite episcopal power to return. On the other hand, an alliance with the Protestant city of Bern promised more freedom.

Farel wanted to transform political convenience into conscientious faith by repentance, moral reformation, and church discipline. In November 1536, the city adopted the *Articles Concerning the Government of the Church*, the *Confession of Faith*, and the *Catechism* that Farel and Calvin had prepared.

The two reformers' program was reformation with a vengeance. Unlike Luther or Zwingli, they attempted to bring the entire community under ecclesiastical supervision. Their ecclesiastical order gave the church authority to discipline its own members for moral or religious infractions. Although Calvin believed that the church existed to preach the Word and administer the Sacrament, the church was also the court of the Kingdom of God.

Geneva did not long support the new order. In 1538 the government clashed with Calvin over the church's right to order its own affairs. When Protestant ally Bern demanded that Geneva accept the practice of using unleavened bread at the Lord's Supper (to show that it was a memorial of Christ's death at Passover), Calvin and Farel refused. Only the church, they argued, could make that decision. After their refusal to serve communion under the new order the Council expelled them.

Farel became pastor at Neuchâtel where he remained until his death, and Calvin went to Strassburg where he fell under Martin Bucer's influence. Bucer, a former Dominican, was an early convert to the Reformation. Although he retained much respect for Luther, his own thought had moved in another direction. Like Zwingli, Bucer believed that the Bible provided a model for both life and worship. But he disagreed with Zwingli's view that the eucharistic elements were *merely* symbolic, and his sacramentology stressed the believer's spiritual communication with Christ in the service, making the Supper a means of grace. Bucer became Calvin's theological mentor. While serving as minister to the French exiles in Strassburg, Calvin studied with Bucer and observed how Strassburg governed the church. Calvin adopted much of Bucer's understanding of the Supper as well.

Meanwhile Geneva had not solved its problems, and those who had exiled Calvin pleaded with him to come back. Calvin hesitated. His life in Strassburg was almost ideal, and he had time to write. Nonetheless, the offer of a substantial salary, a parsonage, and a grant of 250 gallons of wine induced Calvin to return to Geneva in 1541 as the pastor of Saint Peter's Church. The city also promised to accept Calvin's form of church government.

Shortly after his return, the city council adopted Calvin's *Ecclesiastical Ordinances* establishing four orders of ministry: pastors, teachers, elders, and deacons. The ministers and the city council cooperated in electing pastors who also had to receive the people's general consent. While the government was not excluded from church discipline, the Consistory (the ministers and twelve lay elders sitting as a court) had the right to judge some cases independently. In particular, the Consistory had jurisdiction over dancing, card playing, and sexual morals.

Despite the support for Calvin's return, many still questioned the church's right to judge its members apart from the city council. Calvin styled his opponents "libertines" which suggested loose morals. But while Calvin's enemies did disagree with the reformer on some moral points, the dispute was not a squabble over ethics. Calvin's opponents either called themselves "Perrinists" (after their leader, Ami Perrin, a former supporter of Calvin) or "Old Genevans." These representatives of the old order in Geneva were aristocrats who believed that their secular privileges should be recognized in church affairs. In contrast, Calvin's supporters were often newcomers attracted to the city by Calvin's theology.

The Old Genevans won the 1548 elections in Geneva, but they did not expel Calvin or his followers. Instead, the elections inaugurated a five year long struggle over matters of church discipline between Calvin and his opponents. The battle went back and forth with Calvin and the Consistory winning some cases, and the city councils others.

The most serious challenge to Calvin came, not from the libertines, but from Michael Servetus (1511–53). Servetus was a physician who discovered the circulation of the blood, but whose obsession was theology. In 1531 he published his *On the Errors of the Trinity*, and in 1553 his

Restoration of Christianity. Servetus argued that the doctrine of the Trinity was a corruption of the original teachings of Jesus and his disciples. Only a return to Jesus' original teachings, he claimed, would reform the church.

In the earliest correspondence between the two men, Servetus seems convinced that he could persuade Calvin of the truth of his views. At the time, this may not have been farfetched. Calvin, like other Reformed ministers, strongly believed that the finite cannot contain the infinite. Although this idea originated in Reformed sacramental theology, it also justified Reformed simplicity in worship. To some, like Servetus, its application to the Person of Christ may have seemed inevitable, if not logically necessary. Unfortunately, Servetus sent Calvin some pages of his *Restoration.*

Soon Servetus—who had been practicing medicine under an assumed name—lost his cover, and the Inquisition accused him of holding heretical Trinitarian views. Somehow Servetus convinced his judges to let him go, but they received the pages sent to Calvin, conclusive evidence of his guilt, shortly after his departure. The Inquisition then burned Servetus in absentia. Servetus next traveled to Geneva, perhaps hoping to unseat the person who had betrayed him. Instead, Servetus was tried and executed for heresy in 1553.

With Servetus's death, the political tide turned toward Calvin and his supporters. Two years later, the Consistory received the right to try offenders without review by the city authorities.

Throughout his career, Calvin rewrote his *Institutes of the Christian Religion.* The first edition appeared in 1536 and the last in 1555. Whenever Calvin faced a new adversary, he included his refutation of his opponent's position. Since his enemies often attacked Calvin's doctrine of predestination, that section was disproportionately long in the last edition. For many Calvinists, the message of the *Institutes* was the mystery of the divine decrees.

But there was more to the *Institutes* than election. For Calvin, humankind has fallen into a world in which sin has obscured both moral and religious truth. Human life is much like an infinite maze with numerous wrong turns and false paths. God was not content, however, to leave human beings in this desperate condition. From the beginning, God sought specific human beings to hear and speak God's Word. Although the faithful are overcoming sin, the process is incomplete. Divine guidance is needed for the saints to reach their eventual destination in God's Kingdom. Although God may use miracles or other extraordinary ways to do this, Calvin believed that God ordinarily worked through historical or earthly means, especially preaching, Baptism, the Lord's Supper, and church discipline.

Calvin was an international leader; exiles and refugees from many countries flocked to Geneva to hear him. These foreign guests, many of whom became citizens after 1555, also studied the Genevan church because it seemed to prove that a strict form of Christianity could be the backbone of a secular society.

The Broader Reformation

Embattled Protestants in Holland, Scotland, France, and England found Calvin's theology a spur to effective action. The independence of the Reformed church was part of its attraction. While Calvinists wanted to reform both church and state, their theology and ecclesiastical practice allowed them to begin reformation with the church and trust God for its completion. If Catholicism triumphed, Calvinists could still organize their churches, practice their discipline, and preach their message.

Calvinism penetrated Scotland, a poor country that maintained its independence only through an alliance with France. The Protestant movement entered Scottish history violently. Armed individuals, inspired by the martyrdom of the early evangelical preacher George Wishart, assassinated Cardinal David Beaton in 1546. In the repression that followed many reformers, including John Knox (c. 1513–72), were sentenced to the galleys.

After his release Knox served as a chaplain to the young King Edward VI until the king's death and the ascension of Mary I to the throne in 1553 forced him to flee England. Traveling through Germany, Knox arrived at Geneva just when Calvin reached the zenith of his power. The Scottish reformer stood in awe of Calvin's achievement and developed Calvin's doctrine and polity to suit Scottish conditions. Unlike his mentor, Knox believed that the common people could resist unjust authority, especially where their souls were at stake. Scotland had the right to reformation even at the cost of revolution. Further, Knox modified Calvin's church order for a larger nation. In the place of Calvin's Consistory, Knox proposed a hierarchy of church courts that began with the local session and ended at the General Assembly.

In 1559, Knox returned to Scotland and led a revolution. His work was endangered when Mary, Queen of Scots, took the throne in 1560. But Mary's failed marriages and sordid affairs eroded her popularity with both Lords and Commons. In 1567 an armed revolt forced her to abdicate the throne in favor of her young son, James VI. A year later,

Mary escaped from Scotland to England. Although Elizabeth I proclaimed her love for her fellow queen, she imprisoned and executed Mary in 1587 for her alleged participation in a plot against herself.

The breathing spell provided by Mary's misadventures gave the Protestants time to become part of the fabric of Scottish life. The new faith was vigorously preached, reforms ruthlessly carried forward, and a ministry educated and settled. Although the Stuarts reintroduced episcopacy, the nation's religious character was set. Despite almost a century of pressure and two civil wars, Scotland remained firmly Calvinist. Following the 1688 Glorious Revolution, the Presbyterian system was finally established by law.

The history of Calvinism in Holland was similarly a story of bloody struggle and warfare. Philip II of Spain inherited the Netherlands from Charles V, who had held them as part of the Holy Roman Empire. Traditionally this region was governed like Northern Germany, with cities and princes having considerable autonomy. This ended when Philip II resolved to integrate the region into the more centralized religious and political system of Spain. A militant Counter-Reformation Catholicism replaced the region's traditionally tolerant strain of Catholic faith.

Many opponents of Spanish rule were Catholics who favored the older ways. But a handful of cities and counties in the North, led by the German prince William of Nassau, embraced Calvinism. In 1566 the region revolted, only to have the rebellion quickly defeated. Philip II refused to lessen his control of the region and appointed the Duke of Alma, Ferdinand Àlvarez, as commander. Serious repression followed, and the rebellion resumed. Although the Spanish won most of the battles, they were unable to subdue the North which—swelled by a Calvinist migration from the South—secured its independence.

The history of Calvinism in France was also violent. As in Holland and Scotland, the real burst of growth of the new theology came after 1550. Calvinism spread rapidly, particularly among the artisans and small shopkeepers. Simultaneously, the new theology found powerful advocates in the fractious French nobility, including Gaspard de Coligny, the Admiral of France, Henry of Navarre, and Louis of Bourbon, Prince of Condé. Civil War began in 1562 when the Catholic Duke of Guise massacred a Protestant village. The Protestants (who had been preparing for war) promptly marched on Paris. When Paris held, as it would in each of the Civil Wars, the two sides were unable to make significant gains against each other.

In 1572 a peace was declared. The marriage of Marguerite of Valois and Henry of Navarre (1553–1610) on St. Bartholomew's Day (August

24, 1572) was to mark the end of hostilities. However, Queen Catherine d'Medici (1519–84) apparently ordered an attack on the Protestant leader, Admiral Coligny. The attempt failed, and when the Protestants demanded an apology, the queen refused. The Paris mob rioted, and several thousand Protestants died in a single night. The Civil War resumed, led by Henry of Navarre who had escaped from Paris. Despite truces, warfare continued until the death of Henry III in 1588. By law, the Protestant Henry of Navarre was next in succession. After an extended war against the remaining Catholic forces, aided by the king of Spain, Henry IV reconverted to Catholicism. After all, he thought, Paris was worth a Mass. As King Henry announced a policy of toleration, promulgating the 1598 Edict of Nantes that permitted Protestants freedom of worship and gave them control of several armed cities for their own defense.

Calvinism and the Economy

Calvin and his successors were economic conservatives, believing in such medieval doctrines as the just price and uneasy about such commercial matters as interest and profits. Yet wherever it was introduced, Calvinism was popular among those people who were constructing a money economy based on individual initiative and responsibility.

The great sociologist Max Weber believed that there was an intrinsic relationship between Calvinism and capitalism. While Weber understood that this relationship was primarily ideological—Calvinism taught hard work and discipline—Calvinism did more than change people's minds. The new faith released its adherents' energy. Clearly, some of that energy went into wars of liberation. In almost every instance of conflict between the two sides, the Catholics held military supremacy; yet, Protestants held their own and occasionally gained territory. In a similar fashion some energy released by the Calvinist gospel went into the economic order. In 1550 the richest areas in Europe were Catholic and the poorest Calvinist; in 1700, that relationship was reversed.

CHAPTER THREE

ENGLAND'S REFORMATION

The England of Henry VIII (1491–1547) was a poor candidate for reformation. The Tudor monarchy was comparatively new, dating from the victory of Henry VII over Richard III in 1485. Erasmus had taught at Oxford, and he influenced such English leaders as John Colet (1467–1519), Thomas More (1478–1535), and John Fisher (1459–1535). Most English intellectuals were humanists, and, like Erasmus, disliked Lutheranism.

Henry's government rejected Protestantism early. Shortly after Luther's works appeared in Germany, a few scholars, including the future biblical translators William Tyndale (1495–1536) and Miles Coverdale (1488–1568), began to meet at the White House Inn in Cambridge—"Little Germany"—to consider the new ideas. Henry ordered Luther's works suppressed and published the *Assertion of Seven Sacraments* under his own name to show where he stood. The persecution of several individuals sympathetic to reform followed: the courts ordered John Firth burned at the stake in 1532, and Henry's agents assassinated Tyndale abroad in 1536. Robert Barnes followed in 1539. The pope conveyed on Henry the title "Defender of the Faith" to acknowledge Henry's personal fidelity to Rome.

The annulment of Henry's and Catherine of Aragon's (1485–1536) marriage complicated matters. Henry wanted to divorce Catherine for many reasons. Catherine had six children, only one of whom, Mary, survived, and Catherine's childbearing years were at their end. If Henry was to have a legitimate male heir, he would have to find another wife. Secretly Henry was involved with Anne Boleyn (1507–36), his mistress's sister, and wanted to marry her. Henry's psychological disposition also influenced events. Henry VIII usually got his own way, and his ego did not tolerate opposition.

Although Henry's Lord Chancellor, Archbishop Cardinal Thomas Wolsey (1475–1530), was a legate of the Holy See, Wolsey was unable to secure the divorce. Even though Henry held Wolsey responsible for this failure and dismissed him in 1529, it was not Wolsey's fault. Charles V, Catherine's nephew, occupied Rome, and his army was more persuasive than Wolsey's diplomacy.

When statesmanship failed, Henry turned to other means. The king asked Thomas Cranmer of Cambridge (1489–1556) to ask the advice of foreign universities about his case. Interestingly, almost all—including Wittenberg—declared that Henry was not entitled to an annulment. The king then turned to English politics. In 1531 he accused the clergy of submitting legal disputes to Wolsey for adjudication in his role as papal legate, a violation of the Act of Praemunire (1373) which forbade the transfer of cases (and the revenue they generated) from the king's courts to those of the pope. One year later Henry extorted an exorbitant sum from the clergy as atonement for this crime. The money was not incidental; Henry would mine the church to meet his personal expenses. The king also persuaded Parliament in 1532 to declare him the supreme head of the church in England, and in 1533 to pass a bill prohibiting appeals to Rome. When the pope threatened excommunication, Henry asked Parliament for additional legislation. One such act, the 1534 Supremacy Act, added the word "only" to the royal supremacy, making Henry the "only Supreme Head in earth of the Church of England." The same law authorized Henry to use the secular courts to suppress heresy and to end abuses. Sir Thomas More and Bishop John Fisher, strong supporters of the earlier persecution of the Protestants, were charged with denying the royal supremacy and executed.

Henry and his new minister, Thomas Cromwell (c. 1485–1540), devised an effective way to raise funds. They would locate an ecclesiastical abuse and then use it as an excuse to confiscate church property. Of course, all sums collected went to the crown. The seizure of the shrine of Thomas Becket, for instance, required barges to carry the gold and silver booty to London.

The real wealth of the church was its land. In 1535 Henry ordered a visitation that revealed the supposed abuses of the monasteries and nunneries. The next year the smaller houses (those with a revenue of less than 200 pounds a year) were suppressed, followed quickly by the more prosperous houses. The lands were confiscated and sold—often for less than their real value—to the king's supporters.

Henry tired of Ann Boleyn and had her executed in 1536. Then he married Jane Seymour who died shortly after the birth of Edward, the long-desired male heir. At this point, Cromwell persuaded Henry to marry for diplomatic advantage and suggested Anne of Clives. Unfortunately Anne was ugly, and Henry set her aside, in effect pensioning her off. In 1540 Henry had Cromwell charged with treason and executed for his role in the affair.

What changed religiously through Henry's machinations? In one sense, little or nothing. Henry ordered each parish to maintain a copy of the Great Bible which, because it was valuable, was to be chained to the pulpit. The 1536 Ten Articles made some concessions to Protestantism. The Articles mentioned many Protestant doctrines but did not commit to them. Thus, the document said that faith justified, but it also urged Christians to perform good works. In 1539 Henry withdrew these concessions. In the Six Articles Act, Parliament affirmed most traditional Catholic doctrines, including transubstantiation. The service was essentially the same, and the priests continued to be celibate. Since the Crown did not seize the chantries until Edwards' reign, the people continued to have the comfort of masses for the dead. The most visible change was the abolition of monasticism. In effect, Henry VIII had created a reformed Catholicism without the pope.

Edward VI and Mary

The young Edward VI (1537–53) followed his father to the throne. Edward only reigned for six years and never gained his majority, and as a result Lord Protectors (regents) ruled England in his stead. The first was Edward Seymour, Earl of Hereford and Duke of Somerset, who ruled for two years. John Dudley, Earl of Warwick and Duke of Northumberland, followed Seymour. Both Protectors were Protestants who wanted to make England a Protestant country. Interestingly, the new government's first step was to seize the chantries and other ecclesiastical endowments. Henry VIII's foreign adventures had left the crown almost bankrupt, and the Protector desparately needed funds to keep the government afloat.

Finances settled, Edward's governments moved forward with deliberate speed. In 1549 Parliament passed an Act of Uniformity requiring every parish church to use the Book of Common Prayer. This prayer book, written by Archbishop Cranmer, moved toward Protestantism, although it retained many traditional usages. The book was not popular; Protestants found it too Catholic, and Catholics too Protestant. Cranmer and some associates subsequently revised the Book in a consistently Protestant direction. Building on both the ancient church and continental practice, the 1552 prayer book removed all references to the Mass as a sacrifice. The altar was replaced by a table, and ordinary bread replaced unleavened bread. While Cranmer himself probably had adopted a Reformed understanding of the Supper by this time, probably derived from Zwingli and Bucer, the text was ambiguous enough to cover all Protestant interpretations. The Book's language was majestic, suggesting God's presence with the congregation. Parliament adopted this new prayer book in the 1552 Act of Uniformity.

The people of England did not have time to learn the new prayer book, however. Edward VI died in June 1553, and his advisors' attempt to replace Catholic Mary with the Protestant Lady Jane Grey failed. Mary (1516–88) quickly cemented her right to the throne and had Northumberland and Lady Jane Grey executed. The queen intended to make England Catholic again, and in 1554 Cardinal Reginald Pole reconciled England to the Holy See. Many Protestant clergy fled to the continent.

Despite her initial political success, Mary was no politician. When she married Philip of Spain in 1554 few of her subjects were pleased. The English feared that the prince consort might try to become king, and merchants knew that England's commercial interests conflicted with Spain's. Further, Mary relentlessly persecuted Protestants. In her mind, England would not be safe until the architects of the previous government were dead and buried. While the total number executed was not excessive for the time, Mary made the mistake of conducting her burnings in public. When she condemned Archbishop Cranmer to the flames, Mary had him burned in Oxford.. As a result she rapidly became noted for her cruelty. John Foxe's *Acts and Monuments of the Martyrs* (1563) fixed Mary's reputation as a female Nero. Foxe was a skilled writer with an ear for language and an eye for detail whose prose let generations of readers feel the heat and smell the burning flesh of the executioner's victims.

Elizabeth I

After Mary Tudor's unmourned death in 1558, her sister, Elizabeth I (1533–1603), came to the throne in a peaceful succession. Within a few years Elizabeth assembled an effective government both nationally and internationally. England responded well to her firm leadership, and English literature, art, and music flourished during her reign.

Whatever her personal beliefs, Elizabeth understood that Protestants were important supporters of her government. In 1559 Parliament passed two bills, an Act of Supremacy and an Act of Uniformity. The first declared Elizabeth the "Supreme Governor of the Church of England," and the second mandated the use of an amended 1552 Book of Common Prayer. While the Book retained much of the earlier text, many passages that offended Catholics were removed. Parliament passed the Thirty-Nine Articles, a modification of Cranmer's earlier Forty-Two Articles, in 1563.

With few exceptions, Mary's bishops refused the new religious settlement, and Elizabeth removed them from office. In their place, Elizabeth appointed moderate Protestants. The structure of the church, however, was not changed. The Church of England retained the traditional three-fold ministry of bishops, priests, and deacons. Moreover, many medieval practices continued. Church courts, for instance, retained their authority over family law.

Tragically, Elizabeth left the chaotic financial structure of the medieval church in place. The church was financed through traditional tithes, advowsons, glebes, fees, parish rates, and endowments. These financial arrangements left some bishoprics and parishes wealthy and others impoverished. Since many serious abuses of the medieval church, such as clerical non-residence, were related to church finance, these abuses continued. Elizabeth's church was more reformed theologically and liturgically than practically.

If the Elizabethan settlement offended few, it pleased fewer. Many critics were Protestants who wanted further reforms. Initially, their opponents called them Puritans, perhaps, to imply that they believed that a perfect or "pure" church was possible. Puritan problems with the new church varied. Some opposed parts of the liturgy. Early in Elizabeth's reign, many ministers objected to the wearing of the surplice at Holy Communion and to such matters as kneeling at the rail, the use of the ring in marriage, and various practices around baptism. These rituals separated the sacramental life of the church from the preaching ministry and implied that the believer received grace apart from the Word. But this was precisely the point of the settlement. Elizabeth wanted Catholics to feel more at home in the service. She ordered her Archbishop, John Whitgift, to enforce uniformity by whatever means were necessary.

The battle over church order was more important and persistent, lasting until the restoration of Charles II in 1660. In part, the problem was theological. Theodore Beza, Calvin's successor in Geneva, taught that the Bible required a church order composed of elders and deacons. In the New Testament, Beza reasoned, bishops and elders occupied the same office. Since the Reformed believed that whatever the Bible taught, the present church ought to do, this supposed New Testament order was *de jure divino* (by divine right).

The question of clerical equality was not an abstract issue. Those who advocated a presbyterian system of organization wanted to simplify the church, remove the church courts, modernize ecclesiastical finances, and outlaw such ecclesiastically dubious practices as non-residence and pluralism. Church discipline would be local, and presbyteries would only try offenses clearly proscribed in the Scripture. Excommunication was to be the only penalty. Naturally, these reforms would reduce the gap between the highest and the lowest paid ministers, and all ministers would preach and administer the sacraments. Some Presbyterians wanted to retain bishops as administrators.

Presbyterianism claimed some of the most able minds in the English church, including, for example, the Cambridge theologian Thomas Cartwright (1535–1603). Once repression had begun, advocacy for Presbyterianism became less public. But students at Cambridge were taught the system by their tutors and believed that it would eventually be instituted. When the English Civil War erupted in the 1640s, advocates of Presbyterianism dominated the Westminster Assembly, called by Parliament in 1646 to settle religious issues.

Some went beyond Presbyterianism. Robert Browne (1550–1633), for instance, believed that the New Testament churches were independent of each other and had sole control of their own ministry and discipline. Only those who believed could be members of such gathered and covenanted bodies. If this was true, he reasoned in *Reformation Without Tarrying for Any* (1582), then any particular body of believing Christians could adopt whatever measures they needed for their religious life. These convinced believers could, if necessary, leave the established church to secure their aims, although Browne never argued that establishment was evil or undesirable. His opponents called Browne and his followers Separatists. Browne was exiled, but he later conformed and served a parish.

Browne's understanding of church order, however, remained part of the larger English debate. Small groups separated from the English church. After a cat and mouse game with the authorities, these groups typically went into exile, usually in Holland. The small congregation at Scrooby, England, was the mother of many of these churches. The first English General Baptists, formed by John Smythe in Holland, came from this body as did the congregation that migrated to Plymouth in the new world.

Elizabeth I continued episcopacy primarily for political reasons. However, when the Presbyterians attacked the system, some able writers defended the established order. Richard Hooker (1553–1600) in his *Laws of Ecclesiastical Polity*, perhaps building on the views of the continental theologian Thomas Erastus, argued that human beings had the same right to form an ecclesiastical government as to form a secular state. Just as some secular states were monarchies, others oligarchies or republics, and others democracies, Hooker reasoned, churches could also take whatever form they believed rational. Since the organization of the English church corresponded to the larger organization of England, it was the best for that country.

Hooker's approach, favored by church moderates, was not radical enough for all Episcopals. Bishop George Bancroft (1544–1610), for instance, argued that episcopal government was itself required by God. William Laud (1573–1645), Charles I's Archbishop of Canterbury, developed a position that made both ordination and apostolic succession essential to the church. For Laud, tradition had authority in the Church of England, since the church participated in the divine life through the Sacraments. In many ways, Laud's position was similar to that of the Eastern churches who believed that each nation had its own hierarchy and liturgy.

The defenders of Episcopacy had their own ecclesiastical program. While most wanted to maintain the status quo, others wanted to revive older sacramental and spiritual practices. For them, the church was a continuation of the incarnation, the place where the Spirit made Christ present to faith.

Elizabeth held these competing factions together by a variety of means. Although Elizabeth was careful (unlike Mary) not to create martyrs, she did persecute those who threatened her establishment. By law established meant by law enforced. But Elizabeth preferred indirect means. Since both Puritans and Anglicans were highly patriotic, Elizabeth associated her church with England's quest for gold and glory.

Privateers, such as Sir Francis Drake, robbed the Spanish new world fleets at will. Philip II of Spain, disgusted by English piracy and perfidy, declared war. The Spanish plan was simple. A massive Armada would be assembled that would sail from Spain to the Netherlands where the large, seasoned army of the Duke of Parma was to gather. The Armada would then transport Parma's army to the English coast. The plan's cost was astronomical and contributed to Spain's later bankruptcy and decline.

England was not as weak as it appeared. For some years, Elizabeth's navy under John Hawkins' leadership had improved its ships and its tactics. Although tradition has remembered the smaller ships that Hawkins used—a mosquito fleet that could sting and then retreat—his navy included as many large galleons as his opponents', and his carried more fire-power, making them floating gun placements.

When Philip's fleet sailed in 1588 nothing went right for the Spanish commander, Medina Sidonia. Arriving in the Netherlands, he learned that Parma would not meet him with the expected army. Then on the night of August 7, Drake and Howard attacked the Spanish fleet and continued the battle the next day. While the Battle of Gravelines was not decisive, the English forced the Spanish to sail north around Scotland where savage storms weakened the Spanish fleet.

While the Spanish War lasted sixteen more years, England credited Elizabeth with the defeat of the Armada, which subsequently became a symbol of national might. The mythmakers implied that the Spanish defeat came from God's personal intervention in the history of England!

James I and Charles I

When James I (1566–1625) became king in 1603, the Puritans had high hopes, since James was a Scot and a Presbyterian. A delegation of Puritans met the king on his way to London with a petition, supposedly signed by a thousand people, that listed needed ecclesiastical reforms. James was not impressed. Whether or not he actually told the petitioners "No bishop, no king," the slogan expressed his sentiments. Instead of importing Presbyterianism into England, James exported episcopacy to Scotland. By 1625, when his reign ended, James had established bishops in his Northern Kingdom.

James used his patronage to secure high positions for his supporters. However, he made little attempt to remove Puritans from their positions. The Puritans continued to dominate the University of Cambridge and the law schools, called the Inns of Court. In 1618, James published the *Book of Sports* advocating Sunday recreations. Sports were, after all, preparation for war. While the book angered the Puritans, it did not hurt them or weaken their popularity.

James's court was alive with masques and other entertainments designed to win over the nobles. While the Puritans were, of course, offended by these displays of royal luxury, the country gentry and town and city merchants who controlled the House of Commons also took umbrage. In winning the aristocrats, James lost the wealthier common-ers and these people, as much or more than the dukes and earls, had power in England.

When James died in 1625, his legacy to his son, Charles I (1600–1649), included a polarized nation. From the beginning, Charles encountered strong resistance in the House of Commons. In 1629 he dismissed Parliament and did not call another meeting of that body until 1640. Meanwhile Charles came increasingly under the influence of William Laud, whom he made Bishop of London in 1628 and Archbishop of Canterbury in 1629. Laud was the leading advocate of the Anglican party, and he wished to strengthen the Catholic elements in the Church of England.

Laud's religious policies were an attempt to secure uniformity at any cost. For instance, his persecution convinced many of England's most skilled preachers to emigrate to Massachusetts. Few of these religious leaders, including such learned men as John Cotton of Boston, would have left the Church of England otherwise. They were convinced non-separatists. Further, Laud used the Court of the High Commission, also known as the Star Chamber, to suppress his political enemies. The Star Chamber was a court of inquisition that had the right to summon a person and inquire about his or her religious and political activities under oath. Since perjury meant the death penalty and since the court did not have to inform the accused of what evidence it had, people might confess to matters previously unknown to the authorities. The Court's victims often had their ears removed or a hole bored through their tongues. Branding on the cheek with the letters, SL (for seditious libeler), became so common that wags contended that the letters stood for *Stigmata Laudis*.

Charles's bold attempt to rule without Parliament might have suc-ceeded, had he not attempted the further reformation of the Scottish church. In 1637 Charles ordered the Scots to follow a new prayer book which, although based on the Book of Common Prayer, moved in a more Catholic direction. Rebellion followed, and the Scots gathered in Edin-burgh to sign a National Covenant to defend true religion. Charles resolved to take military action against the North, and he called an English Parliament to vote the necessary funds. The first such Parlia-ment refused. Charles disbanded it quickly. The next, the Long Parlia-ment, called in 1640, passed a law refusing to disband without its consent.

The Long Parliament began to reform the church in England almost immediately. Parliament arrested Archbishop Laud, and then abolished episcopacy officially. In 1643 Parliament summoned the Westminster Assembly to formulate the doctrine and worship of the new church. The Assembly worked steadily at its tasks, producing a Directory of Worship, a Confession, a Shorter and Longer Catechism, and a system of church government. Westminster's documents all featured the covenant theology that argued that God dealt with humankind primarily through a series of covenants. In each covenant, God explained what people needed to do to merit salvation, but people failed to keep each new covenant. Finally, God made a covenant of grace in which God both set the conditions for salvation and fulfilled them in Christ.

Civil war broke out between Charles and Parliament. Forces primarily drawn from the north and west of England supported the king. In contrast, an army from the south and east backed Parliament. In 1644 the Parliamentary forces under Oliver Cromwell (1599–1658) defeated the king at Marston Moor and one year later routed the last large royal army at Naseby. After repeated attempts to reach an accord with the king, Parliament executed Charles I on January 30, 1649. After Charles's death, Oliver Cromwell, who became Lord Protector of England, centralized power in his own person, resting that power, not on Parliament, but on the army.

The religious implications of the victory were not clear. While Parliament wanted to establish the Presbyterian system, the army resisted that step. The army favored religious toleration and resisted any Act of Uniformity that would shackle conscience. Each congregation should be able to settle its own religious affairs. However, this did not mean that the army favored or seriously considered the separation of church and state. Cromwell still financed the church through its traditional endowments, and biblical and secular law reinforced each other.

The revolutionary period also saw many new religious movements. Perhaps the most important were the Quakers or Society of Friends who followed the teachings of George Fox. The early Friends were true religious radicals who interrupted worship services to present their perspective. Like the Hebrew prophets, they often acted out their beliefs in public demonstrations. Occasionally, these became too much for even the tolerant Cromwell. When James Naylor rode into Bristol on an ass in imitation of Christ, the Lord Protector had him arrested and flogged.

Cromwell's paradoxically tolerant dictatorship did not last long after the Protector's death. Parliament and some army commanders invited Charles II (1630–85) to return to England, and he did so. Charles himself was a secret Roman Catholic who was willing to make many compromises to retain his crown. The nobles who supported him, however, were not. Taking advantage of an Anglican majority, the royalists expelled the Puritans from the Church of England and subjected them to mild persecution. Puritanism found itself increasingly on the margins of English religious life. When toleration finally came after the Glorious Revolution, the Puritans had become dissenters, divided among several denominations. While the dissenting tradition (later called non-conformity) continued to influence English religion, Elizabeth's compromise had established Anglicanism's preeminent place in English public life.

CHAPTER FOUR

CATHOLICISM SPANS THE GLOBE

Those who remained in the old church after the Protestant Reformation had to respond to the new faith. In part, their response was defensive; measures were taken to confine Protestantism and to prevent its spread. These included the intensification of the Inquisition, an Index of prohibited books, and strengthened relations with Catholic rulers. Historians have often referred to these measures as a Counter-Reformation. The most effective Catholic response, however, was the internal reform of the Church by its own leaders, often called the Catholic Reformation. The Council of Trent (1545–63), for instance, reaffirmed medieval Catholic doctrine and instituted some needed disciplinary canons. Monasticism and mysticism likewise revived. The most important sign that the Roman Catholic Church had recovered its *élan* was the missionary movement; although Roman Catholicism had lost northern Europe, missionaries spread its faith around the globe.

Spanish Catholicism

The struggle to expel the Arabs dominated medieval Spanish history. After Aragon and Castile united in 1479, the newly united armies drove South. Whenever the Catholics conquered a new area, the vanquished were offered a choice between baptism and exile. Since the Spanish distrusted the sincerity of the Marranos (converted Jews) or Moriscos (converted Arabs), the slightest relapse into the old faith, real or imagined, led the authorities to summon the dreaded Inquisition.

In the fifty years after Columbus's discovery of America, Spain commissioned many *conquistadores* who won an empire that began in the southwest of what is now the United States and terminated at the tip of South America. Nor did the conquests stop at the Pacific. In 1521

Spanish explorers entered the Philippine Islands where they established the great trading city of Manila.

The Spanish conquest was brutal. Since Native Americans outnumbered the Spanish knights, the invaders had to exploit their superior mobility (the horse versus llamas and travel by foot) and fire power. The conquerors' attack was similar throughout the new world. They seized a high place, such as Mexico City, fortified it, and used it as a base to raid the countryside. The raids served two purposes. First, the Spanish wanted to eradicate the earlier Native American political organization. Second, the use of terror and cruelty was one way for a handful of soldiers to control the surviving native population.

Catholic Resources for Mission

Sixteenth-century Spanish church leaders had limited, but rich, resources to use in their mission to the new world. Most Spaniards regarded Catholicism as a part of their people's independence and character. Like English Protestants, Spanish clergy taught a post-millennial theology that stressed the triumph of God's earthly kingdom, with Spain as a harbinger of that hope.

Spanish law made the king, who had extensive rights called the *real patronato*, the effective head of the church. Under these laws the crown appointed bishops and was the final judge in ecclesiastical discipline. The king transmitted (or refused to transmit) all communications between the Spanish hierarchy and Rome. The larger church, symbolized by Rome, had authority only in the undefined area of faith and morals.

The sixteenth century was a classical period for the Spanish religious orders which were attracting new members. Such great mystics as Teresa de Jésus of Ávila (1515–82) and John of the Cross (1542–91), received new visions of the Ever-Present God. The union of the soul and the divine, they taught, released new human energies enabling the God-intoxicated person to do the most difficult tasks. This was similar to the way in which faith also animated the Spanish knight. The Spanish author, Miguel de Cervantes (1547–1616), captured this piety in *Don Quixote de la Mancha* (Part One, 1605; Part Two, 1615). The hero, an aging gentleman, resolves to spend his last years in a final quest for glory for king and church. Summoning his faithful page, Sancho Panza, Quixote begins his impossible dream. Whatever should be done, Quixote will do. The summons to convert two continents had much in common with Quixote's adventure, and Spain's religious orders provided two centuries of spiritual knights ready to undertake it.

Ignatius Loyola (c. 1495–1556), the founder of the Jesuits, was one such knight of faith. Loyola was converted while recovering from battle wounds. For a short period, he lived as a solitary ascetic, but soon found that he was an extrovert who needed to work among people. He next resolved to become a priest and enrolled in a boys' school to learn Latin. The Inquisition, doubting the propriety of a hardened veteran cavorting with lads, arrested Loyola. Once released, he went to France where he entered the University of Paris. There he gathered a band of young adventurers, The Company of Jesus, around himself. The band resolved either to go as missionaries to the Holy Land or, if that was not possible, to place themselves directly in the service of the pope. In 1540, they traveled to Rome. Despite real concerns, the pope approved the new order and renamed it the Society of Jesus.

Jesuit spiritual training was rigorous preparation for missionary work. In his *Spiritual Exercises*, Loyola urged the new members to pray in a way that enabled them to see, hear, taste, smell, and feel the great mysteries of the faith. The candidate contemplating hell, for example, was to picture the sufferings of the damned, hear their piteous cries, and smell the burning flesh and smothering sulfur. The director forced the young Jesuit to ask whether any of the damned were in agony because of his failure to share the gospel.

The Jesuits followed a military organization that stressed strict obedience. Loyola used hyperbole when he asserted that a good Jesuit would believe that black was white, if so ordered. Yet the statement was apt; Jesuits went where their superiors ordered them to go and did what they were told to do. With a memo the society's general could dispatch missionaries around the world who would remain in place until ordered to leave.

In an age of state Catholicism, Ignatius' decision to place his society directly under the pope secured the Jesuits' partial freedom from political authorities. As a result Jesuit fathers could and did protest unjust conditions in New Spain colonies without losing their ecclesiastical position.

Friars and Native Americans

Bernard Boyd was the first Roman Catholic priest to enter the new world, ministering briefly in 1493. However, serious efforts at evangelism did not begin until the arrival of twelve Franciscans under Martin de Valencia. In 1505 they established the Mission of the West Indies and began to register converts to the church. In 1510 Dominicans began a similar mission. These two orders sent more than one hundred missionaries a year to the new territories. The Spanish mission to America reported more than ten million baptisms in its first fifty years.

The most serious problem faced by the missionaries was the Spanish colonists' exploitation of the Native Americans. Spanish settlers developed the *encomienda*, a form of slavery, to hold the Indians in bondage. The Friars' position was not comfortable. The king commanded them to minister to both the settlers and to the Indians. Any intervention for the oppressed might lead to white opposition to the mission's work. Many priests, particularly those in the Spanish garrisons, said little or nothing.

Others took up the issue vigorously. In 1512 the crown enacted the Laws of Burgo, providing some minimal protections to the native populations of the colonies, primarily because of Dominican agitation. In 1523 the king ordered Cortés to end the *encomienda*.

Bartolomé de Las Casas (1474–1566) came to America to profit from the new world's wealth. Once he arrived, Las Casas recognized that much of that wealth depended on the oppression of Native Americans and resolved to become their defender. His first effort was to gather Native Americans into free villages and to teach them agriculture. Unfortunately these idealistic efforts failed because of white opposition and Las Casas's poor organizational skills.

Returning to Spain, Las Casas found his vocation as a publicist. In work after work he described the conditions that existed in the new world and proposed correctives to Spanish policy. Las Casas's writings contributed to the 1542 enactment of the New Laws. This legislation restricted the rights of *encomienda* (royal displeasure had not ended the practice). Through his influence at court, Las Casas secured the appointment of bishops that supported the rights of Native Americans. Ironically, Las Casas argued that black slaves from Africa might replace the Native Americans as cheap labor.

Antonia de Valdivieso, Archbishop of Nicaragua, was another crusader for Indian rights. From his arrival in America in 1544 he denounced the abuses of the system and protested conditions repeatedly to the king. In 1550 Juan Barmijo and a band of adventurers killed the bishop, fearing that his preaching might harm them economically. Juan del Valle, bishop of Popayan, called diocesan councils in 1555 and 1558 to condemn the treatment of the Indians. When these failed to secure reform, del Valle returned to Spain to persuade the Supreme Council of the Indies to protect his charges. He died in 1561 on route to the Council of Trent where he planned to lay the case of the Indians before the whole church.

Neither crown nor church ended the oppression of the Native Americans. In desperation the missionaries adopted the *reducciones*, a self-contained Indian colony directly under the control of the priests. In these Christian commonwealths, the Friars hoped to protect their charges from white "Christians" and to teach their people European husbandry. The architectural ruins of these Spanish missions still dot the American southwest.

Christian Institutions

Catholic missionaries believed that Christian institutions would complete the work of conversion begun at baptism. Church leaders built these institutions quickly. Shortly after establishing its power in an area, the Crown appointed bishops who, in turn, appointed priests. The new dioceses held provincial councils to regulate the church area and to enact canon law. Often such meetings debated higher standards for missionary work, including canons calling for a period of instruction before baptism. These councils also required missionaries to conduct religious instruction in the indigenous languages. Competition between religious orders required councils to adjudicate claims to this or that territory.

Universities were established early in the new world. In 1552 the king chartered the Dominicans university at Lima, with other universities soon following. In 1571 the pope granted the new universities in Lima, Santo Domingo, and Mexico, the same rights and privileges as the ancient Spanish schools. The Jesuits here, as elsewhere, maintained excellent academies for the children of the ruling class.

The Bible was available in Spanish, Latin, Greek, and Hebrew versions. Missionaries translated the Bible and prepared catechisms into various Native American languages. Spanish professors and church leaders published extensively on Native American life, language, and culture.

Catholic Faith and American Reality

From one perspective, the Catholic mission to the Americas was a phenomenal success. Besides millions of new members, the church established the four classical marks of catholicity (hierarchy, Scripture, creed, and liturgy) over a territory larger than that of the Roman empire. The new churches were strong enough to survive disaster. When the dissolution of the Jesuit order in 1767 depleted the supply of missionaries, the American churches continued the mission.

The missionaries believed that the Native Americans were childlike savages whose souls were a religious *tabula rasa*. Yet Indian faiths were more resilient than they appeared. Indian religious customs often reappeared in the parasacramental practices of the Latin American churches. On Epiphany, the priest celebrated the mass inside the church building, while the people conducted mock battles, similar to the older reenactments of Indian myth, in the town plaza. Other popular Epiphany devotions included juggling, religious dancing, and leaping. The American experiment also transformed Pentecost. Native Americans and African slaves believed that spirits possessed some human beings and gave them gifts of healing and prophecy.

The cult of Mary enjoyed extraordinary popularity in Latin America. This devotion may have continued an earlier worship of various Indian goddesses. The legend of Our Lady of Guadalupe shows the connection. According to the saga, a Native American peasant received a message from Mary for his bishop, a Spanish noble. The ecclesiastic, offended that heaven might shine on such a lowly one, denied the truth of the man's report and demanded that the peasant bring him a rose (a symbol of Mary) as proof. The peasant prayed, and Mary told him to go to his bishop and unfurl his cloak. Doing so, roses tumbled out and Mary's picture appeared. The authorities immediately built a church on the site, the location of an earlier temple to the fertility goddess.

Spanish clergy, trained to fight heresy in all its forms, resolutely opposed the continuation of any traditional Native American religious practices. Further, the magisterium (the church's teaching office) took measures to preserve the purity of the faith. Thus the colonial Inquisition's records contain numerous instances of trials of Native Americans for "witchcraft" and "magic." The catechisms also condemned other indigenous practices in sharp, unmistakable language. Why then did some syncretism occur? For one thing, every new religion continues and preserves earlier religious practices and beliefs. Other reasons include the inadequate supply of priests to catechize the converts adequately, and the small number of schools for Native Americans. Moreover, the most syncretism occurred in devotional practice, the area where the church historically allowed the most latitude.

Asian Experiments

Latin American missionaries encountered a culture less advanced than their own and assumed that they were bringing civilization to poor, benighted savages. When Catholic priests entered India, China, and Japan, however, they confronted ancient and sophisticated cultures. The European relationship to Asia was defined by trade and the first European outposts were trading posts. The economic relationship suggested that the missionary endeavor had to be one of give and take.

Saint Francis Xavier (1506–52), an original companion of Ignatius Loyola, went to Asia in response to a request from King John III of Portugal for four missionaries for Goa. In 1541 Francis sailed for the colony with a commission as papal nuncio and accompanied by two companions. Arriving in India at Socotra, Xavier discovered a large Christian community whom Xavier baptized according to the Roman rite. Despite his plea to remain, the governor ordered him to continue his journey.

Xavier's mission to Goa resulted in the conversion of the pearl-fishers (who were already nominally Christian), as well as the establishment of a college. Moving south to Ceylon, Xavier had some further success with fishing people. The missionary then traveled as far east as Japan where he established a Christian community at Nagasaki that, despite persecution, still survives.

Xavier's ministry illustrated an important feature of western missions in India: most of the converts were poor, often *harijans* or untouchables. The poor heard words of liberation in the gospel message. However, some missionaries were bothered by the low caste of the converts since they did not believe that the poor could convert others. The official Roman strategy was to convert the ruling classes first who would, in turn, influence the masses.

Robert de Nobili (1577–1656), a Jesuit, resolved to win India's rulers. Hinduism organized Indian life into castes (hereditary social classes), and de Nobili organized his mission along similar lines. Since de Nobili was a European noble, he adopted the dress and manners of a Hindu Brahmin. Further, de Nobili used Indian religious philosophy to interpret the gospel to his hearers and wrote extensively in Tamil, an Indian language. By 1700 the missions to both the lower castes and to the Brahmins had converted more than one million people.

In China the Jesuits were originally well received because of their work as mathematicians and calendar makers. Matthew Ricci (1552–1610) undertook a serious study of Chinese customs, religion, and philosophy. Over the years, Ricci learned to compose Chinese philosophical and scientific works. Ricci also studied the works of Confucius and used Confucian teachings in presenting Christianity to the Chinese.

Throughout Europe, theologians debated the Jesuit missionary strategies and experiments in Asia. The measures' opponents believed that the Jesuits compromised the gospel by sanctifying elements of the older religious traditions. In 1742 the pope condemned the most radical Jesuit practices.

Other Catholic Missions

Not all Catholic countries received the decrees of the Council of Trent. The most important was France where Catholicism needed spiritual and organizational reform. Young priests, often associated with Pierre de Bérulle (1575–1629), conducted an active program of evangelization. A priest would enter a parish, preach repentance, and summon sinners to the confessional and the altar.

St. Vincent de Paul (c. 1580–1660) was a principal leader of this renewal movement. As with other notables, legends developed around his life. For example, the stories claim that Vincent's imprisonment by North African pirates taught him to love the poor and oppressed. Vincent adapted traditional Catholic practices to a changed situation. Traditionally Catholics covenanted together for communal works of piety and charity. Vincent used this tradition to meet the needs of Paris' poorest people. Prayer groups provided wood, cared for orphans and found them homes, and fed the hungry. When war destroyed many farms in Lorraine, Vincent organized a relief effort that provided seed and tools.

De Paul believed that the future of vital religion in France depended on an educated priesthood. To provide such spiritual leaders, Vincent organized a band of priests, the Vincentian Fathers or Lazarists who devoted their lives to priestly formation. The Vincentians separated minor (high school) from major (college and theological training) seminaries. Further, they carefully delineated the stages that each candidate needed to pass through before ordination. A Vincentian theme was the right of a candidate to choose his own vocation, even if the prospective priests' parents had reared him for the priesthood.

French Catholic women had few religious options. They could enter a nunnery and live a cloistered life or they could marry. At most, the church permitted cloistered sisters to teach a few girls reading and writing. The Sisters of Charity, organized by Vincent, offered another option. Although the Sisters promised poverty, chastity, and obedience, they were to go into the world and to meet human needs. The Sisters were successful nurses, teachers, and social workers.

Jean-Jacques Olier (1608–57) was another prominent leader of the French Catholic mission. After a series of successful preaching missions in Brittany, he became pastor of the parish of St. Sulpice in Paris which he made a training center for young priests. His own educational method emphasized the development of a priestly character rather than the abstract knowledge of doctrine and dogma. Olier's Society of St. Sulpice was—like the Vincentians—consecrated to the education of priests. However, the Sulpicians were not a traditional order. Each member was a secular priest who owed his bishop obedience and service.

Jansenists and Jesuits

The French church's relationship with the state hampered its mission. As in Spain, the effective head of the church was the king who maintained minimal connections with the Holy See. The controversy between Jesuits and Jansenists dominated seventeenth- and eighteenth-century French Catholicism. The Jesuits believed that the loyalty of the upper classes to the church had to be maintained. In line with the openly immoral French court, the Jesuits compromised the requirement of true contrition, so that a penitent had only to want forgiveness to receive absolution.

In contrast, the Jansenists were ethical rigorists. Cornelius Jansen (1585–1638), the movement's founder, spent his life studying St. Augustine's writings, especially the Anti-Pelagian tracts. In 1640, after Jansen's death, his friends published his *Augustinus* that argued that the sinner must continually repent and attend the sacraments to receive forgiveness. Jansen's most able defender was Antoine Arnauld (1612–94), whose sister Jacqueline "Angelequé" was abbess of Port Royal, a Jansenist convent. Arnauld's early theological treatises, especially his *Apology for Jansen*, were well received, but he created a furor when he published his *Letters to a Duke*. This work openly attacked Jesuit laxity in the confessional. Blaise Pascal (1623–62), a layperson and leading mathematician, joined Arnauld in the debate. Pascal's *Provincial Letters* combined logic and ridicule to attack the Jesuit moral theory known as "probabilism" (which held that any action might be accounted as moral if it was *probably*, though not *certainly*, legal) by claiming that the Jesuits were willing to proclaim the forgiveness of any sin if the slightest chance (probability) existed that the person had repented. The Sorbonne censured Arnauld for his writings, but Pascal's work was so effective that Pope Alexander VII was forced to condemn "probabilism" in 1665 and again in 1666, and Pope Innocent XI repeated the condemnation in 1679.

Mediators arranged a temporary truce between the two parties in 1668 called the "peace of the church." Neither party was to publish on the issues under debate. In 1672, however, the Jansenist Pasquier Quesnel (1634–1719) published his *Moral Reflections on the New Testament,* renewing the controversy. Quesnel and Arnauld fled to Brussels, and the pope formally condemned *Moral Reflections* in 1708.

Partly because of this internal division, French Catholicism did not participate in the seventeenth-century non-European mission in proportion to its numbers or wealth. French missionaries did enter New France where they explored as far west as the Mississippi and witnessed to many Indian tribes. Montreal became an early center of North American Catholic culture with a college, an Ursuline convent, a hospital, and a Sulpician seminary. The French also translated the Bible into many of the Native American languages of this region.

CHAPTER FIVE

BRITISH NORTH AMERICA: THE AGE OF EXPERIMENT

Under Elizabeth I (1533–1603), England advanced militarily, politically, and economically. History indicated that the course of empire had moved ever westward, and now England—the most western land in Europe—was next in line to wear the imperial purple. The Protestantism that regenerated the national spirit, however, also divided the population. Despite their love of England, many wanted to live without the compromises that they believed sullied English religious life. The "Pilgrims," a small band of Separatists (those who wanted to form churches separate from the Church of England), first found sanctuary in Holland. Disturbed by their children's loss of English, part of this congregation sailed in 1620 to Plymouth in New England to establish an independent colony.

A much larger group of Puritans (those who believed that the Church of England was not Protestant enough, yet who sought to reform it from within) also sought refuge. Archbishop William Laud wanted to rid the English church of Puritans and he used the power of the state, including the dreaded Star Chamber, to this end. The Puritans did not surrender their ideals when they left England; they went on an "errand," determined to create a "city on a hill" to inspire a further English Reformation.

After the Restoration of the monarchy in 1660, Quakers began to enter the colonies. The first Quakers to come to America were missionaries, but Quakers also came to escape persecution at the hands of the English authorities. Although Virginia, the oldest of the colonies, was founded in 1607, its period of growth came in the 1640s. Many Cavaliers (royalists) fled to the New World to escape the Parliamentary armies that defeated Charles I. These settlers were as devoted to the Church of England's pomp and ceremony as the Puritans were to their plain style of worship.

Religion was not the only reason for emigration to the colonies. The literature about America pictured a land with gold and glory readily available. Many came to create or restore an economic fortune or to win renown by military victories. Further, England was a pre-industrial society whose agriculture did not provide sufficient employment for a growing population. Although the laws were stiff and oppressive, crime was rampant.

Many settlers had no choice in the matter since they were bound in one way or another. In addition to African slaves, first introduced in 1619, perhaps a majority of whites entering the colonies did so as indentured servants. Colonial recruiters, often called Spirits, captured women in England and sold them as wives upon their arrival in the new world. Men also were captured and often sold as agricultural workers.

The British Mission

Every colonial charter obliged the settlers to teach the Native Americans Christianity. John Eliot (1604–90), the translator of the Scriptures into Algonquian, gathered his charges into "praying towns," similar to the Spanish *reducciones*. Similarly, Thomas Mayhew established a mission on Martha's Vineyard and Nantucket. Father Andrew White (1579–1656), a Jesuit, began Roman Catholic Indian missions in Maryland.

The English mission to the Native Americans had meager results. The whites rejected or occasionally persecuted native converts. For instance, the New Englanders burned Natick, Eliot's largest Christian village, during an Indian War. However, the most serious stumbling block before the British missionaries was the nature of English colonization. Those Britons who came to the new world wanted to establish permanent settlements. To them, Native Americans were more hindrances to their goals than potential brothers and sisters in Christ. English and Indian wars were brutal affairs with the English settlers pushing the indigenous peoples west, and the colonies often slaughtered those who did leave voluntarily.

Protestantism was not organized for missionary work. The Catholic Church could draw upon an immense reserve of idealistic women and men in religious orders. In contrast, the only recognized Protestant religious leader was the minister, laden with wife, children, books, and secular responsibilities. With the exception of the Quakers, Protestants had no leadership positions for women.

The two dominant traditions—Anglicanism and Puritanism—were not open to the incorporation of new people. The Virginia Cavaliers envisioned a hierarchical society in which authority flowed from the king down to the heads of families. In this society, each person had their appropriate rank, and the only "place" for the Indian (or the African) was as a servant. New England was little better. Reformed Orthodoxy taught an understanding of covenant that encouraged the Puritans to think in "tribal" terms. New converts had to be incorporated into Puritan culture before they could be converted to the faith.

The other non-Christian people in British North America were the African slaves. Although the masters made every effort to suppress the memory of Africa and its culture, most seventeenth-century slave-owners ignored their slaves' religious life. Whites regarded the slaves as an inferior race, the "talking tools" discussed by Aristotle. Serious attempts to convert the slaves did not begin until the eighteenth-century Great Awakening.

The history of Christianity in seventeenth-century British North America, consequently, is the history of Christianity among the white settlers. In their first century in the new world the Anglo-Americans accomplished much: they established congregations and parishes, founded denominations, and established educational structures.

Geography, Settlement, and Faith

The geological variety of North America encouraged diverse religious responses to the new world. From Virginia to Georgia, there was a broad coastal plain, cut by deep rivers, that gently rose to a piedmont, or foothills region. In this area, Europeans settled on large estates or plantations, devoted to the production of agricultural staples. The white families lived a considerable distance from each other, making it difficult, if not impossible, to reestablish the orderly patterns of the English countryside. Religious services were also thin. The clergy served several chapels within a single parish, many believers were unable to attend regularly, and priests often conducted funerals on the estates. While wealthy Virginians educated their children and sent them to the College of William and Mary or to an English university, few schools for the poorer population existed, and most Virginians were illiterate. Few children received adequate catechetical instruction or preparation to enter the ministry.

Despite many pastors' hard work, a decline in religious knowledge and practice occurred, especially among the lower classes. When the Great Awakening began, the revivalists often exploited the erosion of traditional doctrine by urging people to accept a simple gospel that required no intellectual elaboration.

The geography of New England was different. The terrain was rocky, and the mountains were near the coastline. This encouraged people to settle in traditional parishes, called towns as in East Anglia, the home of many Puritans. Although parishes in New England were larger than their English equivalents, the colonists arranged their towns by building homes around a central green or common with a church, and with working fields in the surrounding countryside.

The compact pattern of settlement made New England a conservative society. Despite the potentially revolutionary Puritan theology, New Englanders continued many customs long after people in the old country discontinued them. Town organization also made possible the New England emphasis on church discipline, the maintenance of common schools (the so-called Old Deceiver law, passed in the 1640s, required one teacher for every one hundred families), and the democracy of the town meeting.

The middle colonies (New York, New Jersey, Pennsylvania) had the most diverse settlement pattern. New Englanders, migrating southward, established towns; Quakers preferred urban and town settlement; the New York Dutch established large plantations in the Hudson Valley; and German Lutheran settlers attempted to reproduce the detached farms of their homelands. Some radical German sects experimented with utopian communities. Each of these forms of social organization required a different style of ministry.

Cities were unusual in British North America, but the few that existed were disproportionally influential in religious affairs. Boston did not require its citizens to support any particular congregation, but allowed people to choose affiliation with one or another of the city's churches. The city was the hub around which much of New England's religion revolved. Many of New England's most gifted preachers lived in Boston. Harvard College, located in the adjacent town of Cambridge, was at the center of much New England thought.

Philadelphia, the City of Brotherly Love, was a thriving port, market, and financial center located on the Delaware River. Its booming economy attracted people from diverse religious traditions, including Quakers, Baptists, Lutherans, Catholics, Presbyterians and Anglicans.

The port of New York, which developed more slowly, was also filled with a number of different religious bodies.

Churches in British America

The American experiment with diversity began early. Almost from their first settlement a variety of churches located in the American colonies. These ecclesiastical bodies had multiple origins. Some were European state churches; others, such as the New England Puritans, were ecclesiastical parties excluded by the establishment; others, including Baptists and Mennonites, were European sects. Before the official separation of church and state, most American churches had some experience as a free church or denomination. Southern colonies established the Church of England, for example, but England's mother church was a voluntary body in Pennsylvania, New Jersey, and New England, and Congregationalists, legally favored in New England, were voluntary churches in the middle colonies.

The Anglican Churches

The Church of England had difficulty reproducing its faith and order in the new world. English church government was far more complicated than the word "episcopal" suggests. The system was the outgrowth of tradition, parliamentary statutes, canon law, and personal privileges. The appointment of a priest to a local congregation, for example, depended on cooperation between the patron, the bishop, and the university. First, the universities prepared a man for ministry. Second, when the individual reached the canonical age of twenty-six, a patron nominated him. Finally, the bishop installed him in his church. Canon law granted the priest a life tenure, and he (or his estate) was responsible for the upkeep of the parsonage and glebe.

Since the traditional supports of the Church of England were missing in America, Anglicans made makeshift arrangements. The Bishop of London reluctantly accepted the task of ordaining men for colonial service, although parliament had not authorized him to do so. Despite the establishment of the College of William and Mary, the College of Philadelphia, and King's College, colonial Anglicanism lacked an effective institution for training its clergy. Colonial candidates for the priesthood often had to travel to England for their education. Colonial Anglicanism was short of ministers and relied on immigrants to fill many pulpits.

American ministers were appointed in a non-traditional manner. Since no one owned the advowsons (rights to nominate candidates for vacant ecclesiastical positions) to colonial parishes, Virginia law designated the governor as patron. In Maryland, this privilege was reserved for the proprietor. Since neither official had the time or inclination to fulfill these duties adequately, the Southern churches became *de facto* congregational. The vestry, a minor parish committee in England charged with the poor rates and the maintenance of the church building, became the parish governing board in the colonies.

Finances were another problem. In England ancient endowments, often accumulated over centuries, great and small tithes, occasional governmental grants, and gifts and fees supported the churches. In contrast, the lack of these traditional sources of income forced the Southern churches to rely on church rates (taxes) to pay the minister. Both Virginia and Maryland set aside glebes, farms of about 100 acres, for their clergy.

Thomas Bray (1656–1730), the Commissary of Maryland, spent less than one year in the New World, but that period convinced Bray that the American churches needed substantial help. To provide it, Bray organized two societies: The Society for Promoting Christian Knowledge (S.P.C.K., 1698), and the Society for Propagation of the Gospel (S.P.G, 1701). The S.P.C.K. provided libraries for colonial clergymen to equip them to tutor or to teach a small school and, thus, supplement their incomes.

The S.P.G. was to recruit priests for the colonies and to convert the Native Americans. While the S.P.G. provided a few ministers for the middle and southern colonies, much energy (and funds) went toward founding Anglican churches in New England, the most churched place in America.

Colonial Anglicans had no bishops, and hence confirmation was unavailable and parish priests had to consecrate church buildings and cemeteries. More seriously, no one had the authority to discipline ministers when they deviated from ecclesiastical or moral norms.

New England

The New England colonists had less difficulty establishing an American form of church life. Except for the Plymouth settlers, the New Englanders were non-separating Puritans who wanted to remake the Church of England in a more Genevan mode. Despite harassment during the reigns of Elizabeth I and James I, they had remained loyal to the church. Even when Bishop Laud drove them from England, they did not denounce the Anglican Church as a false or un-Christian body. Instead, they hoped that their American experiment might be an example to the people at home.

The Puritans arrived in the New World short on practical experience. While they knew what they wanted to avoid ecclesiastically, their leaders had not planned the details of church life. Some historians believe that Massachusetts churches learned their polity from the Separatists at Plymouth. Yet the New England Way's basic principle—the authority of the local church to order its own affairs—was implied in the colonial situation. As new towns (parishes) were created, the membership elected officers, ordained elders, and established discipline. Each church was united by a covenant that set forth its faith and practice. While church members were the only people with a vote on the minister, the towns (outside Boston) set the pastor's salary. In the seventeenth century most New England ministers served one parish during their professional career. A handful of New Englanders believed that presbyterianism was a more biblical solution, and in 1707 Connecticut adopted the Saybrook Platform that incorporated some Presbyterian practices.

The distinctive element in Puritan ecclesiology was the insistence that all members be "visible saints." A visible saint was an individual who had stood before the church (in the case of women before the deacons) and related the details of their conversion experience. The requirement was easily fulfilled by most first-generation settlers. Problems came later when many adult children of the saints were not converted and, hence, were ineligible to have their own children baptized. The Puritan solution was pragmatic. The pastors met in 1657 and allowed unconverted persons, if they were the children of saints, to affirm the covenant and have their children baptized. Thus New England churches had two classes of members: those in full communion and those in covenant.

The complexity of New England church life came from the Reformed practice of fencing the table. St. Paul had warned against unworthy participation in 1 Corinthians 11. In Scottish Presbyterianism the session (the governing body of the congregation) issued small coins or tokens to those whose lives (in an opinion of charity) evidenced Christian commitment. In New England the churches supplemented table discipline with rigorous requirements for church membership.

Solomon Stoddard (1643–1729), the energetic pastor of Northampton in western Massachusetts, proposed that the churches open the Lord's Supper to all not scandalous in life. He believed that the Lord's

Supper was one way that God brought sinners to saving grace (a "converting ordinance"). While Stoddard's own congregation followed his lead, few others did.

Seventeenth-century New England worship was plain. The church buildings, called meetinghouses, were simple structures with clear (not stained) glass windows, a small table, and a central pulpit and sounding board. The Sabbath service (morning and afternoon) consisted of a few psalms, a long pastoral prayer, and a sermon of an hour or more that was the center of the service. Sermons were plain in their language, clear in their application, and biblical in their content. Sabbath observation was itself worship. New England's Sunday began at sunset on Saturday evening and continued to sundown on Sunday. The faithful did no work on that day, and families often held private devotions.

The social theory that united New England life was the covenant theology. For the Puritans, God usually dealt with humankind through covenants or agreements. Such agreements with God regulated every area of New England life. Families were "little commonwealths," established by covenants; towns and congregations organized around covenants, and the region was united to God through a covenant. The Puritans believed that God punished social and political entities in this life just as God judged individual malefactors in the next. Thus earthquakes, Indian wars, and other disasters caused both ministers and people to search their hearts for secret sin on days of fasting and repentance.

The covenant theology seemed to demand uniformity, and the Puritans were as willing to punish those who violated the First Table of the Law as those who violated the Second. In 1636, Roger Williams (c. 1603–83) fled to Rhode Island after his arrest for demanding that the colony separate church and state. A year later, the authorities exiled Anne Hutchinson (1591–1643), a popular leader of prayer services, for her deviant views on saving grace. Mistress Anne and her followers also went to Rhode Island.

New England's Puritans reserved their most severe punishments for Baptists and Quakers. In his *Ill News from New England*, Dr. John Clarke (1609–79), the founder of the Baptist Church in Newport, Rhode Island, reported incident after incident of Baptists being whipped from town to town in the Bay Colony. The Society of Friends offended the Puritans even more. If Quaker missionaries arrived in Massachusetts, they were to be whipped publicly and then deported. When these measures failed to keep the Quakers out, the Massachusetts Bay Colony hanged William Robinson and Marmaduke Stephenson on Boston

Common in 1659. Massachusetts officials halted their persecution of the Quakers only after Charles II ordered that accused Quakers be returned to London for trial at New England's expense. Like the Baptists, the Quakers went to Rhode Island where they established prosperous settlements.

While historians still debate the exact rate of New England literacy, the region's men and women were among the most educated in the world. Parents taught children to read at an early age—often by imitating their elders—and the laws required the establishment of schools in every town. Most children could recite the catechism and even poor people committed much of the Scripture to memory. Printing was established early, and despite economic hardships New Englanders purchased many books, especially sermons. Harvard College, founded in 1636, stood at the top of the educational system. New Englanders kept abreast of the latest intellectual developments in England, including the scientific work of the Royal Society, and their ministers published extensively.

Other Churches

Both the Anglican South and Reformed New England attempted to continue the ideal of the *Corpus Christianum* in the New World. Although governments erected strong establishments in Connecticut, Massachusetts, Virginia, and Maryland, dissenters flourished in every colony. Eventually, every colony adopted laws guaranteeing a measure of toleration to its Christian minorities. However, these early establishments were not the whole story. Some settlers came to America planning to establish churches on a voluntary basis. Rhode Island turned out to be more prophetic of America's future than were its larger neighbors and adversaries.

In 1634 the *Ark and the Dove* arrived in the Potomac river with settlers for a new colony, Maryland. The Baltimore family, which owned the colony, believed that they could establish an ideal feudal order in the New World, complete with manors, quitrents, and social ranking. Since the proprietors converted to Catholicism after receiving the grant, the Baltimore's envisioned their colony as a place of refuge for Catholic gentry. Unfortunately many immigrants were Protestants. Despite Maryland's liberal toleration laws, Catholics and Protestants struggled for political power and economic rewards. In the early eighteenth century Maryland changed course, established the Anglican Church, and passed laws prohibiting Catholic worship.

Pennsylvania was the home of many free churches. William Penn (1644–1738), an English Quaker who traded a crown debt for land in America, was a practical idealist. Penn believed deeply in religious freedom—his Holy Experiment—and wanted to prove that it offered faith superior opportunities. To secure this ideal, Pennsylvania had few religious qualifications for voting and made it easy for congregations to secure legal incorporation. Penn also carefully recruited settlers from different religious backgrounds. Not only were Quakers welcome, but Penn's agents sold land to Baptists, Presbyterians, Anglicans, Lutherans, German Anabaptists, and others.

Pennsylvania and the adjacent colony of New Jersey were particularly important for American Presbyterianism. New Englanders migrating into the middle colonies and Scots-Irish immigrants formed the first Presbyterian churches. The Presbyterian missionary Francis Makemie (1658–1708) organized churches in Barbados, Maryland, Virginia, New York, and New England. The first American Presbytery met in Philadelphia in 1706. The Adopting Act (1729) set the terms of subscription to the Westminster Confession and limited the work of the synod to administrative matters.

Baptists, largely from Welsh churches, established their first association in Philadelphia in 1707. The new body adopted the Second London Confession (a version of the Presbyterian Westminster Confession edited to include the Baptist understanding of baptism and the relation of church and state). To educate other Baptists the Association also published its minutes and the works of prominent Baptist theologians.

The various German groups had more difficulty adjusting to life in English North America. The Anabaptists avoided the main settlements and established their own, almost self-contained, communities where they could keep their faith pure. Immigrants from a Reformed or Lutheran background had a more serious problem. In Germany the state had provided the church buildings, appointed pastors, and supervised church life. Missionaries from the Pietist center at Halle, including Henry Melchoir Muhlenberg (1711–87), eventually came and provided the Lutheran settlers with needed ecclesiastical and theological guidance.

CHAPTER SIX

INNER FAITH:
PIETISTS, PURITANS,
AND PRECISIONISTS

The question of authority obsessed the second Protestant generation. As in contemporary Catholicism, theologians defined faith as assent to religious truth. Synods in the various national churches adopted official confessions, and the various states adopted acts of uniformity making these creeds legally binding. Theologians defined Protestantism in terms of the authority of the Scriptures (the Reformation's formal principle) and justification by faith (the Reformation's material principle). From these maxims, they constructed theological systems, filled out by Aristotelian logic, that strained to answer every possible theological question.

Orthodox Protestant theology had little place for the experiential. But in the seventeenth century Puritans and Pietists turned to a more lively faith. Their hermeneutic was simple: Paul's doctrine of justification was interpreted through John's doctrine of the new birth. Since John 3 discussed the Holy Spirit, this understanding of conversion also renewed interest in sanctification.

The synthesis of the Pauline understanding of justification and the Johanine emphasis on the Spirit is the *Pietist principle*. Whenever Pietism became part of Protestant church life, the Pietist principle inspired people to experience a strong sense of God's presence, to work actively for God's Kingdom, and to become involved in evangelism. While outsiders frequently referred derisively to those who held to this style of faith as Puritans, Precisionists, or Pietists, they usually called themselves "the godly."

A Problem in Reformed Theology

Most people associate Reformed theology with the doctrine of election. For the scions of John Calvin, God decreed before the foundations of the world that Christ would save some. Since no Calvinist ever feared a syllogism, it was logical to conclude that God's election of some to salvation meant that God eternally abandoned others. In the earliest stages of the tradition, this teaching caused little anxiety. Most Reformed Christians, including Calvin himself, believed that participation in the visible church could give one confidence in one's election. However, when the Reformed churches turned to the personal—rather than the corporate—dimensions of faith, anxieties rose. Calvinism weakened the individual's spiritual confidence further by distinguishing between saving faith and a merely historical belief. Individuals could believe every word of the Scriptures and be damned at the last judgment.

This anxiety was particularly acute in England. The struggle to "purify" the Church of England naturally made those who participated uneasy. What if one had made the wrong choice? Further, England was the first country in which modernization changed traditional social organization. The newer forms of social life rewarded personal achievement and enterprise. Such social change was painful for many, including those who benefitted from it, and was often internalized as guilt.

Since God realized the dreadful divine decrees through the providential ordering of history, personal biographies were narratives of divine grace. The individual might emotionally experience the Pauline order of salvation (confession of sin, justification, glorification). Since each saint's conversion was unique, the Puritans recorded their conversions in private diaries, sermons, and other documents. The Baptist John Bunyan (1628–88) told of his personal struggle in *Grace Abounding to the Chief of Sinners* (1666), and summarized many conversions in *Pilgrim's Progress* (1678, 1684).

The godly preferred plain preaching, because it depicted the plight of the individual sinner clearly. The Puritan sermon began with the exposition of a specific biblical text, moved to a statement of the teaching (doctrine) contained in the passage, and ended with an application of the passage to the life of the hearer.

To secure conversions, the Puritans needed able and godly preachers. Many were trained at the University of Cambridge, especially at Christ and Emmanuel Colleges. Fellows of these schools often led their students through the conversion experience. Once the students were saved, the Fellows found them positions. Except for Oliver Cromwell

England's rulers favored the moderate and high church wings of the Church. To evade this preference, the Puritans mastered English canon law, placing their preachers wherever they might secure a living. In many parishes Puritan lay people established a lectureship, supported by voluntary contributions, to hire a minister to teach them the Scriptures. In addition, Puritan leaders placed students in the chaplaincies of such institutions as the Inns of Court (schools that taught the common law). The godly also took advantage of such privileges as the right of any cleric to preach at certain landmarks, such as Paul's Cross.

Intellectual issues intrigued the Puritans, and the Puritan insistence on biblical authority may have been a major factor in the rise of English science. However, the Puritans were not speculative theologians. Their genius lay more in soteriology (the doctrine of salvation). The two most influential Puritan theologians were William Perkins (1558–1602) and his student William Ames (1576–1633).

Both Ames and Perkins employed the logic and rhetoric of Peter Ramus (1515–72) in their theology. Ramus, a French Protestant martyr, proposed that theologians abandon Aristotle and adopt a logic that more closely followed the actual pattern of human thought. For Ramus, people thought by dividing topics into dichotomies or pairs of component parts. Naturally, each division could be divided again and again until the whole topic was explored. Although dichotomies were useful as rhetorical devices, Ramus and his followers believed that their analytical use might also clarify the meaning of any material, including the Bible.

Despite Perkins's and Ames's anti-Catholicism, both also found the Catholic "cases of conscience" a useful model for practical theology. The original purpose of the cases of conscience was to guide the priest in the confessional by examining every moral act for the degree of sin involved in its commission. However, when read through Puritan eyes, this casuistry assumed a different meaning. Puritans replaced the traditional Catholic questions regarding moral conduct with inquiries about whether a person was elect.

Perkins and Ames began their analysis of conversion with the conscience, an indwelling sense of right and wrong that neither reason nor emotion could deceive in the long run. Conscience unmasked human pretensions and exposed sin for what it was. Although Perkins and Ames insisted that conscience was God's servant, the implications of their thought went beyond that orthodox conclusion. While Ames and Perkins refused to admit that conscience was the voice of God within, such radicals as the Quaker George Fox (1624–91) did indeed draw that conclusion.

Perkins and Ames described the course of conversion or the order of salvation (*ordo salutis*) in terms of God's effects on the conscience. The process began when God's ordinary providence provided a preacher of the gospel who could stir the sinner's heart. This initial encounter with God mortified the sinner, although human pride sought to deny that experience. In the next stage, the sinner realized that his or her offense was a sin against a holy God and that he or she deserved eternal death for it. Ames and Perkins called this conviction. Sinners under conviction became desperate. They sought security in godly parents, their own devotion to the church, or their willingness to live a holy life. Yet conscience struck down their rationalizations; conviction was not necessarily a mark of grace, and both theologians assumed that many who experienced this preliminary awakening were ultimately lost. At some point God's Holy Spirit intervened and the sinner found religious peace. Some Puritans had a vivid sense of the day and the hour of their salvation, but neither Ames nor Perkins believed that the sinner needed to know when God changed his or her innermost being.

Neither theologian gave infallible signs of saving grace. God worked in mysterious ways to redeem God's own. The best of divines could only describe God's ordinary or usual way of acting. Perkins and Ames did note that the converted sinner usually abandoned conscious sin and lived in obedience to Christ. Holy obedience as a mark of grace was related to the Puritan love of the Old Testament law.

Dutch Precisionists

Seventeenth-century Holland had many similarities to England. The nation passed through a religious civil war that left it permanently divided between a Catholic south (modern Belgium) and a Protestant north (the Netherlands). Further, the Dutch were a trading nation, oriented toward the sea. Like the English, they were beginning modernization in the seventeenth century.

Contemporaries called the Dutch version of the Puritan movement Precisionism. They intended the term, like the English word "Puritan," as an insult. Implicitly, the affront tied the Precisionists to the ancient Donatist heresy. Unfortunately, the term also implied that the Dutch movement was uniform. As with the Puritans, the Precisionists were a diverse group that included people with differing perspectives. Like the

Puritans, they would have preferred that people call them simply "the godly."

Dutch Precisionism's ethos is hard to describe. The movement had five characteristic qualities. (1) An emphasis on an emotional and mystical experience of rebirth. (2) A practical legalism that urged people to strict Sabbath observance and the denial of such worldly pleasures as card-playing and dancing. (3) Programs of complete religious instruction for both children and adults that were ideally conducted in small groups. (4) A strong doctrine of the Christian family and an emphasis on the importance of family devotions and prayers. And (5) a belief that a new form of pious ministerial preparation was needed to replace the often worldly programs of the universities.

The route by which Puritan emphases entered Holland is clear. Besides formal theological treatises, written in Latin, many young Dutch ministerial candidates went to England to observe churches there and to study practical divinity. Further, many Dutch pastors, especially in Amsterdam, knew English, and studied such Puritan stalwarts as John Dod(d), Arthur Hildersam(e), and Lewis Bayle.

William Teelinck, the parent of Dutch Pietism, described his own encounter with Puritanism in his *Housebook*. While in England, the family devotions of his host deeply stirred Teelinck's heart. Their example and his own reading awakened his conscience. Soon Teelinck was under conviction. After an inner struggle, God renewed his faith. When Teelinck returned to Holland, he urged others to experience conversion as well.

William Ames (1576–1663) had a lasting influence on Dutch theology. Ames emigrated to Holland after his strong stands against wearing the surplice and card-playing offended the English authorities. In Holland Ames became a popular university teacher. Ames' *Medulla Theologiae* (*The Marrow of Theology*)—the most widely read Puritan text in Holland, England, Germany, and New England—summarized his Cambridge teachers' theology.

The *Marrow* was thoroughly anti-scholastic. Ames expanded the Protestant doctrine of the inspiration of the Scriptures to include the need for the Holy Spirit to interpret the Sacred Text. Before Ames, most Protestant theologians argued that the biblical message could be understood by anyone who could read the ancient languages. Thus the only difference between believer and unbeliever lay in the reception or application of Scripture. In contrast, Ames argued that only the regenerate knew the true meaning of the Bible. The Book meant one thing to the natural person who saw only its bare bones and another to the spiritual person, able to crack the bones and extract the marrow.

Ames' hermeneutics had important implications for the understanding of the ministry. If only someone with personal experience can correctly interpret the Sacred Text, then religious experience is as important as formal clerical education. While Ames, a true son of the university, did not believe that unlettered individuals ought to teach, he did maintain that only those who could unite piety and learning were fit candidates.

Mystical Heritage

The Dutch filtered Ames' theology through their own traditions. Since the late Middle Ages, practical mysticism was part of Dutch religion. Dirck Coornheert (1522–90), a popular mystical writer, spoke for many when he criticized the cold formalism of the Protestant doctrine of forensic justification. The human heart, Coornheert maintained, wanted more than the forgiveness of sins; it also desires friendship with God and participation in God. Since Ames' theology stressed the Spirit, other Dutch theologians easily combined the Puritan understanding of conversion with this Dutch mystical tradition to create their understanding of the new birth.

Medieval Dutch mystics often formed small groups of lay people and clergy for prayer. The Dutch Precisionists continued this tradition. Jadocus Lodensteyn (1620–77) advocated the use of small groups or *collegia* to develop habits of prayer and Bible study. Lodensteyn actively recruited such groups at the Dutch universities to prepare prospective Dutch ministers in piety as well as in logic.

While in a French monastic prison for heretical views, Jean de Labadie (1610–74), a Jesuit, read Calvin's *Institutes*. Allowed to escape, Labadie went to Holland where he became a popular Precisionist preacher and teacher. An extended controversy with the Dutch authorities led to his exile in Switzerland where his private lectures were attended by many University of Geneva students. However, the Swiss soon tired of Labadie's excesses. They exiled Labadie, who ended his career leading a small house church and communal sect in Amsterdam.

In his *Reformation of the Church Through the Pastoral Office*, Labadie reasoned that the key to the reform of the church was the ministry. Since universities taught only the formal doctrines of divinity, the Dutch should not train their ministers in such institutions. Instead, Labadie proposed the creation of seminaries where the only candidates would be those who had experienced saving grace. A "born again" student body would devote its time to Bible study and spiritual reading. Once the candidates completed the course, Labadie believed that they ought to devote themselves to a practical ministry of pastoral visitation, religious education, prayer meetings, the care of souls, and enthusiastic preaching.

German Developments

Pietism traveled from Holland to the German speaking areas of Europe through the ethnically similar areas of Northern Germany. Theodore Untereyck (1635–93) was typical of the early German Pietists. Trained in Holland, Untereyck organized *collegia* and spent much time in personal religious counseling. Untereyck's preaching led to the conversion of the musician Joachim Neander (1650–80), whose classic "Praise to the Lord, the King of Creation" is still popular.

Later forms of German Pietism developed in the various Lutheran states. Lutheranism did not generate the intense tensions engendered by Reformed theology, perhaps because the sacraments provided Lutherans an objective assurance of salvation. Lutheran ministers might urge fearful parishioners to remember their baptism or to trust the Eucharistic promises.

Like the Dutch, the Germans had a longstanding mystical tradition. As a young scholar, Martin Luther had published the *German Theology*, a mystical classic, and composed devotional works himself throughout his career. Luther's most noted successor as a devotionalist was Johann Arndt (1555–1621), whose *True Christianity* is a spiritual masterpiece still read in Germany. Arndt began his studies in the faculty of medicine. During a serious illness he experienced a call to the ministry. Arndt reacted negatively to the scholastic theology popular in his time, which he believed dealt primarily with theological controversies. In contrast, real preaching touched the heart.

The influence of the mystic Jacob Boehme (1575–1624) on later German developments is difficult to determine. Boehme was an eccentric whose many friends included orthodox Lutherans, radicals, alchemist, and astrologers. From these diverse sources, Boehme developed a system of thought that sought to reconcile opposites, affirm the spiritual nature of the world, and attest symbolism in religion. The state church condemned Boehme after his death and exhumed and burned his body. Nonetheless, those who wanted a more living faith often read Boehme's books secretly.

Philip Jacob Spener (1635–1705) founded German Pietism. Spener was born in a small village in Alsace near Strassburg, a city with a Reformed Church government and a Lutheran theology. After Spener's graduation from the University of Strassburg, he moved to Geneva. There he studied with the great Hebraist John Buxton, and met Jean de Labadie. He also read widely in English Puritan literature, including the works of Louis Bayle and Richard Baxter.

Following his studies, Spener moved to Frankfurt where the city council appointed him superintendent of the city's churches. He organized *collegia pietatis*—small groups of laymen and women—for prayer, bible study, and social ministry. Spener did not use small groups in his later positions in Dresden or Berlin. More important for Spener were voluntary societies to perform religious and charitable tasks. He established societies to maintain homes for those orphaned by the Thirty Years War, to alleviate poverty, and to minister to the Jews. Wherever he was employed, Spener taught catecheticals, confirmation, and Bible classes.

Spener published his program in his *Pia Desideria* (1675), originally an introduction to some sermons by Johann Arndt. The book was biting. The principal problem of the German churches, Spener claimed, was the ministry's low spiritual state. The clergy had substituted assent to dogmatic theology for biblical faith and were more concerned with their private disputes than with the Scriptures. German churches needed to return to the Bible, Spener thundered. Pastors should read the Scriptures publicly aloud every day for the illiterate, make the Bible the subject of all preaching, and teach it to any person who was interested. Ministers needed to spend more time ministering to their people, especially through visitation and pastoral care, and less time on their literary pursuits. Further, they needed to speak frankly about such matters as the German sin of drunkenness and to demand that their people reform their lives.

Spener's strong words provoked much opposition. The theologians of the University of Wittenberg, which prided itself on its unbending orthodoxy, found more than 200 errors in Spener's writings. Orthodox ministers frequently denounced him from the pulpit. Fortunately for Spener, he was a personal friend of the king of Prussia.

August Hermann Francke (1663–1727), whose influence extended from Russia to New England, was an important disciple of Spener. Francke became a Pietist almost by accident. As a young Hebrew professor at the University of Leipzig he angered his senior colleagues by establishing a class in the Hebrew Old Testament. When Francke's course enrollment exceeded the number in his colleague's class, taught from the Latin translation, the Faculty dismissed the young upstart. Francke visited Spener while looking for work and fell under the older pastor's spell.

Spener used his influence with the Prussian king to have Francke appointed rector of the new royal university at Halle. Francke immediately began a reform of university education, replacing lectures in Latin with lectures in German and modernizing the study of law and theology. In conjunction with the university, Francke organized one of the first schools of education and opened a school for girls.

Francke wanted to make Halle a model Christian university. He established an orphanage nearby that inspired other Christians, including George Whitefield, who founded a similar institution in Georgia. When the king of Denmark appealed to Halle for missionaries to send to India, Francke responded by enlisting Bartholomaus Ziegenberg and Heinrich Plutschau and establishing a society to support their work. Together with Karl von Canstein, a relative, Francke organized the Canstein Bible Society to make copies of the Bible available to every German home. Using new technical methods, the Society could sell New Testaments for only a few pennies and complete Bibles for little more.

Francke continued Pietism's alliance with the Prussian government and broadened the movement to include many members of the nobility and officer corps. One reason for Pietism's popularity may have been its role in the modernization of Germany. Pietism stressed the individual, promoted education, and taught self-discipline. Equally important, Pietism's postmillennial optimism promoted confidence in the future.

South German Pietism

Although inspired by Spener and Francke, south German Pietism was distinguished by its thoroughgoing biblicism. Johannes Albrecht Bengel (1687–1752), a teacher at the Cloister school at Denkendorf, devoted his life to the study of the Greek New Testament. In 1734, he published his own version of the text with an introduction that set forth his principles for resolving conflicting readings. While much of Bengel's method appears conservative today, many of his critical rules, including the axiom that the most difficult reading is preferred, are still followed.

Bengel, unlike most Pietists, was a convinced premillennialist who believed that he could decipher the chronology of the Book of Revelation.

After an exhaustive study of the various dates in the Bible, Bengel concluded that Christ would return early in the nineteenth century.

Christoph Oetinger (1702–82) began another more speculative stream in South German Pietism. Oetinger believed that the new world-view, associated with Newton and modern astronomy, required a new metaphysics. For him, God worked in and through the process of nature. Hence people might find God in the depths of their experience, especially, their apperception of the natural world. Later German philosophers and metaphysicians, including Hegel, found fruitful suggestions for their work in Oetinger's analyses of the brave new world of science.

CHAPTER SEVEN

THE ENLIGHTENMENT

The phrase "The Enlightenment" is a grand historical generalization that refers to a shift in the attitudes of European and North American cultural leaders. The Enlightenment began with the 1687 publication of Sir Isaac Newton's (1642–1727) *Philosophiae Naturalis Principia Mathematica* and ended roughly with the 1789 French Revolution. Immanuel Kant (1724–1804) used the term *Aufklärung* (literally, "clearing" or "cleaning up") to describe the intellectual changes. As Kant understood his times, humankind's tutelage to authority was over, humanity had "come of age," and people were ready to take responsibility for their own thought and belief.

The Enlightenment's keynote was science. The advances made in natural philosophy astounded both intellectuals and ordinary people. New mathematical techniques, especially calculus, dispelled many cosmic mysteries. Further, the microscope revealed a universe that the unaided eye could not see. All areas of human investigation seemed ready to deliver their secrets, and people began to apply the methods of scientific reasoning to medicine, economics, politics, and religion.

Enlightenment Motifs

Although the leading Enlightenment thinkers did not agree with each other, they often appealed to six common concepts.

1. *Reason*: Although eighteenth-century authors frequently referred to Reason with a capital letter, they rarely defined the term's meaning precisely. In much eighteenth-century literature, the term meant simply thinking about something. That which was "reasonable" involved the use of ordinary human intelligence or common sense.

Yet the term also had a more technical connotation. Reason might refer to the type of thought associated with Sir Isaac Newton's mathematical physics, commonly called induction. Inductive reasoning requires the thinker to find a common thread in a mass of data. Induction proceeded analytically. To solve a problem, one broke it down into its component parts. A complex phenomenon was assumed to be composed of smaller units that might be understood more easily. Reason was also critical. The word "criticism" comes from the Greek word *krinein* meaning to judge or to separate. The rational person separated or judged ideas or data to make the common elements more clear.

2. *Autonomy*: Belief in Reason was closely connected to belief in autonomy. Autonomy referred to the need for human beings to trust their individual judgment about intellectual, moral, and spiritual matters. In other words, individuals should not accept authority without examining the evidence independently. Autonomy did not mean that all individuals could know everything about the world. Instead, it meant that human knowledge could be attained through universally available means; that is, through a solid method of investigation.

3. *Nature*: Eighteenth-century literature frequently referred to the need for human beings to live in accord with Nature, to study Nature, or find the secrets of Nature (again, the use of capitalization in "Nature" is significant). A natural explanation did not include supernatural realities. When the Enlightened said that illness was natural they meant that neither demons, bad karma nor divine punishment caused sickness. The Natural was whatever agreed with scientific law and to live in accord with Nature was to work with natural law and not against it. Thus technology testified to the power of Nature.

Particularly toward the end of the period, a few thinkers used the term "natural" to refer to anything untouched by civilization. Literature often pictured Native Americans as Noble Savages with a morality uncorrupted by the chicanery of Europe. In a similar vein landscape painting was valued because it revealed the essence of Nature. In *Émile*, Jean-Jacques Rousseau (1712–78) explored this understanding of Nature. Rousseau argued that civilization had corrupted the primitive original human state, and humankind had to return to a simpler time to find its true potential. But this could only be done if the individual relinquished his or her freedom and surrendered to the common will.

4. *Tolerance*: The eighteenth century was an age of tolerance. The terrible religious wars, heresy trials, and witch-burnings of the seventeenth century convinced many that individuals had a right to their own beliefs. Both the mind and the conscience should be free from govern-

mental coercion. Most believed that all religions contributed to public morality, and that the state, consequently, did not need to distinguish between them.

Intellectuals did not base their confidence in tolerance on a lack of belief. Rather, they affirmed tolerance because they thought that truth would sooner or later banish error. The model was science where the publication of better theories quickly replaced older understandings. The progressive nature of science was assumed to apply to metaphysics and religion. Modern people would improve their understanding of ultimate reality just as they had improved their understanding of physics. The most radical advocates of tolerance, such as the Scottish philosopher Adam Smith (1723–90), argued that governments should extend toleration to the economic realm.

5. *Optimism*: The savants' faith in the human future was often misunderstood. Philosopher Gottfried Wilhelm Leibniz (1646–1716), the co-inventor of calculus with Isaac Newton, taught in his *Theodicy* (1710) that this was the best of all possible worlds. Leibniz probably meant by this that the world was as just and fair as God could make it, given the restrictions of moral and natural law. Yet some people understood him to say that this world was in principle perfect. Voltaire mocked this reading of Leibniz in his novel *Candide* (1759), in which undeserved and meaningless evil strikes the hero repeatedly.

The position that Voltaire caricatured so effectively was a minority view. Most eighteenth-century thinkers confined themselves to the belief that, while evil could never be completely overcome, people could improve the world. A true philanthropist (lover of humankind) would construct hospitals, aid the poor, extend education, and reform the mechanism of government.

Again the model for such philanthropic efforts was science. Just as our worldly knowledge had improved, so might the human condition. There was some evidence to support this view. Eighteenth-century middle-classed people were better fed and housed than many nobles had been earlier. Both art and music were available to a wider audience than ever before. Education, particularly in such Protestant countries as Prussia, Scotland, and Holland, had made great strides, and these states (along with Britain's New England colonies) were almost universally literate.

6. *Humanism*: In the eighteenth century educated men and women knew classical literature as well or better than the writings in their own languages. The great authors of Greek and Latin antiquity believed that

human beings were the measure of all things and that, therefore, the "proper study of man was man."

The thinkers of the eighteenth century often expressed their humanism through their deep concern with politics and political theory. Intellectuals revived ancient debates about the best form of government. For instance, enlightened or benevolent despots believed that only a strong government, similar to that of the great "Sun King" of France, Louis XIV (1638–1715), was equal to the present task of government. Frederick the Great of Prussia (1713–86) used his almost unlimited power to make his North German kingdom an advanced European state.

The American revolutionaries were excellent Enlightenment political theorists, and the United States Constitution was the best summary of their conclusions. Further, the writings of such men as Thomas Jefferson (1743–1826) and Benjamin Franklin (1706–90) contained acute analyses of the problems of governing a large, diverse nation.

Humanism also referred to the humanities. German professors developed the seminar, a small group of teachers and students, to help future professors master the increasingly complex methods of research. In such groups the students also helped their professor explore the large amount of data available on different subjects.

Representative People and Movements

René Descartes (1596–1650) began his career as an officer in the French army, and then moved to Holland where he developed analytical geometry and made major contributions to the theory of exponents and negative roots. Descartes' operative understanding of science was the clarity and precision of mathematical ideas. Yet, Descartes knew that most human thought falls short of the mathematical ideal. In his *Discourse on Method*, Descartes argued that people had an obligation to doubt everything that they could. If we did so, he maintained, all we could know with certainty was God's and our own existence. From this simple foundation, we should be able to derive all other knowledge. Descartes' system posited a dualism of inner assurance and outer skepticism.

Although Leibniz was more than Descartes' follower, he pursued a similar philosophical approach. Like his French counterpart, Leibniz was a brilliant mathematician, captivated by the beauty and rational coherence of numbers. Since the world must be composed of logically irreducible elements, which Leibniz called monads, we could learn all truth by exploring the relationships between these logical atoms. Hence the ultimate goal of science was a system that related everything to the whole universe.

Leibniz's disciple Christian Wolff (1779–1754) simplified his thought and made it available to academic audiences. Wolff believed that philosophy needed a logical system that contained all present and future knowledge. While Wolff knew that vast territories were yet unexplored by reason, he believed that it was only a matter of time before scientists completed a cognitive model of the universe.

The second major philosophic stream was British empiricism. Using the new physics as their intellectual model, English and Scottish philosophers limited knowledge to what people learned from ordinary human experience. Although Francis Bacon (1561–1626) has often been cited as the originator of this perspective, empiricism developed from the work of John Locke (1632–1704), an English physician and political philosopher. Locke reasoned that human beings were born with no preexisting knowledge (in an often quoted phrase, he called the mind a *tabula rasa* or clean slate) and learned everything through their own or others' experiences.

David Hume (1711–76), a historian and conservative political theorist, argued that Locke was insufficiently analytical. What we experience is limited. For example, when one billiard ball hits another, we say that the first ball "caused" the second to move. This is not necessarily so. All that we have seen is a sequence in which event B follows event A temporally. The explanation of this relationship as "causation" may be only a mental habit.

The third stream may be called literary philosophy. In the eighteenth century artists, musicians, and writers began to free themselves from the patronage system and present their works on the open market. Many lived on the brink of economic disaster, and the intelligentsia (as they were later called) had to be well-informed to survive.

The French writer François-Marie Arouet de Voltaire (1694–1778), known simply as Voltaire, combined knowledge, an excellent style, and clear analysis in his writings, which earned him a substantial living. Voltaire was largely responsible for the introduction of English philosophy and science into France. In addition, he made a major contribution to historiography in his *The Age of Louis XIV*, an early cultural study.

Gotthold Ephraim Lessing (1729–81) held a position in German literature similar to that of Voltaire in French letters. Lessing was a dramatist whose essays were largely responsible for the German discovery of Shakespeare. His best-known play was *Nathan the Wise*, an appeal for toleration, in which the story of three brothers is told. The father had inherited a magic ring from his ancestors that guaranteed that its holder would possess true virtue. When the time came to pass the ring to the son of his choice, the father gave rings of identical appearance to all three brothers. Naturally, the brothers fought over whose ring was the true one, but the conclusion was obvious: each should live as if his own ring were real.

The poet Alexander Pope (1688–1744), whose "An Essay on Man" (1733) summarized contemporary philosophy, followed a similar course. Like Lessing and Voltaire, Pope had a reputation as a wit, and his "Dunciad" (1728–43), a mock epic, poked fun at the pretensions of his fellow writers.

Knowledge was no longer reserved only for an elite class of scholars but shared by all educated people. In 1771 the first edition of the *Encyclopedia Britannia* appeared. Despite government opposition, the French philosophers published their *Encyclopedia* one year later. While the editors of the encyclopedias simplified complex technical information for their readers, the popularity of such expensive works showed the deep middle-class desire for more information.

Reason and Religion

Some Enlightenment thinkers believed that the new philosophy and science supported traditional Christianity. Others believed that these discoveries meant that the church had to modify many of its central tenets. A few advocated more radical religious changes, including the replacement of Christianity by a more rational faith.

The new theologies can be traced back to the seventeenth-century Cambridge Platonists, an informal group of Cambridge dons that included Benjamin Whichcote (1609–83), John Smith (1618–52), and Ralph Cudworth (1617–88). These Cambridge philosophers wanted a theology that would not engender the revolutionary excesses of Puritanism. They found it in a mystical rationalism that avoided the extremes of atheism and fanaticism.

The Cambridge Platonists deeply influenced the Latitudinarian movement. The theme of the Latitudinarians was that reason and faith worked together to produce a life marked by balance, morality, and manners. Archbishop John Tillotson (1630–94), a popular Latitudinarian spokesperson, divided religion into natural and revealed. According to Tillotson, natural religion taught belief in one God, the necessity of virtue, and rewards and punishments. He argued that these affirmations could be verified by anyone who thought seriously. Hence, natural religion was the yardstick to use to measure claims to revelation, since a rational person would not support any religion that ignored these affirmations or did not teach them at every opportunity. Revealed religion completed natural religion by adding teachings about salvation and the afterlife.

John Locke's 1695 *The Reasonableness of Christianity as Delivered in the Scriptures* argued that all religious statements can be divided into three classes: statements in accordance with reason, statements opposed to reason, and statements above reason. An example of reasonable religious statements might be the existence of God; of unreasonable statements, the existence of witches; and of those beyond reason, the doctrine of the Trinity. Obviously, Locke theorized, a reasonable person must accept the first and reject the second class of statements. A reasonable person, Locke believed, could only believe the affirmations above reason if evidence existed for their truth. For Locke, such evidence existed in the teachings of Jesus which God validated through prophecy and miracle.

Whether deliberately or inadvertently, Tillotson and Locke raised the Christological question. Many eighteenth-century thinkers rejected the traditional doctrine of the Trinity and replaced it with a doctrine that stressed Christ's humanity and the unity of God. Most such persons remained in the established church, but Theophilus Lindsey established an independent Unitarian church in London in 1773.

Deism was a radical solution to the Christological problem. While some historians have identified Deism with belief in a "watchmaker" god who created the world and left it to run on its own energy, most deist writings were not concerned with God but with revelation. Although Edward Lord Herbert of Cherbury (1583–1648) is often identified as the first deist, eighteenth-century Deism was an extension of arguments found in John Locke's writings. In *Christianity Not Mysterious* (1696), John Toland (1670–1722) argued that revelation was not needed, since God had given humankind all it needed through reason. Matthew Tindal (1655–1733) struck a similar note in his *Christianity As Old As Creation*. Tindal argued that all religions contained a true picture of God and moral duty and only the few teachings common to all religions were obligatory on all people.

Perhaps because the deists were skeptical about revelation, they pioneered the historical and critical approach to the Scriptures. Most doubted the veracity of the miracle stories or offered rational explanations of the biblical narratives. David Hume, the Scottish skeptic, argued that no miracle story, no matter how well authenticated, was believable.

Hume reasoned that since a miracle was a violation of the laws of nature and since the laws of nature were summaries of our experience, to believe in a miracle was to deny one's own senses.

Culturally, Deism marked the beginning of a separation between Christianity and cultural life that has characterized much modern experience since. Before Deism, one could assume that the leaders of European culture were Christian. After Deism, such assumptions were no longer valid.

Apologetic Theology

In response to Deism, Christian theologians developed a new philosophical defense of Christianity. In *The Analogy of Religion, Natural and Revealed, to the Constitution and Course of Nature* (1736), Bishop Joseph Butler (1693–1752) presented the disingenuous argument that both Christianity and Deism had only probable arguments from nature. The real question, consequently, was which possibility conformed more to our experience. Butler presented many analogies to Christian theology from nature. These included biological irregularities, the apparent death of caterpillars, and unexplained phenomena, in order to show that Nature is more in line with biblical irregularities than with the rational Deist God.

Less influential, but far better argued, was William Law's (1688–1761) *The Case of Reason Against M. Tindal*. Law was a high churchman and non-juror whose *A Serious Call to A Holy and Devout Life* is a devotional classical. In his debate with Tindal, Law reasoned that Tindal and other religious liberals had misunderstood the Christian doctrine of God. The biblical God was not philosophy's unmoved mover or a deduction from earthly phenomena. This God was a mysterious being, beyond space and time, who was made known only by revelation. God did not reveal truths to aid our religious understanding; rather, God was the Truth. Further, Law pointed out that the word "nature," a favorite of the deists, had many definitions. If nature means what any being does without effort, the faith of millions of ordinary Christians proved that Christianity was "natural" to the human race.

The rational supernaturalists (sometimes called the physico-theologians) argued that nature provided evidence of design by an intelligent being. In some ways, the argument rested on an analogy. If one found a watch on the beach, one would assume that someone had made it. When we discover greater wonders in nature, such as the human eye, we may conclude that a rational being made these as well. Although his work was not original, William Paley (1743–1805) was the most famous exponent of this position. His *View of the Evidences of Christianity* (1794) was a minor classic that ministerial candidates studied for almost a century after his death.

Neologians and Scientific Theologians

Although the Enlightenment made its primary impact on Great Britain (including its North American colonies) and France, it also affected Germany. At this time, Germany was emerging from the devastation of the seventeenth-century religious wars. The governments of the various "lands"(or states) were catching up economically, socially, and militarily with the more enlightened nations of the West. Enlightenment philosophy with its emphasis on science, progress, and education was an ally in this struggle.

The Enlightenment affected German churches in a variety of ways. One was the regularization of church procedures. Beginning with Prussia, the various governments established state-administered examinations for the ministry that measured whether a prospective minister had attained a certain level of knowledge. Church bureaucracies adopted more rational organizational and financial procedures and revised ecclesiastical law in conformity with enlightenment ideals.

The German liberal theologians, commonly called the Neologians, sought to reinterpret Christianity according to the intellectual canons of the time. Johann Spalding (1714–1804), who studied with Christian Wolff and read widely in English rational theology, believed that the main purpose of religion was to produce virtue. His son-in-law Friedrich Sack (1738–1817), court preacher in Berlin, often spoke of religion as a moral style of life and a means of social elevation. For Sack, the good pastor was as concerned with public health as public prayer. The targets of the Neologians' intellectual reforms were those Lutheran teachings that they believed were survivals from the Middle Ages, including a personal devil, the eternality of hell, the substitutionary atonement, biblical infallibility, and the real presence of Christ in the sacrament of the altar.

Although the Neologians were important in the eighteenth century, the new scientific (the German word *Wissenschaft* and its derivatives has no precise English translation) theology had more lasting impact. What the scientific theologians attempted to do was to separate theological studies from their confessional base and approach religious issues apart from any preexisting commitments. Part of this effort was the division of theology into separate "disciplines" with their own methods. By the end of the century, theological encyclopedias commonly tried to show the relationship between the separate studies of Old and New Testament, Church History, Dogmatics, and Church Law.

Johann L. von Mosheim (1673–1755), although personally deeply religious, pioneered the new direction in the study of church history in his *Institutes of Ecclesiastical History* (1726) and his *History of Heresy* (2 vols., 1746–48). Mosheim used the same method of analysis and research in contemporary political history. His accounts of the doctrine of the Trinity included full discussions of the political alliances at the great councils. In biblical studies, Johann Ernesti (1707–81) completed his pioneering *Institutes of New Testament Interpretation* (1761). Johann Semler (1725–91) published his important history of the canon in his *Treatise on the Free Investigation of the Canon,* (published in four parts between 1771 and 1775).

The new scientific treatments of theology marked a new professionalism. By 1800 many accepted the belief that the best studies of the Christian tradition were those that followed the general rules of humanistic research.

Popular Enlightenment

The populace did not learn of many of the more advanced ideas of the Enlightenment until much later. Yet the new intellectual directions did influence popular Christian practice. Church buildings, whether Protestant or Catholic, were built on classical lines and the ornate decorations of the baroque period went out of fashion. Sermons tended to discuss ordinary human affairs rather than classical orthodoxy's abstractions. All churches shortened services and included more congregational singing and participation.

Christianity became more sentimental under Enlightenment influence. Christmas ceased to mark the awful mystery of the incarnation and became a festival for children, marked by family traditions and gifts. In Germany the decoration of the Christmas tree became part of the season. Worshipers wanted to experience their faith and to have a personal relationship with God that was independent of the authorities in church, state, or university.

Almost every western country accepted some measure of religious dissent as part of the human condition. The most liberal governments passed Jewish emancipation laws as a needed social reform, even if they often failed to repeal older discriminatory legislation. The churches also had to find voluntary ways to secure their members' loyalty and enlist them in the Christian cause. In this sense, toleration affected every aspect of church life. For example, evangelism (neglected by most ecclesiastical leaders for almost a millennium) became a necessity as did a larger measure of lay leadership. The Enlightenment forced the churches to become a "popular" movement.

CHAPTER EIGHT

THE NEW WINE OF EVANGELICAL FAITH

Nicholaus Ludwig Count von Zinzendorf (1700–1760) and the Moravians sparked a pietist renewal movement in Germany that influenced other evangelical leaders, including John Wesley. Originally the Moravians were a branch of the Hussites (followers of John Hus), the *Unitas Fratum* persecuted in Bohemia and Moravia. When Zinzendorf met their leaders they lacked a permanent home. Zinzendorf offered these pilgrims sanctuary on his property subject to the condition that they commune in the state church. Aside from this, the Moravians were to retain their own customs, elect their own pastors and bishops, and live a communal life. Their new Saxon settlement was named *Herrnhut*, "the Lord will protect."

Orphaned at an early age, Zinzendorf was reared by his grandmother, Henrietta von Gersdorf, a stern pietist, who funded many pietist voluntary associations. As a child Zinzendorf wrote passionate love letters to Jesus in which he promised to give his life for his Master's cause. However, Zinzendorf's childhood piety shattered when his tutors introduced him to modern scientific and literary thought. He experienced periods of doubt throughout his life.

Like others who have wrestled with doubt, Zinzendorf struggled to find religious security through Christian activism. While a student at the Universities of Halle and Wittenberg (where he was sent by his uncle to cool his spiritual ardor), he organized small groups of students for prayer and missionary work. Zinzendorf called one such *ecclesiola in ecclesia* ("little church within the church") "The Order of the Mustard Seed" to reflect his conviction that a handful of faithful Christians might revive the whole church.

Following graduation, Zinzendorf toured the various centers of Christian activity in Europe instead of taking a traditional *Wanderjahr* (year of traveling). When the Count returned, he married Erdmuth Dorothea von Reuss. On their honeymoon the two young people dedicated their marriage to the coming of the Kingdom. Shortly afterwards Zinzendorf and his friends Johann A. Rothe, pastor of the Bertelsdorf church, Melchoir Schäffer, pastor at Görlitz, and Francis von Wattewille formed a committee to work for a Christian revival in Germany.

The Moravian refugees fit into these plans. While Zinzendorf allowed the Moravians to elect their own officers, the Count became their leader shortly after they settled on his estate, and D. E. Jablonski, the Berlin court preacher and Moravian bishop, gave Zinzendorf episcopal consecration in 1737.

Zinzendorf inspired the Moravians to undertake two different ministries. First, the Moravians worked to renew the European state churches. Sending missioners to various European cities, the Moravians established small groups for preaching and prayer. The purpose of these meetings was not to win converts to the Moravian movement, but rather to regenerate the state churches from within by reviving individual piety and devotion. In their meetings the Moravians shared their love of church music, taught a personal form of Bible study, and urged people to come to Christ.

Second, the Moravians carried the gospel to foreign lands. Rather than sending individuals, the Moravians moved an entire community. Their hope was that the Moravian colony would convince unbelievers of the truth of Christianity by their example as well as their preaching. Missionary communities were sent to Greenland, North Carolina, Pennsylvania, and South Africa.

The Moravians divided their communities into choirs, and every member had a place in the church's worship. They also revived many ancient church practices, including the love feast or *agape*, the Easter Sunrise Service, and the watchnight service.

The Count, especially in his early years, focused on Christ's blood and wounds, picturing the atonement in personal, almost sentimental language. Each person's sins had wounded the Lord. His exaggerated language about the cross contributed to his exile from Saxony in 1736 to 1747. But Zinzendorf also pioneered ideas that later became modern commonplaces. He rejected the orthodox identification of theology with authoritative doctrines, understood as truths drawn directly from the Scriptures. Instead, Zinzendorf argued that true religion was a matter of the heart; that is, of the emotions, feelings, and sentiments. Every attempt to explain the inexplicable had only relative value. Thus, creeds and confessions have a paradoxical status. They are true in their witness to a past generation's Christian experience; they are false, since Christ is always more than the past church affirmed.

Zinzendorf's response to modern science was a thorough Christo-centricism that almost ignored the doctrine of God. The Count (like Luther) believed that God hid God's self from human eyes apart from the divine self-revelation in Christ. Therefore all theological statements should refer to Christ directly or indirectly. What is important is not that Christ is like God. Rather, what the believer needs to know is that God is like Christ.

Zinzendorf also affirmed the "feminine" characteristics of God by calling God not only Father, but also Mother. The Holy Spirit was the nurturing principle within the Godhead, and a favorite metaphor was that the Kingdom was a holy family in which all believers are the adopted children of their divine parents.

A Brave New World

In the seventeenth century an agricultural revolution began in England that gradually spread to the rest of Europe. This revolution stressed the rational application of fertilizers, the systematic rotation of crops, and the concentrated application of animal power. The new agriculture worked best on large fields and required less labor than traditional methods. Landlords created larger fields by moving the traditional peasants off the land. When a peasant's lease, often issued for two or three "lives," expired with the death of the last heir, the landowner did not renew it.

Former peasants lost more than a livelihood. Traditional rural life was an ordered society in which individuals had a "place" in the social order—an order which eighteenth-century rural life mirrored. The landowner's family, the rector's wife, and a few other people of quality sat in the front of the sanctuary. Behind them, neat rows of yeoman and rural servants, often dressed in smocks, stood or knelt. At death, the church buried the wealthy in the church, while the churchyard graves of the poor were reused every five to ten years.

Each social class had its own privileges and obligations. When the new agriculture forced people to emigrate, these comfortable social relationships were disrupted, leading to a felt alienation from society and the church. Often individuals' sense of personal self-worth and economic value were pummeled. The best plowman in Dorset became only one face in the crowd seeking work.

When the uprooted did find work, the manufacturers and mine owners who employed them often paid low wages. The new industrial classes had few traditional privileges: they had no guild membership, few legally guaranteed holidays, and received services from only a handful of charities. Further, although their incomes apparently increased, they now lived in an economy where everything they used, including food, shelter, and fuel, required payment.

Gin symbolized the new social order. Traditional English alcoholic beverages, such as beer and porter, were naturally fermented and comparatively weak. In contrast, gin was a manufactured product that was 40 percent alcohol or more. Since gin could be manufactured on a mass scale, the drink was inexpensive, costing about a penny a glass. For many alienated from the social order, it seemed better to drink themselves into oblivion than to face daily life.

The revival which spread across the British Isles at this time enabled people to shift their identity from the external security provided by social tradition to an internal sense of self-worth. For evangelicals, every individual was a beloved son or daughter of God. In addition, the congregations and para-church organizations created by the revival developed the individual discipline needed to make people socially mobile.

British Revivals

Although friendly observers spoke about the eighteenth-century evangelical revival as a miracle, the revival continued many earlier movements in English religion. The predominant influence was Puritanism, but other groups also contributed. For instance, the "high church" party in Anglicanism contributed an emphasis on personal holiness, a sense of special vocation or call, and a strong doctrine of the Holy Spirit. The "low church" taught the classical Protestant doctrines of justification by faith and the priesthood of the believer. From the (Ana)baptists came an emphasis on voluntary faith and the New Birth. The Lollards may have also given their mite in the evangelical stress on every individual reading the Bible without note or comment.

The tiny principality of Wales was an important center of the early revival. Wales had its own language, customs, and religious traditions. Griffith Jones (1683–1761), rector of Llanddowror, strongly supported the Society for the Propagation of the Gospel. When a revival broke out in neighboring parishes, Jones worked for revival in his own congregation. Determined to make the Bible available to the illiterate, Jones organized a "traveling school" that moved from church to church teaching people to read, using the Bible as its text.

Books provided by the Society for the Promotion of Christian Knowledge led Howell Harris (1714–73), a school teacher, to experience grace. After Harris's conversion he became an itinerant preacher in Wales, often teaming with Daniel Rowland, a convert of Jones and a powerful preacher. The Anglican church refused to ordain Harris because his services were so emotional that the bishop questioned his mental stability. Nonetheless, Harris continued to preach and to organize his followers into small prayer groups. Eventually Harris and his followers left the establishment and joined the Calvinistic Methodists.

Selina Hastings (1707–91), Countess of Huntingdon, participated in both the Welsh and the English revivals. Her money supported the outreach of the most important Welsh revivalists. In addition to Howell Harris' ministry, the Countess sponsored much of George Whitefield's work. She contributed heavily to Whitefield's American tours, purchased the Tabernacle where Whitefield preached when he was in London, and served as the trustee of Whitefield's colonial charities after his death. No good cause escaped her notice, and she spent an estimated £1,200,000 to spread the gospel.

A less extensive revival occurred in Scotland where the "Marrow men," inspired by Edward Fisher's *The Marrow of Divinity* (as edited by Thomas Boston), were noted for the fervor of their sermons. Unlike many Scots, the "Marrow men" believed that a felt conversion was an important part of an individual's religious life. George Whitefield began conducting missions in Scotland in 1741, and in 1742 the great revival at Cambuslang occurred. Religious journals (an eighteenth-century innovation) reported the Cambuslang revival, and people in Germany and in New England followed developments there. About the same time a notable revival occurred in the town of Kilsyth. Most of the Scottish revival, however, was invisible, with evangelical preachers envigorating one congregation at a time.

England Aflame

The greatest eighteenth-century revival occurred in England. While it benefited from the work of many energetic leaders, including George Whitefield (1714–70), the greatest preacher of his generation, the key figures were John (1703–91) and Charles (1707–88) Wesley. John was the organizer who gathered the newly converted saints into societies for mutual growth. Charles, a gifted English hymnist, provided the music that inspired many to commit their lives to God.

The cradle of John's and Charles's religious life was their parents' home in Epworth. Although Samuel and Susanna Wesley were from dissenting stock, both held passionately to "high church" and "Tory" principles. They resolved that their children would likewise be strong supporters of the established Church of England.

Susanna was a severe disciplinarian. From their infancy Susanna surrounded her eleven children with rules that she expected them to obey instantly and without argument. If the children did anything, they had to do it correctly. For example, Susanna once dismissed a servant for giving the children an unauthorized sweet between meals. To impress the importance of the principle that their sin contributed to other's pain, Susanna forced the children to witness the firing.

An incident in John Wesley's childhood permanently affected his ministry. In 1709 the parsonage at Epworth burned, and the flames trapped John in an upper room. After his parents gave him up for dead, a neighbor rushed in, grabbed the child, and threw him into the waiting arms of his father. In his later preaching, Wesley illustrated salvation by comparing sinners to brands snatched from the burning.

John Wesley and his brothers were gifted students, and their parents believed that they should receive the best education that they could afford. After attendance at the better "public" schools, Samuel, Charles, and John were sent to Oxford (the "high church" university as compared to "low church" Cambridge). While at Oxford the group that came to be called the "Holy Club" gathered around John and Charles. This group met together for prayer and Bible study, and practiced the semi-monastic disciplines of fasting, confession, and frequent communion. To set an example for young men preparing for holy orders, they followed a regiment of good works, featuring visits to prisoners and a social ministry to the poor. Some students mocked the group by calling them "Methodists," a term that possibly referred to a type of medicine that used purges and laxatives. The Wesleys made the insult a mark of honor.

While at Oxford John Wesley mastered Greek and Latin, learned to write in a clear, concise English style, and established lifelong scholarly habits. Besides these academic skills, Wesley studied the tradition of Christian holiness. His reading encompassed authors as diverse as the ancient Egyptian desert fathers, William Law, and Thomas á Kempis. These studies taught Wesley to appreciate the monastic concepts of mystical union with Christ, holiness, and perfection.

In his search for a vocation, Wesley volunteered to go as a missionary to Georgia, an experimental penal colony for felons. His period in America was disastrous. His preaching was dull, lacking the common touch. Further, his personal life was a quagmire. When the young woman he was courting married another, Wesley excommunicated the woman and her husband. Accused of abusing his ecclesiastical power, Wesley was held under house arrest until he finally "escaped" across the border to Charleston.

The Georgia experience depressed Wesley. The young cleric had consecrated his life to Christ, and his failure could only have happened because his faith was weak or nonexistent. Events seemed to confirm this morbid interpretation. He could not forget that, during his trip to Georgia, he had been terrified by a storm at sea and cowed below deck as the winds howled. The memory of the calm composure of a group of Moravian passengers, gathered to praise the storm's Lord, continued to mock him.

When he returned to England in 1737, Wesley entered a taxing round of prayer meetings and personal introspection, desperate for some assurance that all was right with his soul. During this search he often asked the Moravian missionary Peter Böhler for advice. The counsel that Wesley received was traditional: Böhler told him to preach Christ until he believed his own sermons. Wesley's *Journal* reports that at a religious society meeting in Aldersgate Street on May 24, 1738, while someone was reading Luther's Preface to the Epistle to the Romans, God "strangely warmed" his heart and assured him of the forgiveness of his sins, although subsequent *Journal* entries show that he did not receive lasting peace at that moment. A further turning point came when Wesley was drawn into a revival that his good friend George Whitefield began near Bristol. People responded to his messages, crowds grew, and many experienced the new birth. The tone of his *Journals* changed. Wesley's spirits rose; his despair lifted, and he never looked back.

Wesley's assurance spoke to an intellectually and socially insecure age. The enlightened raised many serious questions about faith, and neither reason nor tradition helped many find a vibrant piety. The heart might bypass the head, at least for a season, and find comfort. Further, Wesley's vocational insecurity was commonplace. The men and women who heard Wesley were those whom economic change had shaken free of traditional social roles: miners, small shop keepers, workers, and clerks. Like Wesley, these people were not sure of their place in this world or the next, and they feared failure and its consequences.

Wesley's preaching sparked revival. His sermons, which often stressed the nearness of death and judgment, urged people to accept the grace of God. Often, especially in the early years, the audience responded with great emotional fervor: some were struck down in the Spirit; others fell to their knees in contrition; and many cried for mercy or wept for joy. Wesley's *Journals* reported healings and other miracles.

Unlike more Calvinistic awakeners, Wesley wanted his converts to "go on to perfection," to become holy. As early as 1739 Wesley organized his converts into societies and classes. Ever mindful of backsliding, Wesley tightly disciplined each group. The class leader accepted each member after an examination of his or her experience. However, if individuals wanted to retain their admission tickets, the leader needed evidence that they were remaining faithful in their stewardship of time, money, and effort. In addition, each member had some task or position that was for the good of all.

Wesley did not want the Methodists to become an independent church. His vision of the organization was very similar to Zinzendorf's understanding of the Moravians. The Methodists were to be an evangelistic order within the Church dedicated to leading others to the fullness of Christian experience.

Wesley appointed people as his "helpers" or "assistants" from the society's membership. Many had only an elementary education. Like other contemporary employers, Wesley regulated almost every detail of his workers' lives. The ideal helper lived according to the *Discipline*, a distillation of the rules announced at the various conferences. Wesley assigned each assistant to a circuit, and he made frequent changes, based on his sense of the needs of the various societies. While historians often describe the early circuit riders as preachers, a more accurate term might be "exhorters." Wesley expected his circuit riders primarily to be soul-winners and organizers.

In America, Methodism did not become a separate church until after the Revolutionary War. Then, faced with a rebellion in the ranks, Wesley joined other presbyters of the Church of England in ordaining ministers (elders) for America. Methodism in England did not become an independent denomination until after Wesley's death.

A Religion of Experience

Wesleyanism was a religion of experience and not necessarily of theology. Wesley's theological language was traditional. Like other high church leaders, Wesley desired to teach only what he believed that the church had always taught. Such Wesleyan words as "perfection," "holiness," "pardon," and "discipline" had a long history, and Wesley used them in accord with their historic meanings. For example, he used the monastic term "perfection" both in the Latin sense of a style of life free from known sin and in the Greek sense of total or complete love of God and neighbor. Since Jesus had urged his followers to be perfect as their Father was perfect, such a life must be possible for more than the spiritual elite.

Occasionally Wesley's theological language led to some confusion. For example, Wesley claimed to be an Arminian. The Arminians were originally a party in the Reformed Church of Holland that wanted to revise Calvinism's doctrine of election. In time, Arminianism had become associated either with the high and dry rationalism of the most formal English churches or Unitarianism. Wesley was not an Arminian in the usual eighteenth-century sense of the term. In fact, Wesley's theology of salvation was similar to the Semi-Augustinianism taught by the Council of Orange. As Wesley understood the matter, prevenient grace—grace that Christ gave to everyone—was sufficient to enable each person to accept or reject God's offer of salvation. The cross weakened the power of original sin, and all that God required of individuals was that they allow Christ to win the final victory in their lives.

Wesley's soteriology (doctrine of salvation) is best understood through the evangelist's personalism. For Wesley, God created humankind for relationship with God and others, and the most rewarding relationships are those which individuals enter freely. Just as in human friendships, one person or another must takes the first step, so it is in our relationship with God. In Christ, God reaches a hand out to us, but human beings must respond by putting their hands in God's.

Unfortunately Wesley, like many of his contemporaries, loved controversy and debate. Early in his career, he attacked the Moravians for their "quietism." Later, he verbally assaulted his good friend George Whitefield for his belief in predestination. The battles may have done some good, in that Wesley supported his movement through his work as an author, and the controversies encouraged people to buy more journals, tracts, and pamphlets.

The Broader Revival

The "people called Methodists" were not the only eighteenth- century English evangelicals. George Whitefield, the best-known eighteenth-century preacher, conducted important revivals throughout the British

Isles and in America. His London Tabernacle, located near the theater district, was a city landmark.

Like Whitefield, most Church of England evangelicals remained (or became) strong Calvinists. The center for much Church Evangelicalism was Cambridge University, where a strong tradition of Puritan scholarship and devotion was present. In addition, William Grimshaw (1708–63), vicar of Haworth, was a strong evangelistic preacher. Augustus Toplady (1740–78), of Broad Hembury, was a strong defender of Calvinistic theology and the author of the hymn, "Rock of Ages." Many upper-class evangelicals worshiped at John Venn's parish of Clapham. The "Clapham Sect" was an important center of benevolence and reform.

John Newton (1725–1807) lived an adventurous life before his conversion. A ship's captain and slave trader, Newton traveled throughout much of the world and experienced several shipwrecks. One led to his own temporary enslavement by an African tribe and helped change his mind about the morality of slavery. The hymn "Amazing Grace" reflects his own spiritual journey.

Evangelical influence was most evident in worship. In all but the most formal congregations, the hymn book supplemented the Book of Common Prayer as an aid to worship. Such hymn writers as Isaac Watts (1674–1748), Charles Wesley, William Cowper (1731–1800), John Newton, and others laid a firm foundation for the development of an English tradition of congregational music.

CHAPTER NINE

A GREAT AND GENERAL AWAKENING

Of the English possesions in the new world, the middle colonies established their social patterns later than New England or the South. Although the Anglican and Dutch Reformed Churches had some legal status in the southern four New York counties, no middle colony had an established church. The area was the most ethnically and religiously diverse in the new world. William Penn (1644–1718), the proprietor of Pennsylvania and Delaware, recruited settlers from Ireland and Germany to settle his colony. The former Dutch port of New York became a cosmopolitan center with colonists from many European countries and slaves from Africa.

In Germany, the government provided buildings, hired pastors, regulated schools, and chartered charities for the Lutheran and Reformed Churches. Perhaps because these state churches were so well-administered, Germans had great difficulty establishing churches in the New World. An able ministry was the most serious problem. When the Germans gathered congregations, "irregular pastors" with varying qualifications often took leadership. Some were former school teachers with less than the university education required for ordination at home, who nonetheless did a credible job. Yet others were charlatans, more concerned with fleecing the flock than feeding the sheep.

In time, European societies and churches sent missionaries. The Swiss Reformed pastor Michael Schlatter (1716–90) was an able frontier evangelist who traveled throughout Pennsylvania and Virginia organizing churches and appointing pastors. To maintain some church discipline, Schlatter formed a *coetus* or Presbytery to regulate the ministry. Philip William Otterbein (1716–1813), who arrived in America in 1752, was another effective Reformed missionary. After the Revolution, Otterbein participated in the ordination of the first American Methodist ministers.

The Lutherans responded more slowly than the Reformed to appeals from their co-religionists. No missionaries arrived until the Pietists at Halle received word that Zinzendorf planned to work among the German colonists. In response, the Halle leadership sent the orphanage superintendent Henry Melchior Muhlenberg (1711–87) to the new world.

Like Schlatter and Otterbein, Muhlenberg was an effective itinerant preacher who could gather and inspire a crowd, and he was also an experienced organizer of voluntary associations. Muhlenberg reorganized Pennsylvania Lutheran congregations as legal corporations, complete with constitutions, trustees, and officers. To protect the churches against "irregular" pastors, Muhlenberg organized a Ministerium or ministers' conference to examine, approve, and ordain candidates.

Theodore Jacob Frelinghuysen (1691–1748), a North German Pietist, came to America to minister to the Dutch settlers in New Jersey's Raritan Valley. Frelinghuysen preached wherever he found listeners, whether in a barn, a field, or a church. His preaching stressed simple gospel themes: the ruin of human nature by the Fall, personal responsibility for sin, the danger of hell, and the availability of grace. Frelinghuysen reenforced his demand for a new birth by maintaining high moral and spiritual standards for the Lord's Supper.

Under Frelinghuysen's preaching, the New Jersey Dutch experienced a wide-spread revival. Like other frontier revivals, the conversions were often emotional, with Dutch pastors taking sides for or against the new religious movement. Behind the theological questions over the revival, other issues may have influenced the debate. The pro-revival churches were more willing to participate in colonial culture and abandoned Dutch language in worship earlier.

The Dutch revival spread to the Presbyterians, who were at this time composed of two ethnic strains: Yankees and Scots-Irish. The English government originally settled Scots in Ulster to protect Protestant interests. The move did not benefit those immigrants. Northern Ireland was desperately poor in resources, and its English landlords practiced rent-racking; that is, charging a rent equal to the land's production.

Although both the New Englanders and the Scots-Irish accepted the Westminster Confession and Catechism, the two groups understood these documents differently. The New Englanders were biblicists who believed that the confessions were to serve simply as guides to biblical teaching. Any pastor or congregation might dissent from them, if the

Bible appeared to teach something else. In contrast, the Scots-Irish believed that the confessions accurately summarized the Bible's teachings. To disagree with Westminster was almost to disagree with the Scriptures themselves.

The two parties compromised in the 1729 Adopting Act by balancing the power of the synod and that of the presbyteries. Although the synod could legislate for the whole church, local presbyteries adjudicated all laws. Thus presbyteries decided whether a candidate had met the synod's standards or not and could demand as strict or as loose subscription to the confessions as it wanted. In effect, American Presbyterianism was an agreement to cooperate on the synodical level despite local theological disagreements.

William Tennent (1673–1746) was a priest in the Anglican Church of Ireland who joined the Presbyterian Church when he immigrated to America. More important than denomination affiliation for Tennent was a burning desire for practical godliness. While serving the village of Neshaminy, Pennsylvania, Tennent realized that the Presbyterian Church had a shortage of learned ministers and established a school in his manse to meet this need. The program of the school was essentially that of any English college: classics, some mathematics, and rhetoric. What made the school unique, however, was Tennent's strong emphasis on conversion and righteous living.

Gilbert Tennent (1703–64), William's son and a graduate of the Neshaminy school, was called to minister in New Brunswick, New Jersey, where he quickly fell under Frelinghuysen's influence. Imitating the Dutch leader, the younger Tennent traveled throughout the colony, organized churches, helped congregations find pastors, and supplied vacant pulpits. In 1738 he was instrumental in creating the New Brunswick presbytery which joined pastors and elders who supported the revival.

Just at the time that Tennent's ethnic revival was peaking, George Whitefield (1714–70) toured the colonies to raise money for his orphanage in Georgia. Although the Georgia venture began small, Whitefield hoped that it might become another Halle with a college, various charities, and a press.

While Whitefield won numerous converts, the evangelist often denounced other ministers for their lack of zeal. His logic was simple: the fact that religion was at such a low state meant that pastors had not done their duty. Not even Harvard and Yale, the pride of the New England ministry, escaped his denunciations. Whitefield's preaching and personal style fascinated Gilbert Tennent, who became a close friend of the evangelist and imitated the good and the bad features of his mentor's ministry.

The Presbyterian revival was controversial from the beginning. To the more conservative Scots-Irish, the awakener's "enthusiasm" masked unsound doctrine. Thus in 1736 the old guard passed a synodical resolution tightening requirements for subscription, and in 1737 they urged the synod to prohibit itinerant preaching. As the controversy deepened, Gilbert Tennent became angered. In 1740 he preached a sermon entitled "The Danger of An Unconverted Ministry" at Nottingham, Pennsylvania. In that address, Tennent accused his enemies of being whited sepulchers who concealed a lack of piety behind right dogma. Such ministers had dead churches, because dead men preached to them. The message's application was obvious. Godly people should flee any congregation opposed to the revival and join an evangelistic congregation.

Tennent's injudicious remarks confirmed the conservatives' worst fears. When the Scots-Irish arrived first at the 1741 meeting of the synod, they passed a resolution excluding the New Brunswick Presbytery from the church. The action divided Presbyterians into two denominations: the Old Side and the New Side. In 1745 the New York Presbytery, formerly neutral, joined with the revivalists in the Synod of New York.

The two churches competed intensely, and education was the decisive battlefield. The Old Side lost. Although the conservatives had the outstanding leadership of Francis Alison (1705–79), they did not have the capital to found a college, and only established an academy. The New Side was more fortunate, inheriting a chartered college.

David Brainerd (1718–47) made some unwise statements about the authorities at Yale shortly after his conversion, upon which the college promptly expelled him. Despite Brainerd's public repentance, Yale refused readmission. The more evangelistic alumni petitioned Governor William Franklin of New Jersey for a charter. When the charter arrived, the Yale men invited the New Side Presbyterians to join the board of the new College of New Jersey (later Princeton University). The college drained the New Side of its leadership. Such popular and learned preachers as Jonathan Dickinson, Aaron Burr (father of the more famous politician of the same name), Jonathan Edwards, Samuel Davies, and Samuel Finney died within a few years of assuming the school's presidency. In 1766 the trustees called as president the Scottish Evangelical John Witherspoon (1723–93), who made the College a center for the study of Scottish common sense philosophy and scholastic theology.

In 1758 the two sides negotiated peace. The Old Side had declined in numbers and prestige, and many of its Scots-Irish supporters had merged into the general population. In contrast, the New Side had grown rapidly both numerically and financially, and its leaders had matured. Gilbert Tennent had shown a new spirit in his 1749 *Irenicum Ecclesiasticum* (subtitled "A Humble, Impartial Essay Upon the Peace of Jerusalem"). Whitefield, whose example was always important to New Side pastors, also reached out to his former opponents. The final terms favored the New Side and included a declaration that vital piety was as important a qualification for ordination as orthodoxy.

New England

The New England revival may have begun in partial response to the half-way covenant—the practice of allowing a form of church membership to those who, although baptized, had not committed themselves to the "full" covenant of discipleship so important to the Puritans. Solomon Stoddard (1643–1729) of Northampton, Massachusetts, solved the problem by adopting two contradictory positions. First, Stoddard maintained that church membership, including admission to Communion, ought to be open to anyone who wanted it. In a not-Reformed—but memorable—phrase, Stoddard called the Supper "a converting ordinance." Second, Stoddard preached a type of evangelical Calvinism, as set forth in his *The Safety of Appearing* (1687), that stripped sinners of all earthly security and required them to throw themselves on Christ's mercy.

Stoddard's energetic preaching allowed him to have it both ways. Periodically, Northampton's young people passed through a season in which most experienced saving grace and joined the church. Stoddard trained Edwards to expect a resumption of these harvests, and Edwards developed his theology of conversion before the awakening began. Edwards' first two published sermons, "God Glorified in the Work of Redemption" (1731) and "A Divine and Supernatural Light Immediately Imparted to the Soul" (1734) outlined his revival theology. In them Edwards argued that conversion added a sixth sense, analogous to the other five senses, that enabled sinners to experience the excellency of divine things. In some ways it was similar to our experience of beauty in a great work of art or music.

In 1738 Jonathan Edwards published *A Faithful Narrative of the Surprising Work of God in the Conversion of Many Hundred Souls* . . . which contained a clinical account of the 1734/35 revival. A revival began among the youth of the town following the 1734 death of one of their number. Edwards took this event as an occasion to preach a vigorous series of messages on justification by faith that inspired religious experiences in children, the middle-aged, and older people. From Northampton the Awakening spread along the river as different ministers intensified their preaching of the need for supernatural grace.

This early revival ended as quickly as it began. In 1737 Edwards' uncle, Joseph Hawley, began to doubt the possibility of his own salvation and—after a period of acute depression—committed suicide.

Whitefield's Ministry

George Whitefield's September 1740 visit to Boston began a new wave of revival in New England. Before his arrival, Whitefield planted stories about his success in Boston newspapers and had printers make his *Journals* available. When Whitefield himself got there, the evangelist drew such large crowds that he had to move his meetings from the churches to Boston Common. After a month, Whitefield went west to visit Edwards to discuss the *Faithful Narrative*. Whitefield then proceeded south through Connecticut, preaching as he traveled. In the next seventy-three days he traveled more than eight hundred miles and preached one hundred and thirty sermons. His success convinced Whitefield that he should send Gilbert Tennent to Boston to continue the work there. For the next three years revival continued throughout Massachusetts and Connecticut.

Whitefield's easy eloquence set an example for his imitators and admirers. Even Jonathan Edwards, whose doctrinal preaching ordinarily was abstract, followed the new fashion temporarily. Edwards' sermon "Sinners in the Hands of An Angry God," preached at Enfield, Connecticut, in 1743 is an example of the Whitefieldian style. "Sinners" is filled with artfully constructed images, carefully selected symbols, and lively exegesis.

Whitefield's example also influenced David Brainerd, who was engaged to marry one of Edwards' daughters. He made the error of denouncing his tutor at Yale (witnesses reported that he said that his teacher had no more grace than a chair), the offense for which Yale expelled him. Deeply conscious of the offense he had caused, Brainerd became a missionary to the Indians in New Jersey and died of tuberculosis. His *Diary*, edited by Edwards, became a popular evangelical classic. Eleazer Wheelock, also inspired by Whitefield, established Moor's Charity School for Indians. Later, the school moved to Hanover, New Hampshire, and became Dartmouth College.

Whitefield's example did not always have such positive effects in New England. James Davenport (1716–57), the scion of an old New England clerical family and a Presbyterian pastor on Long Island, left his parish to become an itinerant preacher. Davenport claimed to be able to tell the saved from the damned, and his sermons were ill-organized and delivered in an almost incoherent shout. In 1741 the Connecticut authorities arrested Davenport and returned him to Long Island. A year later, Davenport went on another tour and was arrested, tried, and escorted home again. Many believed that he was mad. In 1743 Davenport exhausted Connecticut's patience. After a particularly emotional campaign, Davenport urged his converts to bring their vanities, such as cards and expensive clothing, to a pier in New London. He then piled them together and burned them. The authorities appointed Solomon Williams and Eleazer Wheelock to return Davenport to Long Island and to pray with him until he was no longer dangerous. They were able to bring Davenport to repentance, and in 1744 the evangelist published his *Confessions and Retractions*, publicly apologizing for his errors.

High emotional conversions, whether intended or not, were common during the Great Awakening. While eighteenth-century people expected tears as a demonstration of strong sentiments, the new converts went beyond the permissible. Some shouted, fainted, cried out for mercy, or developed other hysterical symptoms. Detractors of the revival quickly tied these popular excesses in the same bundle with the behavior of such "leaders" as Davenport.

Charles Chauncy (1705–87) knew many anti-revival clergy in New England and corresponded with them about the revival in their parishes. When Chauncy had sufficient evidence, he published it in 1743 as *Seasonable Thoughts on The State of Religion,* a *Faithful Narrative* in reverse. Chauncy's work is filled with accounts of arrogance, hysteria, poor manners, and theologically ludicrous quotations.

Jonathan Edwards began his defense of the revival when he delivered his 1741 Yale commencement address "The Distinguishing Marks of a Work of the Spirit of God." Edwards admitted that the revival mixed good and bad religion. Yet Edwards insisted that an impartial examination would show that the revival had many scriptural marks of a work of God. In 1743 Edwards enunciated many of the same themes in his *Some Thoughts Concerning the Revival,* where he gave more evidence of the revival's divine origin: transformed lives, improved morals, the better observance of Sunday, the increase of missionaries to the Indians, and other signs of the coming of the millennium.

In 1746 Edwards published his last formal defense of the revival, *A Treatise on Religious Affections*. The work moved beyond the earlier recitations of empirical evidence that characterized his earlier writing and dealt with the nature of religion. According to Edwards, religion consists primarily in affections or emotions. The skilled pastor needed to distinguish between those affections that were truly supernatural and divine in origin and those that were merely human. For example, affections that inspired actions contrary to the will of God in Scripture could not be holy. But many affections provided no evidence one way or another. If a Scripture came to mind at a seasonable moment, it might mean that the experience was from God. But the devil also quoted the Bible for his own ends—an important reservation. Edwards went on to argue that the Scriptures contained twelve characteristics (signs) of saving affections which climaxed in that elevated love of God, nature, and humankind which Edwards later called the "consent of being to being itself."

The large number of converts during the Great Awakening convinced Edwards that his grandfather's policy of admitting members without an account of an experience of saving grace was unbiblical. His congregation disagreed and dismissed him from his pulpit. In 1751 Edwards became a missionary to the Native Americans stationed at Stockbridge, Massachusetts. While serving there Edwards wrote his philosophical works, including his *Treatise on the Freedom of the Will*, his masterful *The End For Which God Created the World*, and the speculative *The Nature of True Virtue*. While such abstract tomes seem far from the issues raised by the revival, they often dealt indirectly with the issues he discussed earlier.

In Edwards' time, many rationalists said that human accountability depended upon the ability of individuals to make moral decisions. Yet Edwards was convinced that the Reformed doctrine of election was true. In a highly technical argument, he reasoned that humankind was both responsible for its actions and bound to act in certain ways. The core of the argument was Edwards' contrast between natural and moral inability. The normal operation of physical law caused physical inabilities. For example, humans cannot leap over houses or lift horses. In contrast, moral inability came from the functioning of the human mind and soul. Our human wills are bound to our sensible experience. Since Locke had shown that humans only know what they have learned from experience and since our experience begins without God, humans do not understand the moral implications of their actions. However, if God enters the mind and gives humankind a new sense, our new nature can perceive God's presence and practice true virtue (love).

Edwards' system implied that God was everywhere and in everything, although rarely perceived. In the twin essays *The End For Which God Created The World* and *The Nature of True Virtue*, Edwards developed the logical consequences of this position. God had created the world to manifest God's self, and God draws the created order continually back to its center, the Glory of God. What God demanded of all creatures, consequently, was that they consent to being as such. Such consent or disinterested benevolence was the highest form of love and united God, humankind, and nature in a harmonious whole.

Schism

Many newly awakened persons left their local congregations to form what were known as Separate congregations organized around more revivalistic church covenants. Usually, such local schisms occurred after a sermon by the pastor questioning or condemning the revival movement. New England's ecclesiastical laws had not envisioned such a situation. The various Acts of Toleration detailed procedures for licensing Baptist, Church of England, and Quaker congregations and exempted members of these churches from taxes raised to support the established church.

Since these Separate congregations accepted the Westminster Confession, they were not legal forms of dissent. Although no one suffered bodily harm, minor persecution occurred. Separate pastors were harassed under the laws prohibiting itinerant ministers, and the authorities seized property for ecclesiastical taxes and sold it for a fraction of its value.

Many (perhaps the majority) eventually returned to the established church. Others searched the Scriptures for guidance in their present situation. Since the Bible only recounts the baptism of converts, the Separate Congregational churches often debated baptism for years. Almost inevitably, either the whole congregation or a part of it would restrict the Lord's Supper to those baptized as adults.

Rather than resort to self-baptism, these Congregationalists often asked a local Particular (Calvinist) Baptist minister to administer the ordinance to them. Particular Baptist pastors also participated in the ordination of Separate pastors. As a result many of the Separate congregations, which had not begun as Baptist, became part of the Baptist fold. In the seventeenth century Baptists were a small, almost minute, minority. With these new additions, they became one of the largest American denominations.

Isaac Backus (1724–1806) was typical of the new Baptist leaders. Backus left the Congregational Church in a dispute over the awakening and became the pastor of a Separate church. In 1757 Backus joined those who wanted a covenant restricting the Lord's Supper to those baptized as adult believers. Backus made his major contribution to Baptist life as a defender of the separation of church and state. His *Tyranny Exposed and Liberty Described* (1778) and *An Appeal to the People of the Massachusetts State* (1780), based on the political philosophy of John Locke, were classic expressions of eighteenth-century thought on the nature of church-state relations.

Southern Exposures

The revival in the South began with a small band of people in Hanover County, Virginia, who experienced saving grace while studying Whitefield's sermons. Although the Hanoverians did not have a denominational identity, the Presbyterians took responsibility for their pastoral care and sent Samuel Davies (1723–61), an effective evangelist and organizer, to unite the six existing congregations into the Hanover Presbytery. The Presbytery then aggressively evangelized the western part of Virginia.

Shubal Stearns (1706–51) and Daniel Marshall (1706–84), his brother-in-law, migrated into western North Carolina in 1754. The site that they selected at Sandy Creek was ideal for evangelism, since it was at the crossroads of highways that ran in all directions. Within twenty years, the small band at Sandy Creek established forty-two churches in Virginia, North and South Carolina, and Georgia, and ordained 125 ministers.

The Separate churches were enthusiastic. Their preachers often preached in a "holy whine." During their services converts were often "struck dead in the Spirit" (passed out from religious excitement) or experienced uncontrolled shouting and loud weeping. Almost every member had some official office in the church, and women served as deacons, elders, and exhorters. Separate Baptists practiced nine rituals: the Lord's Supper, baptism, the love feast, the dedication of children, the holy kiss, foot washing, the anointing of the sick, the right hand of fellowship, and the laying on of hands.

The Separates experienced severe persecution, especially in Virginia. In that colony the authorities frequently imprisoned and occasionally whipped Baptists. Mobs disrupted worship services and threatened to lynch the minister, if he or she persisted in preaching. Since Virginia society was generally tolerant, this savagery begs for some explanation. Perhaps the ruling classes perceived the Baptists as a threat to the social order. Baptist ministers witnessed to slaves and welcomed black people (at least in the early years) at revival services. Women, who had fewer rights in Virginia than in the middle or New England colonies, also figured prominently in the movement.

The steadfastness of Virginia Baptist preachers made an important contribution to religious liberty in the state. The spectacle of persecution sickened many planters, including James Madison (1750–1836). After the Revolution, these planters passed laws separating church and state and securing liberty of conscience.

CHAPTER TEN

RELIGION AND THE AMERICAN REVOLUTION

The French and Indian War (known as the Seven Years War in Europe) marked the beginning of the American colonies' turn toward independence. When the war began in 1754, the French held Canada, had established trading posts through much of the Mississippi Valley, and had made alliances with many larger Indian tribes. In addition to the traditional calls to arms, the Protestant clergy employed eschatological symbols to describe the conflict as a struggle between God's New Israel and the Antichrist. As the worldwide struggle shifted toward Great Britain, the combined colonial and British armies had increasing military success, taking Louisbourg in 1758 and seizing the greatest prize, Montreal, in 1763. The Treaty of Paris, signed in that year, ceded Canada to Great Britain.

As often happens, one war laid the foundations for the next. Once the fighting ended, British politicians faced an almost unpayable national debt. Additional funds were also required to expand the Royal Navy to defend their territorial gains. With homeland taxes at a historic high, prime ministers expected the comparatively untaxed colonials to contribute.

The American Revolution

At first glance, the American Revolution had little to do with religion. The dispute began over a constitutional question: whether the British government could tax the colonists to raise revenue or only to regulate trade. The two openly religious issues were comparatively minor: an Anglican bishop for the colonies and the toleration of Catholicism in Canada.

During the eighteenth century, the Church of England grew rapidly in the colonies, reflecting developments in England where dissent was declining. In addition, many wealthy Americans found the Church of England with its stately worship an alternative to the Awakening's "enthusiasm." When American Anglicans requested a bishop, Presbyterian and Congregational ministers protested the measure fearing that a bishop might encourage more people to become Anglican. Despite the noise, the British government never supported the proposed bishopric and sought to avoid any religiously divisive issues.

The Quebec Act (1774) inflamed these same ministers. The law guaranteed Roman Catholics the exercise of their religion in Canada and granted the Roman Church certain legal privileges. Egged on by Protestant clergy, colonial politicians branded the law an "intolerable" act and demanded its repeal. The colonial hatred of the Quebec Act was so great that Jefferson included it among the grievances in the Declaration of Independence.

Law and Gospel

American Protestants inherited a long tradition of political preaching. From the time of Ulrich Zwingli and John Calvin, Reformed ministers actively promoted civil righteousness and advised both magistrates and people on current events. English Puritan divines had supported the 1640s Civil War avidly. In 1688 established and dissenting clergy jointly demanded the abdication of James II. New England law required ministers to preach on public occasions and on thanksgiving and fast days.

Although lacking the advantages of establishment, Presbyterian ministers were deeply involved in middle colony politics. In Pennsylvania the two factions in the legislature were the "Presbyterians" and the "Quakers." Although Presbyterian influence was not as strong in New York and New Jersey, it was present in those Long Island and northern New Jersey towns modelled after New England.

The Reformed clergy were important political educators who transmitted the "Real Whig" ideology that the Americans used to support their cause. Although this system of public philosophy was theistic, it owed as much to the Enlightenment as it did to Scripture. Thomas Hollis, an English dissenter, gave Harvard College an extensive collection of radical books in political philosophy that were read by students and local clergy. In the middle colonies the colleges required a course in moral philosophy during the senior year. At Princeton, John Witherspoon's senior ethics course taught that government depended on the consent of its citizens. James Madison, the father of the Constitution, took Witherspoon's course, and Alexander Hamilton credited King's College (present-day Columbia) with his political awakening.

Between the 1765 passage of the Stamp Act and the 1776 Declaration of Independence, published political sermons recited a litany of colonial grievances. Typically, the ministers rehearsed the course of events, pointed to the constitutional and legal principles involved, and appealed to God (or to Nature's God) to redress the balance.

The Revolutionary War

After the British evacuated Boston following Howe's 1775 "victory" at Bunker Hill, little fighting occurred in New England. The dominant Congregational clergy strongly advocated political independence, and their sermons claimed that America's mission was to establish liberty, civil and religious. Puritan ministers frequently used New England theological traditions, including the covenant theology, the jeremiad, and the millennium, to support their political convictions. If the people would repent of their sins, return to the God of their ancestors, God would aid American arms and establish the American Zion. The Presbyterians echoed the same themes. To the British, the Reformed clergy were Washington's "black regiment."

In both New England and the middle colonies, the Anglican clergy were often Tory or pro-British. Although many Anglicans ministers criticized Britain and demanded redress of grievances, they believed that their ordination oaths required them to support the king. Painful experience convinced many New England Anglicans that English misrule was better than Puritan tyranny. The region's Patriots harassed Anglican pastors and people for refusing the oath to the new government or praying for the king.

In Pennsylvania and New Jersey a handful of Anglican clergy supported the Revolution. Most hid their opposition until the British army arrived, when they could safely declare their loyalty. The Southern religious situation was more complicated. About a third of Virginia's clergy elected the patriotic side of the struggle and faithfully supported the war. The rest either returned to England or disappeared. Most Anglican ministers south of Virginia supported the Patriots. In contrast, most Highland Scots and their pastors passionately supported the crown. Likewise, Virginia's recently persecuted Baptists favored the Revolution.

The historic peace churches—the Quakers and Mennonites—were in a quandary. Their leaders opposed participation in the war on either side and advocated a peaceful resolution to the crisis. Many were, however, loyal to the crown. The members of the peace churches were grateful to Britain. The crown protected their rights, often against their more orthodox neighbors, and they were not sure what an independent America might demand of them. The Baptist historian, Morgan Edwards, felt the same way.

Christian Losses

War is not good for religion. Military service disrupts Christian habits, and the troops confront moral temptations avoidable at home. Despite the so-called laws of war, armies often destroy churches in battle or use them for military purposes. In this war the churches lost members and property, and the colleges that educated future clergy closed or declined dramatically in enrollment.

After the war ended, ministerial writers complained that infidelity was growing. "Infidelity," had two meanings. First, it referred to those religious beliefs that minimized the role of Christ, such as Deism or Unitarianism. Second, it referred to a slacking off of church attendance. Clerical perceptions were affected by national trends that made religion appear in radical decline. For instance, parishes often appeared empty because the membership left for the west. Since the new governments were land rich but currency poor, they used western lands to pay their war-debts, including the army's unpaid wages. American religion's statistical distribution had also changed. Before the Revolution, the largest denominations were the Anglicans, the Congregationalists, and the Presbyterians. Afterwards, the Baptists and the Methodists grew spectacularly.

Yet the clerical Jeremiahs were not completely in error. The nation's mood was different, and religion was not held in as high esteem as before the war. Those colleges that trained many Presbyterian, Congregational, and Anglican pastors faced shrunken enrollments, and fewer graduates entered the ministry. In some schools, rationalism was a common fad with the students addressing each other with such nicknames as Voltaire and Diderot.

Deism also appears to have increased. Although contemporaries believed that French army officers brought Deism to America during the war, its sources lay closer to home. America had its own variations on the Enlightenment radicalism. English radical Whig philosophy, not

Christian theology, provided the primary justification for the war. While the Declaration of Independence appealed to faith in the Creator, anyone might find their own faith, if any, in its inspiring words. Further, the Constitution did not mention God, except in the president's oath of office, and nowhere credited the divine as the source of the nation's existence or prosperity. Instead, the document asserted that "the people" had created the new government.

Many Revolutionary leaders were Deists, including John Adams, Benjamin Franklin, Thomas Jefferson, and probably George Washington. Whether because of possible controversy or because they considered religion a private matter, most were reticent to proclaim their views in public. Before the war Deism was a matter for the private drawing rooms of wealthy planters and merchants. Afterwards, people discussed the new philosophy openly.

The Revolution ended censorship, allowing radicals to publish their books. In *Reason the Only Oracle of Man* (1784) Ethan Allen (1738–89), the hero of Ticonderoga, urged Americans to reject the Bible or any other claim to revelation. Elihu Palmer (1764–1806) went even further and attempted to found a church on the principles of "republic religion." Thomas Paine (1737–1809), the propagandist of the American Revolution, issued his 1794–95 *The Age of Reason*, which ministers regularly condemned from the pulpit.

The "liberal" wing of Congregationalism also spread radical ideas. By 1800 every Congregationalist minister in Boston was a Unitarian. Six years later, Unitarian advocates controlled the most important teaching positions at Harvard College. Henry Ware (1764–1845), who became Hollis Professor of Divinity in 1804, gave the movement some intellectual leadership, but William Ellery Channing (1780–1842) was its most effective spokesperson.

Orthodox American Christians acted quickly to check unbelief. They provided a Christian account of the creation of the United States that stressed the Christian faith of the founding fathers. Such legends as Washington praying in the snow at Valley Forge became stock sermon illustrations. Further, ministers rewrote the nation's colonial history as a Christian preparation for nationhood. The clergy stressed the religious motives of the early settlers, expanding the story of New England's covenant with God to include the whole nation. In their hands the motive for all immigration to the colonies became religious. The clergy also evoked post-millennial theology. The new nation was born just as God was ready to establish God's Kingdom.

Liberty: Civil, Religious, and Legal

During the Revolution, the Patriots demanded liberty, both civil and religious. When the war ended, American Christians reorganized their churches in line with this ideal. Different regions and different states moved at their own speed in enacting new ecclesiastical laws. The United States became a denominational state where churches competed for members while often cooperating to influence public life.

The most dramatic change was the disestablishment of the Anglican churches in Virginia, North and South Carolina, and Georgia. Except in Virginia, disestablishment meant a multi-denominational Christian republicanism. For example, in the Carolinas the state constitutions spoke of the people's Christian commitments and required belief in God to hold important offices. In Maryland, the legislature repealed laws prohibiting Catholic political participation, but a generation passed before Jews were given the right to vote there.

Virginia's disestablishment of the Anglican Church was more complete, perhaps because the Church has been more successful in that state. Shortly after the war began the Virginia legislature suspended clerical salaries, although it left other ecclesiastical laws on the books. Thomas Jefferson, who had a lifelong disdain for the clerical professors at William and Mary, closed that college's divinity school by executive order. When the war ended, Patrick Henry and other conservative Virginia politicians urged the state to adopt a general assessment or tax that the state might divide proportionally among the churches. In response, James Madison wrote his famous *Memorial and Remonstrance* urging complete religious liberty. Eventually the Virginia legislature passed Jefferson's radical "Act Establishing Religious Freedom," making Virginia the most secular of the original thirteen states.

The New England states modified their establishment laws to make it easier for dissenters to secure exemption from religious taxes. In all other respects, their establishment of religion continued into the nineteenth century. Interestingly enough, Unitarianism may have been a major factor in Congregationalism's disestablishment in Massachusetts. In the 1819 Dedham Case, the state Supreme Court ruled that a town might hire a Unitarian pastor, even if the church opposed the measure. Orthodox support for the establishment waned after that, and the Massachusetts legislature repealed the laws establishing the churches in 1833.

Outside Virginia, the states followed a legal pattern that continued earlier middle colony precedents. The legislatures allowed churches (both denominations and local congregations) to become legal corporations. In simple terms, this meant that the churches were legal persons. Beside legal standing (the right to sue and be sued), the state allowed ecclesiastical bodies to hold property perpetually and to limit the church's liability to the value of its (and not its members') property.

No state purged its laws or political practices of all Christian influences. The legislatures and courts continued to open with Christian prayer, and chaplains were part of the army and navy. Courts enforced Christian morality, especially regarding family life. Some evidence exists that the Christian influence on legislation increased in the nineteenth-century when the churches secured laws protecting Sunday, prohibiting prostitution, excluding pornography from the mails, and outlawing abortion. When towns and cities established public schools, they were openly Protestant in ambience and curriculum, a fact that Catholics believed justified the construction of their own schools.

The First Amendment to the Constitution was written to keep the federal government from interfering in religion. The statement that "Congress shall make no law respecting an establishment of religion," meant that Congress could neither establish a church where none was established nor disestablish a religion where one was established (as in New England). In addition, the constitution guaranteed the free exercise of religion.

After the Civil War, the nation amended the constitution to protect former slaves by requiring the states to extend the Bill of Rights to all citizens. Yet First Amendment cases were rare before 1940. Since then, the central issue has been the balance between the constitution's guarantee of the free exercise of religion and the prohibition of establishment.

Religion Reorganizes

Changes in church polity (government) are rarely exciting, but such alternations in ecclesiastical structures affect individuals' experience of their religion. After the Revolution, denominational leaders reorganized their churches on a national basis. While only a few denominations were evenly spread throughout the nation, these national structures helped the churches maintain a national vision.

During the colonial period American Methodists were few and considered themselves an "evangelistic order" or "church within the [Anglican] Church." Their motto was "he who leaves the Church, leaves the Methodists." When the Revolution began, Wesley supported the

British government and called his preachers home. Most Methodist exhorters obediently returned, but a handful stayed who were occasionally persecuted as Tories.

The establishment of peace created new problems for the young movement. The Anglican churches on which the Methodists had depended for the Sacraments were in disarray, and their recovery was doubtful. Moreover, the self-understanding of many Methodist leaders had changed. The remaining circuit riders saw themselves as loyal citizens of the new republic and wanted an American church, responsive to American needs. In practical terms, this meant the right to administer the sacraments. After extensive transatlantic correspondence, Wesley surrendered to their demands in 1784. He ordained Richard Whatcoat and Thomas Vasey for service in America and appointed Thomas Coke (1747–1814) and Francis Asbury as "superintendents." At the "Christmas Conference," held at Baltimore's Lovely Lane Chapel in 1784, the gathered ministers elected Coke and Asbury and formally adopted and modified the *Discipline*. The same conference ordained some circuit riders as presbyters and others as deacons.

The new polity was flexible and national. The Methodists, although small in nmbers at the time, planned to spread scriptural holiness over the whole nation. The conference derived the office of "superintendent" (renamed by Asbury "bishop") from Wesley's authority in the English societies and classes. The bishops were able to place their ministers where the greatest need existed and to see that crucial areas were not neglected.

The Anglican churches also had to find a new polity. In the South, the officials in each state governed its own established church. In contrast, the Northern churches were almost congregational in structure, with each parish self-governing. In a sense, no one planned the new order; it just happened. The first step was when a "convention" of Connecticut priests elected Samuel Seabury (1726–96), a former loyalist, as their bishop and sent him to England for consecration. When the English bishops refused—pleading that the law did not authorize them to act for the Church outside England—Seabury went to Scotland to seek consecration from the non-jurors. The non-jurors were descendants of those Scottish bishops who refused the oath of allegiance to William and Mary. The non-juring bishops consecrated Seabury in 1784, but his consecration had its price. In exchange for recognition, Seabury agreed to urge his fellow Americans to accept some Scottish practices in their new prayer book.

Meanwhile, Anglicans in the South and the middle states formed their own conventions. In 1785 a convention representing Virginia, Pennsylvania, and New York elected William White (1748–1836) and Samuel Provoost (1742–1815) bishops. The two went to England for consecration. This time Parliament cooperated and passed a law authorizing the Church of England to consecrate White and Provoost.

The ancient canon that three bishops are needed to consecrate a new bishop forced White and Provoost to negotiate with Seabury for a united church. The discussions were long and involved. Seabury represented a high church tradition that stressed conformity to the ancient church. Seabury was particularly concerned about the place of the Athanasian Creed in the new denomination. He also wanted to secure the revisions of the Communion Service that he had promised the Scottish bishops. White and Provoost spoke for the more low church ministers of their regions. White and Provoost wanted more lay participation in the government of the church, and they believed that the church should be as theologically comprehensive as possible.

The final compromise was artful. Seabury won most of the formal theological issues, although the church did not make the Athanasian Creed obligatory. At the same time, White and Provoost secured a major role for the laity in the governance of the church. The new episcopal constitution located most ecclesiastical power in the vestries who had the right to select their own rectors, to set ministerial salaries, and to regulate their own membership. The bishops were symbols of the church's continuity with the past and expressions of its present unity with more sacramental and theological authority than administrative power. A House of Delegates and a House of Bishops, who had to agree on any proposed church legislation, completed the national structure. Unlike England, the number of dioceses was undefined. The church could found new bishoprics whenever the growth of the church required them.

The Presbyterians only made minor changes in their form of government. A new constitution provided for a General Assembly to act as a national judicatory and allowed the Presbyteries to establish new synods when needed. The basic role of the presbyteries or synods was unchanged. In a similar development, the Dutch Reformed Church broke its last remaining governmental ties with Holland, and adopted a national organization similar to the Presbyterian church.

New England Congregationalists were too bound by their commitment to local church government to form a national church body. In 1801 the Connecticut Congregationalists agreed to join with the Presbyterian Church in a Plan of Union for the evangelization of the West. The Plan allowed frontier congregations to elect a minister from either denomination and send representatives to both judicatories. Later, the Congregationalists used their national missionaries societies as a *de facto* form of national church organization. The Baptists and later the Disciples of Christ followed a similar pattern.

A Silent Revolution

The American Revolution marked an important transition in American Protestant history. Before the war, the most numerous Protestant churches were the Congregationalists, the Presbyterians, and the Anglicans. After the war, the Baptists and Methodists expanded quickly and soon outnumbered the older denominations. By 1830 the Methodists were the largest Protestant body.

No single cause accounts for this religious revolution. Especially in the South, the decline of Anglicanism created a religious vacuum. Where no Anglican minister was available, people went to the nearest church. Both the Baptists and the Methodists ordained sufficient ministers to provide services throughout the South and West.

Baptists and Methodists also attracted frontier residents, because of their strong ecclesiastical discipline. Baptist and Methodist congregations insisted on high moral standards, and both churches frequently excommunicated members for sexual irregularities, for violence, and for drunkenness. Settlement expanded more rapidly than government, and the new residents needed strong local organizations to impose some moral order.

Baptists and Methodists also appealed successfully to democratic sentiment. While the ministers of the largest colonial churches were part of the upper and professional classes, the ministers of the newer denominations identified with the common people. Both recruited their clergy from the lower middle classes, and each denomination provided positions of leadership in the local church for their active members.

CHAPTER ELEVEN

THE AGE OF EVANGELISM

From 1790 to 1860 American Protestantism experienced growth and renewal. Evangelism flourished for two reasons. First, the United States was a free market in religion, and congregations had to recruit and retain their own membership. If another congregation offered a more attractive theology or a better choir, people might move their membership. Sunday schools and other benevolent organizations helped in this competition by making congregational life more interesting and varied.

Second, the new revival aimed at the transformation of the nation. The churches wanted a Protestant America safe from the (perceived) dangers of barbarism, rationalism, and Catholicism, and one that would continue the older Puritan dream of an errand into the wilderness. Americans were to be a royal priesthood, inspiring a similar devotion to true religion and free government in others.

The national mission was less successful than the church's outreach to individuals. In much of the country the rapid expansion of Roman Catholicism made America a more diverse nation than Protestants wanted. Further, the revival only partially checked the rise of rationalism and skepticism. Heterodox Christians and nonbelievers dominated the nation's intellectual life. Such savants as Ralph Waldo Emerson (1803–82) urged people to move beyond Christianity and form a religion in keeping with their own souls's needs.

Local Revivals

After the eighteenth-century Great Awakening, Christian leaders hoped and prayed for God to bring a new wave of revivals. Many contemporary observers believed that a new wave of conversions began in Connecticut during the 1790s.

Most revivals were local, confined to an individual church or town. Typically the minister would proclaim the beginning of a special season of grace. As the revival spread, some pastors invited such popular evangelists as Asahel Nettleton (1783–1844) to lead services. A revival in one town inspired revivals in adjacent towns and villages.

Methodists depended on the local revival. The circuit riders entered a town, gathered an audience, preached, and organized a society or congregation. The next preacher reentered the same town or village and reinforced the work. Their hope was that each visit would refuel the fires of the earlier revival. Although they did not itinerate, Baptists also conducted extensive (and ideally continuous) local revivals.

After the Revolution, Virginia's mother church was in desperate straits. More than a third of the clergy had fled, legal establishment had ended, and Deism was popular among the upper classes. Bishops Richard Moore (consecrated 1813), William Meade (consecrated 1829), and John Johns (consecrated 1842) held frequent meetings for special prayer and renewal. These revivals often led to the organization of missionary societies, and Virginia Seminary, located in Alexandria, became the national center for Episcopal foreign missions abroad.

Catholics also had revivals, called parish missions. Local priests invited preachers, often individuals noted for their oratory, to preach a series of sermons. Like their Protestant counterparts, Catholic awakeners emphasized eschatological themes and ordinarily ended with an invitation for the worshipers to confess, renew their Baptism, and take the sacrament. These meetings helped form parishes among new immigrants.

The American foreign missionary movement began with a prayer meeting, held by Samuel Mills (1783–1811), at Williams College. Mills and his friends formed the Society of the Brethren, a band of young men pledged to go abroad. In many ways, the Brethren were like other college fraternities. They had their own rituals and kept their records in code. Both Luther Rice (1783–1836) and Adoniram Judson (1788–1850) pledged their lives to foreign missions while members of this society.

The Awakening of 1858, popularly called the "prayer meeting revival," was a series of unrelated urban revivals. In these revivals, small groups of lay people met together for prayer and mutual support.

The Camp Meetings

The camp meeting was a revival, often at a local church, attended by people who traveled some distance to the services. Since people exerted so much effort to attend, the audience often camped out so that they could take part in more than one session. The first camp meetings happened by accident. After a failed ministry in North Carolina, Presbyterian James McGready (c.1758–1817), a Presbyterian pastor, went to Logan County, Kentucky, where he organized his fellow ministers to pray for a new awakening. In 1800 McGready announced a sacramental meeting at Red River Church. To McGready's surprise, a large denominationally diverse audience, including several ministers, answered his call. Although the services began in the church, the ministers quickly moved outside to reach the crowds. The camp meeting movement spread and meetings were held at Gaspar River and Cane Ridge.

The first camp meetings were emotional. Converts were "slain in the spirit" (lost consciousness); broke out in uncontrollable dancing, laughing, or singing; and even fell to all fours and barked ("treeing the devil"). Tears and shouts of victory were common. Although critics charged that more souls were begot than saved, little evidence exists of widespread immorality.

The Presbyterians reacted negatively to the camps' emotionalism, lack of discipline, and Arminian theology. After much controversy, the denomination withdrew from the meetings. In contrast, the Methodists sponsored camp meetings and developed rules for the camps. Under their leadership, the more extreme emotional conversions were discouraged, and the meetings conducted with more order.

The nation's westward expansion generated new religious movements. Thomas Campbell (1763–1854) and his son Alexander (1788–1866) organized The Christian Church (Disciples of Christ). The new denomination began when the Seceder Presbytery disciplined Thomas Campbell for offering the Lord's Supper to non-Seceder Presbyterians. Thomas Campbell, soon joined by his son, organized the Christian Association of Washington County, Pennsylvania, in 1809, based on sole authority of Scripture. "Where the Bible speaks, we speak; where the Bible is silent, we are silent." Hence the Association had no use for denominations, confessions, or creeds, believing that such structures and practices had no biblical basis.

The Campbells' theology developed rapidly. After they decided that infant baptism was unscriptural in 1812, they joined the local Baptist association. But the Campbells soon battled their new brethren. Most frontier Baptists were strong Calvinists who believed that no human act was necessary to salvation. They parted company with the Campbells on the question of whether obedience to Christ in baptism was a necessary component of the process of salvation. The dispute ended with about one-third of the Baptist churches withdrawing to join other followers of the Campbells in the Disciples of Christ.

Barton Stone's pilgrimage was even more complicated. Stone began his ministry as a Presbyterian and participated in many camp meetings. When the Presbyterians moved to discipline their more enthusiastic ministers, Stone withdrew from the Synod of Kentucky in 1803 and helped form an independent Springfield Presbytery. A year later that body published its last will and testament in which signers resolved to avoid all denominational names. In the future, they were to call themselves "Christians" and recognize the Bible as their sole authority. Their common biblicism made it easy for Stone's and the Campbells' followers to unite with one another.

Professional Revivalists

The revival was also spread by professional evangelists such as Charles Finney (1792–1872). At age twenty-nine, Finney experienced a dramatic conversion. Although a rising young law clerk, Finney renounced his legal career and began to preach in upstate New York, leading revivals in New Hartford, Rome, Utica, and Rochester.

Finney called his style of revival, "the new measures," although his revivals were similar to Methodist meetings. Each revival was carefully prepared. The people were taught new "gospel hymns," and a large choir—often drawn from several congregations—was recruited to help with the music. Finney formed teams of people to pray for sinners, often by name, and to visit door-to-door. Although Finney usually began his revivals on Sunday mornings, he protracted (extended) the meetings and held weekday and evening services. Every effort was made not to arouse extreme emotion.

Finney's revivals were controversial among Presbyterians and Congregationalists, because he seemed to have changed the Gospel to encourage revival. The evangelist believed that God would save those who made a decision for Christ. In a famous phrase, he said that the Bible commanded people to make themselves a new heart. In his 1835 *Lectures on Revivals,* Finney stated that anyone who followed the right techniques might bring others to conversion, since religious commitment was similar to other human decisions.

Finney had many imitators, including Jacob Knapp, Daniel Nash, Luther Myrick, and Jabez Swan. None of these men were of Finney's stature, and their revivals more resembled sacred "medicine shows" than Christian services. Daniel Nash often preached wearing a black veil; Swan was noted for the emotional excesses of his meetings, and Knapp, a master showman, was accused of financial improprieties.

Theology and Revival

In 1829 Albert Barnes (1798–1870), a Presbyterian, preached a sermon entitled "The Plan of Salvation" advocating a revivalistic theology and suggesting that original sin was not by itself enough to keep a person from accepting Christ. Conservatives accused Barnes of heresy and carried their case to the General Assembly. Although Barnes was acquitted in 1831, the issue was far from closed. The theological issue was complicated by two polity questions: first, whether presbyteries included all churches in a given geographic area or whether some churches were free to form their own judicatories; and second, whether Presbyterians should continue to cooperate with Congregationalists in missionary efforts.

From 1834 to 1836 the revivalists maintained and even strengthened their political position in the General Assembly. The high-water mark of evangelical influence in the General Assembly came in 1836. In that year, the pro-revival party secured the Assembly's official support of the American Board of Commissioners for Foreign Missions and established Union Seminary in New York in cooperation with Connecticut Congregationalists. Then suddenly power shifted. In 1837 Western conservatives forged an alliance with delegates from the South and excised (removed) the midwestern Plan of Union Presbyteries. For the second time in less than a hundred years two Presbyterian churches (now called the Old and New School) existed.

In New England the controversy primarily revolved around the theology of Nathaniel Taylor (1786–1858), professor of theology in Yale's Divinity Department. In his 1828 *Concio ad clerum*, Taylor suggested that the doctrine of original sin only taught that sin was inevitable, not that it was necessary. Human beings are like people running across a bridge with many gaps. Eventually the runner will fall into the water, but he or she can avoid any particular hole. If so, then human beings, despite their inevitable fall into actual sin, still retain sufficient integrity of will to turn from sin to Christ. In Taylor's famous phrase, we retain "power to the contrary."

Churchly Opposition to Revivals

The Anglo-Catholic party in the Protestant Episcopal Church offered a compelling alternative to revivalism. The new high church theology began at Oxford University in England under the theological leadership of John Henry Newman (1801–1890) and Edward Pusey (1800–1892). In their influential *Tracts for the Times,* a series of learned articles published between 1833 and 1843, the new high church theologians argued that the Church of England was the heir of the ancient Catholic Church and the Reformation. American Anglo-Catholicism was centered at New York's General Seminary and in the northwestern dioceses.

Lutheranism also had a significant high church party. The Lutheran churches of Pennsylvania and Maryland had accepted many aspects of revivalism after 1800, and some congregations practiced something like Charles Finney's "new measures." By 1830, however, new immigrants from Germany brought a renewed Lutheranism that "recovered" many half-forgotten aspects of sixteenth-century faith, including the Real Presence of Christ and baptismal regeneration. After the more revivalistic Lutherans proposed confessional revision in the 1840's, the confessionalists established their own seminary at Philadelphia to counter the prevailing errors. Simultaneously, a more radically confessional group, largely composed of immigrants from Saxony, established their own denomination, the Missouri Synod.

John Williamson Nevin (1803–66) and Horace Bushnell (1802–76) were two of the more influential antirevival voices among Reformed Christians. In the *Anxious Bench,* Nevin maintained that revivalism neglected the church's historic message that Word and Sacrament mediated Christ to the believer. Nevin strongly emphasized the corporate dimension of faith, and the mediation of grace through the sacraments.

Horace Bushnell took a similar position in his *Christian Nurture* (1847). In this extended essay, Bushnell admitted that some people, particularly those dominated by sin, needed an emotional conversion. But, Bushnell reasoned, most Christians learned faith from their parents, their church, their community, and their nation. Hence they never know a time when they did not know Christ or reject evil. Instead of making children into sinners again so that the revival can save them, Bushnell argued, we should strengthen the Christian influences on the young.

The Mission to the Nation

The creation of a Christian America was as important to the revivalists as the conversion of individuals. The revivalists passionately believed that the United States was a "Christian Nation" with a divine mission to spread the twin gospels of Protestantism and republicanism around the world.

The missionary movement was central to this strategy. National interest in the missionary movement predated the first American missionaries. American Baptists avidly followed the work of William Carey, a British Baptist missionary to India, and organized societies to raise money for his support.

The American missionary movement began when Samuel Mills (1783–1818) and his colleagues from the Society of the Brethren presented their plans for foreign service to Moses Stuart, Professor of Bible at Andover Seminary. After earnest prayer, Stuart and his colleague, Leonard Woods, presented the proposal to the Massachusetts General Association (Orthodox Congregationalist), which chartered the American Board of Commissioners for Foreign Missions. The American Board was initially an interdenominational sending agency, similar to the British missionary societies of the period. In 1812 the board's first missionaries left for Asia. Shortly thereafter the board sent missionaries to the Sandwich Islands and to the Near East. By 1860, the American Board was among the world's largest missionary societies. In time, American societies were organized for home missions, education, Sunday schools, and publishing. Other denominations quickly established a similar national structure with societies and agencies for home and national missions, Christian education, and other good causes. Similarly, the parish became an alliance of different organizations that met together for common prayer on Sunday.

Historians often credit Robert Raikes (1735–1811), a British newspaper publisher and social reformer, with popularizing the Sunday school. Raikes' primary concern was the large number of children that had no place to go on Sunday and who did not attend school during the week. Inspired by some early experiments, he opened a school in his home parish that taught reading from the Bible. Churches established schools throughout England and the United States. However, the spread of literacy soon transformed their mission into providing elementary Christian teaching.

Ordinary Christians often made the Sunday school into their own "church within the church." The Sunday schools were particularly important in the South and West. Only the wealthiest town churches in these regions could afford a full-time pastor who preached every Sunday. Other churches were quarter-time (once a month), half-time (twice a month), or three-quarters time (three times a month). In these situations the regular meetings of the Sunday school and the various societies were more fundamental to people's religious life than the regular worship service.

Unfortunately, the Sunday school—like many other aspects of the revival—was a great simplifier of Christian truth. When the Sunday schools replaced catechism, American evangelicals' knowledge of Christian theology declined. Sunday school flattened many of the most profound Christian truths into moralistic commonplaces.

The Sunday school and the missionary societies also provided women with a place for Christian service. Although nineteenth-century American churches were predominantly female, most denominations prohibited women from serving as pastors. But they could serve in the Sunday schools and in the various missionary societies. By mid-century, the missionary societies recognized women workers as an essential part of the foreign missionary enterprise and appointed some women (including single women) for service abroad.

Fighting Evil

One goal of the Evangelical Awakening was the reformation of the nation's morals. Yale students formed moral societies as early as 1797. The Methodist emphasis on sanctification added a new sense of urgency to this older tradition. Many Americans came to desire holiness or perfection for themselves and a more moral nation for everyone.

The nineteenth century saw a revolution in family life. In earlier times, most people lived and worked in the same location. Families lived on farms or in small buildings with the living quarters above and shops beneath. Both parents disciplined children and contributed to the family economy. In the nineteenth century, a separation between home and employment occurred in most cities and towns. In response, the churches pictured the ideal family with the woman at home caring for the children and the husband away at work.

Evangelicals pressed for laws to protect the home, particularly laws regulating sexual activity outside marriage. One crusade, for example, was to outlaw prostitution which some cities had tolerated or regulated. Other drives included attempts to prohibit the sale and distribution of pornography. As medicine advanced, Christians demanded that the government limit or prohibit the sale of birth control devices.

The temperance crusade was part of the new stress on family life. Industrialization and mechanization increased the dangers from alcohol as machines increased the need for close human attentiveness. Further, an apparent correlation existed between such domestic problems as wife and child abuse and alcohol use. Christian concern with temperance began in the eighteenth century when Wesley and his followers asked whether a Christian should use alcohol. Lyman Beecher (1775–1863), the best-known American evangelical leader, attacked the intemperate use of alcohol in 1811, and later concluded that drinking alcohol was a sin. In some states evangelicals organized to prohibit the sale of alcoholic beverages by law. In 1846 they secured the first statewide prohibition law in Maine. Before the Civil War, thirteen states had their own laws prohibiting the sale and use of alcohol.

The Bible seemed to assume that alcoholic beverages were part of life, and Jesus apparently used wine at the Lord's Supper. In response Moses Stuart, professor of Bible at Andover Seminary and America's leading exegete, argued that the Bible distinguished between two types of wine: one fermented and one unfermented. According to Stuart, Jesus had only used the unfermented variety. Over the course of the next fifty years, arguments such as Stuart's reformed church practice. At first those who wished to avoid alcohol substituted sugar water for wine in the Lord's Supper, but when technology made grape juice a practical market item, Presbyterians, Congregationalists, and Baptists used it at the Lord's Table.

The temperance crusade may have helped to inspire the whole range of reforms that contemporaries called "ultraisms." Some evangelicals extended the arguments against alcohol to include tobacco, and others used them to condemn all stimulants, especially coffee and tea. Ultraists also sought to regulate food by advocating whole wheat flour and discouraging the eating of meat.

The Rise of the Sects

The age of evangelism was also a great age of sectarian growth in the United States. A radical branch of Quakerism founded by Ann Lee (1736–84), the Shakers, established several celibate communities along the frontier. The name came from the Shaker's use of a holy dance as a way of suppressing sexual desire. John Humphrey Noyes (1811–86), the founder of the Oneida Community, went to the opposite extreme. In his community, every woman and every man were spiritual husbands and wives of each other who were free to have sexual relationships with whomever they pleased.

The most successful of the new religious movements was the Church of Jesus Christ of Latter Day Saints, or Mormons, founded by Joseph Smith (1805–44). Smith claimed to have received a vision that told him where he could find some ancient golden tablets and the glasses needed to translate them. When Smith followed the angel's direction, he read a wondrous story of the coming of Christ to the new world, the immigration of the lost tribes of Israel, two empires of Indians, and the slaughter of the Christian believers. This new revelation, published as *The Book of Mormon*, answered many questions that evangelicals were asking in upstate New York. These included such matters as the lawfulness of coffee and tea and the proper mode of baptism.

Persecution forced Smith and his followers to move further west, first to Ohio, then to Missouri, and finally to Illinois. At each stage in this pilgrimage, Smith received new revelations. These revelations made his group more distinct from evangelical Christianity. These included a belief in the preexistence of souls, in polygamy, and in the ultimate divinization of individual believers. After an Illinois mob murdered Smith, his followers, now led by Brigham Young (1801–77), fled to Utah where they established their own desert Zion.

CHAPTER TWELVE

BLACK PEOPLE
IN A WHITE WORLD

Europeans did not invent the African slave trade. Sub-Saharan African wars often ended with the winners enslaving the losers and, if possible, selling the captives. The Arabs often served as middlemen in these transactions. After 1500 the new world demand for slaves apparently encouraged an increase in African wars. Dutch traders brought the first African "servants" to Virginia in 1619, and subsequent English military victories over Holland and Spain made Great Britain the dominant trader in the North Atlantic. New England entrepreneurs exchanged slaves for sugar, made the sugar into rum, and used the rum to purchase more slaves.

African slaves seemed an ideal source of cheap labor. Africans were technically advanced enough for many slaves already to possess important agricultural skills. Further, they were marked by their skin color. If white servants escaped, they melted into the general population; however, wherever Africans went, people recognized their bondage or, if legally free, their former bondage. Escaped slaves were easily rounded up and returned.

American slavery was chattel slavery; that is, the owner owned the slaves' bodies, similar to the ownership of horses, cows, or mules. Since the fruit of chattel belong to the owner, slavery made children slaves as well. While laws protected the slave's life, governments rarely punished whites who murdered their own slaves, especially if the slave died after a beating for disobedience.

Masters employed slaves in labor intensive tasks: clearing forests, planting and curing tobacco, cultivating rice and indigo, washing, cooking, and housekeeping. Some slaves became skilled artisans and worked as blacksmiths, wheelwrights, and coopers.

131

The Conversion of the African Americans

During the seventeenth century Protestants made little effort to convert their black servants, perhaps because under English law baptism conveyed social as well as Christian freedom. Although Virginia and the other colonies passed laws that explicitly said that baptism did not effect a person's social status, the new laws did not change planters' attitudes.

The first major effort to convert the slaves was made during the Great Awakening. Although Whitefield preached to audiences that included slaves, the Baptists were the first to recruit large numbers of African Americans. Blacks attended the same revivals as whites and often had similar emotional conversion experiences. Later, the Methodist revivals converted many slaves as well.

Evangelicalism was popular among slaves, because it was a religion of dignity and hope. The Baptist and Methodist exhorters preached that every individual had the right and the obligation to accept Christ. Further, the preachers told many biblical stories, especially the stories of Moses, Samson, and Daniel, which taught that God vindicates those who call upon God's name. Evangelical preaching also provided the slaves with a treasure chest of eschatological symbols: the second coming, the fiery chariot, the day of jubilee, and the last judgment.

Baptist and Methodist evangelicals urged every believer to lead others to Christ. Converted African Americans took this obligation seriously. When people "got religion," they returned to their plantation and shared their testimonies with other slaves. Testimonies were one origin of the black-led "brush arbor" prayer meetings that gave African American Christians an opportunity to lead services for other slaves.

By 1800 most white Christians accepted the obligation to tell their slaves about Christ. In devout households, masters invited slaves to join the family devotions and the master or mistress provided some religious instruction. Many masters allowed (or forced) their slaves to attend Sunday services. This was not always inviting: the slave balconies often had manacles to prevent escape.

Nonetheless, the white churches provided African Americans with some religious education. Although Southern laws prohibited teaching slaves to read, slaves heard the Bible at worship, and many memorized long biblical passages. Churches also employed slave missionaries who went to the plantations and held special evangelistic services. The first were appointed by the Society for the Propagation of the Gospel in the eighteenth century. In the 1840s and 1850s Columbia Theological Seminary professors took a special interest in the evangelization of the African Americans. After its 1844 separation from Northern Methodism, the Southern Methodists also devoted personnel to this ministry.

Two Christianities

Two forms of Christianity co-existed in the slave quarters. Many whites believed that Christianity was an effective means of social control. The masters often hired preachers who took their texts from passages which read "servants obey your masters" or "do not steal." Part of the message was that God made some masters, others slaves. Few slaves were attracted to this faith. But the slaves had their own access to the gospel. On the larger plantations slaves held meetings at night apart from white eyes. These services were frequently emotional, and may have provided an emotional cleansing from the problems of the day.

In these meetings, slaves known for their piety or knowledge of the Bible would recite (or if they were fortunate, read) the Bible to other slaves, preach, and lead in prayer and song. Unfortunately, we do not have transcriptions of these sermons, although they may have been similar to post-Civil War African American preaching. We do, however, have much slave music, called spirituals, which were collected and published shortly after the Civil War. These songs should be interpreted on two levels. On their surface, the spirituals are similar to white Gospel music. Often based on a scriptural text, they describe the believer's journey heavenward, praise God's continual mercies, and witness to the peace that passes all understanding. However, the spirituals also carried a word of freedom. A song like "Steal Away to Jesus" could be heard as a call to salvation or as a summons to escape.

Restrictions on Black Religious Freedom

Masters did not allow their slaves to practice their religion freely. After the 1831 rebellion led by Nat Turner (c. 1800–31), whites often prohibited unsupervised black preachers from speaking to other African Americans without a master present. All Southern states made it a crime to teach slaves to read.

Chattel slavery made it difficult to practice Christianity. Slaves could not be legally married, and often the only marriage ceremony was when a couple jumped over a broom together. Even these informal commitments depended on the owner. A master might sell husbands and wives separately, and slave dealers often marketed children before they reached maturity. In Virginia and Maryland, where plantations were often unprofitable, some owners may have bred slaves for the market.

The owners did not allow slaves to assume office in a local white church. Even where a separate black church existed, as in Richmond, Virginia, the law required the pastor and other officers to be white. When slaves attended white churches, custom strictly segregated the services with African Americans served separately at the Lord's Table. Naturally, the authorities did not allowed slaves to participate in church meetings.

Free Black Churches

Not all African Americans were slaves. Although it became more difficult as time passed, owners might emancipate slaves, and a few masters continued the ancient practice of rewarding faithful servants with freedom in their wills. In some areas masters allowed slaves to take jobs off their plantations. Although the master received a share of the wages, a few saved enough to purchase their freedom. New England abolished slavery completely, and the Middle Atlantic states passed laws gradually emancipating their slaves. Some slaves emancipated themselves by fleeing to the North or to Canada.

Free blacks were not content to remain in segregated churches without the privileges of full membership. Sometime between 1773 and 1775 African Americans (perhaps slaves) established a Baptist Church at Silver Bluff, South Carolina, and soon other black Baptist churches existed. Two of the most important of these were the Abyssinian Baptist Church in New York and the African Baptist Church in Richmond, Virginia.

Richard Allen (1760–1831) was typical of many black church founders. Allen earned his freedom in 1777 and became an ardent Methodist. When the congregation at St. George's Methodist Church in Philadelphia humiliated Allen, he and his friends withdrew to form the Free African Methodist Society which later organized itself as the Bethel Methodist Church. Bethel asked Francis Asbury to ordain Allen as an elder. African Americans in other cities formed their own congregations, and these congregations united in 1816 to form the African Methodist Episcopal Church.

A similar secession from the John Street Methodist Church in New York, led by Peter Williams, Sr., resulted in the formation of the Zion Methodist Church. This congregation later joined the Wilmington Union Church of Africans, pastored by Peter Spencer, to create the African Methodist Episcopal Church, Zion.

Some free blacks favored the organization of separate congregations within the larger white denominations. Absolom Jones, who had formed the Free African Society with Allen, believed that this was the best route to follow. William White, the Episcopal bishop of Philadelphia, ordained Jones and allowed him to organize his own congregation, St. Thomas's. Peter Williams, Jr., the son of Bethel's founder, followed a similar road to Episcopal ordination.

By 1820 independent black congregations existed in most cities. The African Baptist Church of Savannah, Georgia, for example, had more than two thousand members, and the African Baptist Church of Richmond more than one thousand.

The leaders of these free African congregations held the same doctrine and practiced the same rituals as the white churches, and their congregations also participated in such movements as the Sunday school, foreign missions, and Bible distribution. Lott Carey (1780–1828), converted in Richmond in 1807, purchased his freedom to become a missionary to Liberia. In 1821, Carey went to Africa where he was martyred in 1828.

The antebellum free black churches were important for four reasons:

1. They were significant centers of evangelism and missions. More converts were made in the nineteenth-century black churches than in India or China. The conversion of the African Americans is among the most important success stories in the history of the modern church.

2. These congregations proved to African Americans (and to some whites) that black people could successfully organize and maintain important cultural institutions. Black churches built black pride.

3. The antebellum black churches created a core of black leadership. Most black leaders before and after the Civil War were church leaders. Black clergy played an important role in the antislavery crusade. When the Civil War ended, the earlier free black churches helped the former slaves create their own churches.

4. Antebellum black congregations attained high standards of theological and moral orthodoxy. Although some African influences remained, African American churches held fast

to the essentials of evangelical teaching. For comparatively uneducated people, the mastery of these complex doctrines was a substantial intellectual achievement.

The Impact of Slavery on White Christians

Slavery affected every area of Southern life. Although only a few whites owned slaves, most whites in the South helped maintain the slave codes. Many ambitious young Southerners aspired to become slave holders. The "Southern way of life" was an important byproduct of slavery. Whites supported slavery because the "peculiar institution" sustained their most deeply held social and political values, particularly, an aristocratic style of life. This style of life also influenced gender identity. The ideal Southern woman was a person of leisure who spent her life in needle work, music, and entertaining. Southern women were to continue the family line by having legitimate children, and an elaborate moral code stressed virginity and fidelity. Although Southern males often put women on a pedestal and talked about the virtues of Southern womanhood, Southern women were almost as restricted as the black slaves.

The social effects of slavery made the South regionally distinct. While the North was exploring the possibilities of democracy, the South continued aristocratic habits inherited from England. In their own minds, Southern planters held a social place similar to that of the great English Lords or the Prussian Junkers. Consequently the South lagged behind in such democratic reforms as universal manhood suffrage, free compulsory education, the creation of colleges and universities, and the legal recognition of women's rights.

Even among Baptists and Methodists, originally lower-class churches, slavery shaped congregational life. Long before the principal denominations (Baptist, Methodists, and Presbyterians) divided on regional lines, Southern Evangelicalism developed differently from its Northern counterpart. Successful pastors saw themselves as gentlemen, and they distrusted Northern evangelical attempts to transform society. The doctrine of the "Spirituality of the Church," developed by Presbyterian theologians, taught that God commissioned the church only to provide for humanity's spiritual needs. Consequently ecclesiastical leaders should not discuss any political or social topic in their sermons or synodical deliberations. In practice this limited sermons to evangelistic appeals or doctrinal exposition.

The White Conflict Over Slavery

Almost from the beginning, some American Christians believed that slavery was morally wrong. Samuel Sewall (1652–1730), a judge at the Salem Witch Trials, published *The Selling of Joseph: A Memorial* in 1700, arguing that the Bible did not condone slavery. By the 1770s, the slavery issue was hotly debated in the New England states. Although Jonathan Edwards had owned a black servant, his theological followers were among slavery's strongest opponents. Samuel Hopkins, a leading New Divinity theologian, passionately opposed slavery, although he ministered in Newport, Rhode Island, the nation's largest slave port. Jonathan Edwards II also expressed strong antislavery sentiments. During the Revolutionary crisis, many Patriots concluded that to protest a three penny tax on tea and to continue to own slaves was inconsistent. By the end of the Revolutionary War, the New England states had freed their slaves and were solidly antislavery.

The situation in the Mid-Atlantic states was more complex. Anthony Benezet (1713–84) and John Woolman (1720–72), two Quaker leaders, toured the nation urging their fellow society members to renounce slavery as a sin. In 1776, the Yearly Meeting of Friends followed their recommendations, and the Quaker denomination became solidly anti-slavery. Many Southern Quakers, particularly in eastern North Carolina, moved north or west to escape the slave system. During the Revolutionary War the middle states adopted laws requiring gradual emancipation. In general, these laws required some slaves to remain in service for life, while freeing their descendants when they reached a certain legal age. For example, Pennsylvania required the children of slaves to be twenty-eight before the law emancipated them. These laws slowly ended slavery in the region, although some slaves still existed in New Jersey during the Civil War. Ironically, some owners took advantage of the period of servitude to sell their slaves in the South.

Anti-slavery sentiment was also strong in Virginia during the post-revolutionary decades. Many planters confessed their uneasiness with the system, and aristocrats from Virginia and Kentucky were influential in the establishment of the American Colonization Society in 1817. The society proposed to compensate slave holders and to send the former slaves to Africa. The society acquired Liberia for this purpose, and some African Americans emigrated there, becoming that country's ruling elite.

Other Southerners did not share the Virginians' uneasiness. At the 1787 constitutional convention, South Carolina's delegates worked to secure legal privileges for slavery. Because of their sharp negotiations, the new constitution counted slaves as three-fifths of a person for representation in the House of Representatives and the Electoral College.

The Issue Becomes Radical

Both proslavery and antislavery positions hardened in the 1830's. Although slave revolts in Virginia and South Carolina had an impact on the new attitudes, the 1833 abolition of slavery in the British empire also contributed. British evangelicals' struggle against slavery began when John Wesley and John Newton embraced the cause. William Wilberforce (1759–1833) was the leader of the Parliamentary forces that finally passed the bill. English evangelicals urged their American cousins to follow their lead and work to wipe out slavery root and branch.

Some American evangelicals shared the English concerns. Arthur (1786–1865) and Lewis (1788–1873) Tappan, business people whose personal fortunes supported many evangelical causes, were also strong supporters of abolition. When Lane Seminary's Trustees insisted that abolitionist students end their interracial ministry among Cincinnati's African Americans, the students refused and transferred to Oberlin. To encourage the students, the Tappans' recruited Charles Finney to teach them theology.

Theodore Weld (1803–95), the leader of the Lane students, became an abolitionist in 1830. He organized a band of antislavery revivalists, called the Seventy, who preached the necessity of immediate abolition throughout the North. In addition, Weld wrote *The Bible Against Slavery* (1837) and *Slavery As It Is* (1839). The latter provided Harriet Beecher Stowe (1822–96) with the information that she used to write *Uncle Tom's Cabin,* (1852), the most successful antislavery tract ever written.

While Weld and others devoted much attention to the Old Testament regulations of slavery, the teachings of Jesus were at the center of their argument. Slavery was inconsistent with the love that Jesus commanded. Further, people could not keep slaves without violating other divine laws, especially those protecting the sanctity of the family.

Southern proslavery opinion solidified. The invention of the cotton gin and the expansion of cotton cultivation made plantation slavery more profitable. Further, Nat Turner's 1831 rebellion led many Southerners to fear that loss of control over the slaves might lead to a blood bath. Slave codes were strengthened, and Southern representatives demanded that the Federal government support slavery by extending the right to own slaves to the territories.

Southern churchmen, including the Episcopal Thomas Dew and the Baptist Richard Furman, fashioned a religious justification for slavery. In part they argued that slavery was a natural good, since aristocratic societies improved human art and letters. Further, Southern churchmen claimed that since Africans were racially inferior, slavery was the most humane way to regulate the relationship between the races.

Every proslavery book included exhaustive examinations of the biblical teachings on bondage. Unlike their Northern counterparts, Southern theologians concluded the Scriptures permitted slavery and cited the Old Testament, Paul's letter to Philemon, and the injunctions for slaves to obey their masters as evidence. Since God's Word never permitted any immoral action, God must consider slavery moral. Nonetheless, some Southern theologians agreed that slavery as it existed needed reform to conform to such biblical mandates as the sanctity of marriage.

The Southern scriptural argument depended on a simple hermeneutic. The Scriptures were authoritative, clear, and infallible, and, hence, all passages equally expressed God's will. Thus, a commandment in Deuteronomy might guide Christian morality as well as Jesus's teachings and Philemon was as important as Galatians. Southerners treated any questioning of this hermeneutic as though it were a denial of the Bible itself.

The Churches Divide

Abraham Lincoln was more right than perhaps he knew when he said that no house divided against itself can long stand. The division of the evangelical churches foretold the coming of the political Civil War.

Slavery contributed to the 1837 division of the Presbyterian Church into Old and New School branches. The Southerners joined the Old School which professed neutrality on slavery and other political issues. Old School Princeton Seminary was the only Northern Seminary where proslavery students felt welcome.

The Methodists divided in 1844. Two schisms of antislavery Methodists had already occurred in 1841 (the Wesleyan Methodist Church) and in 1842 (the Methodist Wesleyan Connection). Simultaneously, other Northern Methodists held informal meetings to discuss the future stance of the church. At this crucial juncture, petitioners asked the General Conference to rule on whether James O. Andrew of Georgia, a slave owner, might continue to serve as a bishop. When the Conference voted 110 to 68 that he could not, the Southern representatives asked for an amicable separation. In 1845 a Conference at Louisville, Kentucky, established the Methodist Episcopal Church, South.

Baptists divided over a similar issue. In the 1830s, the Triennial Convention (a national Baptist body) agreed to neutrality on the slavery issue. To Northerners, a neutral convention meant that the convention would not appoint slaveholders to positions financed by the common purse. On the other hand, Southerners believed that neutrality meant that both slaveholders and non-slaveholders could hold any office. When the trustees of the American Baptist home missionary society refused to appoint a slave owner, James R. Reeves, to a position of service, Alabama Baptists demanded that the Triennial Convention clarify its policy on the the issue. Unable to maintain a non-committal stance any longer, the society finally issued a clear answer: no such persons would be appointed.

The Southerners called for a special meeting at Augusta, Georgia, in May 1845 to organize a new denomination. After those deliberations, Baptists in the South replaced the many Northern missionary societies with a single agency, the Southern Baptist Convention.

Since the 1787 Constitutional Convention, Southern politicians had blocked antislavery legislation by threatening to leave the union. Southern clergy played a similar game in their denominational organizations. When the Southern ministers threatened once too many times, the national denominations called their hand. Both sides were surprised when the Southerners carried out their threat. In 1860 the political leaders of the South tried the same tactic with, unfortunately, the same results. When the North refused to cave in, the South withdrew. This time the North greeted the schism not with anathemas, but with troops.

CHAPTER THIRTEEN

MISSIONS TO THE NONWESTERN WORLD

Missionary work was part of the early nineteenth-century religious revival. Although governments contributed little money to the new missions, the industrial revolution made Europe and the United States wealthy. Missionary advocates believed that they could tap this new wealth to do voluntarily what governments had previously done. It was the age of the gift and the volunteer.

Christianity and Empire

During the nineteenth century, Western nations established political and military control over much of the globe. Missionaries depended on the European military for protection and support. Further, many areas did not welcome missionaries until European or American gunboats forced the local rulers to do so.

Japan's experience was typical. In the seventeenth century Japan outlawed Christianity and limited Western trade to a few Dutch trading posts. American Commodore Matthew Perry (1794–1858) "opened" Japan to foreign influence by entering Tokyo Bay in 1853 with an American fleet. The first American consul to Japan was Townsend Harris, a devout evangelical, who conducted church services in his home. Harris continually urged the Japanese to admit missionaries to the country. Although Japan renewed its anti-Christian measures from 1867 to 1873, American diplomatic and military pressure secured their repeal.

In Africa, missionary explorers such as David Livingston established the "claims" that Europeans used to justify their later conquests. Once missionaries entered an African area, their home governments took over the area to protect them.

Indigenous peoples correctly assumed that the missionaries represented the economic and political interests of their governments. In 1838 war broke out between China and England when China outlawed the drug trade, dominated by Britain, and destroyed an English opium cache at Canton. The 1842 treaty ending the war protected both drug dealers and missionaries in five Chinese ports.

French behavior after the defeat of China in the Second Opium War further poisoned relationships between the Chinese and the churches. After the occupation of the city of Tientsin (Beijing), the French built a large church *Notre Dame des Victories* on the site of a former Imperial Temple and forced the captive Chinese officials to witness the church's consecration.

Such actions created a deep distrust of missionaries among patriotic Chinese. When antiforeign revolts occurred in 1897 and 1900 (the so-called Boxer Rebellion), the missionaries were a special target of Chinese anger. The rebels executed several thousand missionaries, along with many Chinese Christians, and took more than one thousand hostages in Peking. Escaping missionaries sought refuge in the "Treaty" ports where European and American fleets protected them. After an angry exchange of notes, a British, French, Japanese, German, and American joint army invaded. The Chinese were outgunned. As punishment, the allies forced China to pay a $333,000,000 indemnity to the victorious powers. When the Chinese Communists took power in 1949, one of their most popular acts was to expel all Western missionaries.

The missionaries were also implicated in the destruction of non-Western governments. In 1820, American Board missionaries arrived in the Sandwich Islands (present-day Hawaii), an important naval and trading station. By 1830 the missionaries were among the most powerful residents of the islands and owned vast estates. Despite the protests of their Boston-based board, the missionaries were the real powers behind the Hawaiian throne. The United States annexation of the islands in 1893 legally recognized the long-standing American domination of the islands.

Cultural Imperialism

The Christian mission was also aided by indirect or cultural imperialism. European wealth and technical expertise had prestige abroad, and ambitious young people in less developed areas often wanted a

Western education. Further, many nationalists believed that Western industrial technology was essential to economical development. The churches used the study of science and languages to attract young men to church-related colleges where they also received required religious instruction.

Some missionary spokesmen were sensitive to the dangers of "cultural imperialism." Rufus Anderson, secretary of the American Board, Francis Wayland, President of Brown University, and Henry Venn, secretary of the (British) Church Missionary Society deeply distrusted the tendency to confuse "civilization" with Christianity. They urged the churches to make their goal the "three-selfs:" self-governing, self-supporting, and self-propagating indigenous churches. Not all missionary leaders agreed. William Newton Clarke (1841–1912), the author of a major American missions textbook, *A Study of Christian Missions* (1901), proclaimed proudly that all people should become Christian, because Western culture was the best that the world knew. German theologians Adolf von Harnack (1851–1930) and Ernst Troeltsch (1865–1923) defended Christian missions by noting the west's capacity to regenerate indigenous cultural life.

William Hocking's *Re-Thinking Missions: A Layman's Inquiry After One Hundred Years* (1932) almost identified the Christian mission with the spread of Western civilization. Although Hocking made many useful criticisms of the American missionary effort, the *Inquiry* all but called for an end to conversion as a missionary goal. In its place, Hocking believed the church should put education in Western technology, literature, and morality.

Anglo-American Missions and William Carey

William Carey (1761–1834), an English Baptist cobbler, learned Latin, Greek, Hebrew, and Dutch while working at his bench. Deeply interested in foreign lands, Carey addressed his fellow Baptists in 1792 on the need for foreign missions. Preaching from Isaiah 54:2, Carey entitled his sermon, "Expect Great Things From God; Attempt Great Things For God." When he finished, the ministers agreed to establish a foreign missionary society. A year later, Carey sailed for India with Dr. John Thomas, a physician.

Carey's ministry in India began painfully. The English cobbler expected great crowds of people to flock to hear the Gospel. Instead, the Indians greeted Carey with indifference and hostility. In 1800 he moved to Serampore where John Marshman and William Ward joined him. The first years at the new location were among the most successful in Carey's career. He became a professor at Fort William College, a school dedicated to both Indian and Western learning. In 1801 Carey published his Bengali New Testament which he followed in 1809 with a translation of the whole Bible. Later, Carey translated parts of the Bible into twenty Indian languages and prepared grammars of the principal Indian tongues.

The Carey Mission inspired other missionary organizations. Evangelicals from different denominations formed the London Missionary Society in 1795, and members of the Church of England created the Church Missionary Society in 1799. At much the same time the Society for the Propagation of the Gospel began to work in Asia.

The American Board of Commissioners

The American Board of Commissioners for Foreign Missions was the most important American sending agency. New England Congregationalists established the society after an 1810 appeal from students and faculty at Andover Theological Seminary. From 1810–65 the American Board sent out forty percent of all American Missionary personnel, and the board's secretaries were the most widely respected American authorities on missions. The board's first ministry was in Bombay, India, which expanded to include much of Southern India. It also served fields in Hawaii, the Near East, Micronesia, and Africa.

The first success of the American Board was the mission to Hawaii. Henry Obookiah (d. 1818), a Hawaiian, came by way of trading vessels to New Haven, where he became a local celebrity. Obookiah was a close friend of Samuel Mills, and Mills used Obookiah's reputation to establish a school for non-Europeans at Cornwall, Connecticut, to equip them for service at home. After Obookiah's 1818 death, the board sent its first mission to the islands.

Hawaii began to change religiously when the missionaries arrived, and within a few years the missionaries had converted many chiefs. They also translated the Scriptures, established schools, and urged the government to outlaw prostitution, gambling, and alcohol. In 1836 the Hawaiian mission began a mass evangelization that converted most of the population. The American Board of Commissioners declared the mission a success in 1863 and turned the islands' churches over to the Hawaiian Evangelical Society.

The American Board also sponsored missions to the Middle East, especially, modern Lebanon and Syria. These missions made very few converts, and those few faced persecution and social discrimination. Donald Bliss founded the Syrian Protestant College, later the American University of Beirut in 1866, to provide a place for Arabian and American cultures to met.

A Worldwide Anglican Episcopate

During the nineteenth century, Anglicanism spread to every continent. Although much of this expansion came from the rapid maturation of the "white" dominions (Canada, Australia, New Zealand), missionary work among non-Christian peoples also played a part. In 1787 the Church of England ordained Charles Inglis, a former American Tory, as the first Bishop of Nova Scotia. Five years later in 1793 the bishops also consecrated Jacob Mountain as Bishop of Quebec. New consecrations followed rapidly. Other Anglican churches also consecrated missionary bishops. For instance, in 1844 the American Protestant Episcopal Church consecrated William Boone for service in China. By 1854 there were more than thirty Anglican bishops in missionary areas, and by 1882, seventy-two. At present the Anglican communion has some seventy provinces and 430 dioceses.

Appointment as a colonial bishop often transformed the new prelate. In 1814 the church consecrated T. F. Middleton (1769–1822) bishop for Calcutta. When he was first appointed, Middleton saw his work primarily as caring for English administrators and army offices. As he struggled with his duties, Middleton realized the need for evangelization and established Bishop's College in Calcutta to train new missionaries and to educate Hindus and Muslims in Western ways. The college was the most important Anglican theological center in India. Bishop Reginald Heber, Middleton's successor, identified the Bombay episcopate more closely with missionary work.

Anglican missionary work developed its own pattern. The appointment of bishops was the first step toward the ultimate establishment of autonomous churches. Each bishop established needed Christian institutions and provided for training an indigenous clergy. As the work grew the church consecrated new bishops. Eventually the bishops recognized one bishop as the metropolitan. At that point, the new church was ecclesiastically ready for self-government (whether it happened then or not).

The new worldwide Anglican communion was similar to the Eastern Orthodox churches. Each national church was independent of every other, and local bishops had responsibility for the administration of the churches in their dioceses. In 1867 the Archbishop of Canterbury invited the other bishops to meet with him at his London palace, Lambeth, to consult about the case of John Colenso (1814–83), the Bishop of Natal who had radical views on the authorship of the Bible. Thereafter the bishops agreed to meet at Lambeth every ten years to exchange information and to affirm their spiritual unity.

The Lambeth Conference helped popularize the Lambeth Quadrilateral, an Anglican plan for church unity. William Huntington (1838–1918), an American Episcopalian, argued that four principles were essential for Anglican participation in a united Church: the ancient creeds, the Scriptures, the sacraments of Baptism and Holy Communion, and the historical episcopate. America's Protestant Episcopal Church adopted these four principles as official policy in 1886, and the Lambeth Conference affirmed the quadrilateral in 1888. While the quadrilateral did not spawn the ecclesiastical mergers that its supporters anticipated, its four articles did help unify the increasingly diverse Anglican communion.

India

In the eighteenth century the British East India Company governed India. The officers of the company militarily defeated some Indian princes, established alliances with others, and used trade to enforce their will. The East India Company opposed missions because it believed that they would hinder trade or encourage revolt. A major Parliamentary campaign by the Clapham Sect secured the East India Bill (1813) allowing missionary work. When Parliament placed India under British sovereignty following the 1857–59 Sepoy mutiny, the Indian government was in a better position to encourage missions, but English power was not uniform throughout the subcontinent. Indian princes retained much power in different regions, and they could encourage or discourage missionary work.

American Baptist work in India began slowly, and for a time its leaders considered closing its small station at Nellore. But the mission baptized its first convert in 1841 and soon entered a period of dramatic growth. In 1866 a major movement towards Christianity began among the Madigas, a lower caste people. In 1876, a famine year, the Madigas churches baptized 8,691 persons. American Baptists were also successful in Assam with the Garos, the Rabhas, the Abors, and the Miris, who were all hill people, and animists.

In nearby Burma the American Baptists also established vital churches among the Karens, another primitive people. The Karens had a tradition that their ancestors had possessed a sacred book containing all the secrets of life. In 1828 George Dana Boardman (1801–31) and Ko Tha Byu, an early Karen convert, opened a missionary station at Tavoy. Boardman and Ko's mission was a striking success, and Karen Baptists became ecclesiastically independent of the United States.

The Baptist experience with the poor and *harijans* ("untouchables") was typical. The churches' greatest success was in winning members of the lower castes. India's strict caste system fixed a person's social and economic status at birth, and those on its fringes were almost totally excluded from civil life. Since the caste system was legitimated by Hinduism, the only way for a person to break its chains was to change religions and to ally with the powerful British. The Christian churches also provided the psychological and social security poorer Indians needed to advance in the more market-oriented economy encouraged by England. In addition the churches founded many social ministries, especially education, to give their poverty stricken members a chance to advance. Ironically the churches did not maintain a consistent witness against the caste system, and occasionally acted as if missionaries (or Britons) were a separate caste themselves.

The churches had more difficulty reaching India's ruling elite, especially the Brahmins. Alexander Duff (1806–78), a Scottish missionary, made three missionary tours of India. On the first of these Duff joined forces with a disaffected Brahim, Ram Mohan Roy, and formed a Calcutta college that studied Western thought. Duff's school used English as its language of instruction and attained university status. Duff believed that Christianity so penetrated Western thought that exposure to the one was necessarily exposure to the other. However, many students attended Duff's school only long enough to learn sufficient English to work with the British *raj*.

Frederick Tucker, an English convert of D. L. Moody, tried another approach to the evangelization of the upper classes. Joining the Salvation Army, Tucker dressed his officers in the traditional garb of Indian holy men. Shodding them in sandals, Tucker had them wander from town to town with begging bowls.

In some ways, the churches made their greatest impact on India through their influence on the British government. Largely because of Christian pressure, the *raj* outlawed *suttee*, the ritual suicide of a widow on her husband's funeral bier. In addition, the government acted to end the exposure of infants, the murder of aged parents, and temple ritual suicide. In 1947 India outlawed "untouchability" and took some steps to weaken the influence of caste on public life.

China

Christianity entered China many times before the nineteenth century. Other than a few Jesuit missions and Eastern Orthodox churches, however, the early missions did not survive. China was one of the world's oldest political units, and the Chinese tended to see all foreigners as inferiors. Most believed that the west had little to offer.

The first Protestant missionary to reach China was Robert Morrison (1782–1834), a nonconformist, appointed by the London Missionary Society. Since Morrison could not travel to China on an East India ship due to the Company's ban on missionaries, he took an American ship to Canton in 1807 where he mastered the language. In 1819 Morrison completed his translation of the Bible. Morrison spread knowledge about China in England, and Samuel Wells Williams (1812–84), a missionary of the American Board, also tried to publicize his new land. Williams' *The Middle Kingdom* was the standard nineteen-century discussion of China in English.

J. Hudson Taylor (1832–1905) organized the China Inland Mission, an important early faith mission (a kind of mission in which the missionary was supported in whole or in parts by funds which he or she raised). Taylor experimented with self-support early in his ministry when he left the Chinese Evangelization Society and asked his friends to support his work directly. In 1865 Taylor further developed the principle of self-support in the China Inland Mission. Since most boards wanted to work near the coast, Taylor sent his missionaries deep into the Chinese interior. When Taylor's missionaries entered a province, they explored the territory while preaching. By 1905 the China Inland Mission had work in all of China's western provinces and had entered Manchuria, Mongolia, and Tibet.

The most successful missionary institutions in China were Christian schools and colleges. Confucianism had a deep respect for learning, and Chinese society traditionally rewarded scholars with high governmental office. Equally important, many Chinese realized that they needed Western technology to protect China against Russia to the north and Japan to the east. From 1900 to 1914, Protestants established an influential string of universities, including Lingnan University, St. John's University (Shanghai), the University of Nantung, and Peking University.

The cultural missions in China attracted many liberal Christians. In 1918 Augustus Strong of Rochester Seminary published his *A Tour of the Missions*. Strong charged that the missionaries in China had exchanged the Gospel for social service. In 1921, Presbyterian W. H. Griffith Thomas, who had helped start the Bible Union of China, presented a paper that attacked the growth of modernism among Chinese missionaries. Both documents helped spark the modernist-fundamentalist controversy of the 1920s, one of the most bitter ecclesiastical battles in American history.

Africa South of the Sahara

In 1850, Africa was the last unexplored area in the habitable world, but during the next half century, Britain, France, Germany, and Belgium created vast empires that stretched the length of the continent. The primary base for missionary activity in Africa was South Africa. Although the Dutch originally colonized South Africa, the Congress of Vienna awarded the territory to Britain in 1814. When the Dutch settlers concluded that British policy favored the black population, the Boers began the Great Trek north to Natal. After Britain seized that area, the Dutch founded the Orange Free State and Transvaal in 1850. The discovery of vast mineral wealth in these two states, especially diamonds and gold, led to another British invasion. After the British defeated the Boers in a series of bloody battles, they reintegrated the Boer settlements in the Union of South Africa in 1910.

Two other primary bases were Liberia and Sierra Leone. Antislavery leaders established both Liberia and Sierra Leone as refuges for freed slaves who wished to return to Africa, and each had a black leadership deeply influenced by Christianity.

In 1840 the London Missionary Society appointed David Livingston (1813–73), a Scottish medical doctor, for service in South Africa. In 1849 Livingston traveled as far north as Lake Ngami, and in 1852 he resolved to open the whole interior to Christian missions. He pressed up the western coast to Sào Paulo de Loanda and then returned. On the way back, Livingston discovered Victoria Falls. Livingston returned to England where he received a hero's welcome and helped to found the Universities Mission to Central Africa.

Livingston returned to Africa to find a way into the interior that missionaries could easily follow. When Livingston returned to England again in 1864, he spent much time lecturing on the evils of the slave trade as he had observed them, contributing to the British resolve to end the traffic. Livingston's last exploration, begun in 1866, was a search for headwaters of the Nile. When reports that Livingston was lost reached New York, James Gordon Bennett, Jr., the editor of the *New York Herald*, sent the explorer Henry Stanley to search for him. Stanley did find Livingston, who refused to return with him to the coast. Shortly after that Livingston died, and his African workers brought his body to the sea where they turned it over to the Royal Navy.

Missionaries reduced many African languages to writing, established hospitals and schools, and built cities. Besides their constant war against the slave trade, the missionaries interceded with their governments to prevent many abuses caused by the white exploitation of the continent's resources.

CHAPTER FOURTEEN

MODERN EUROPEAN ORTHODOXY

During the Middle Ages the Eastern Roman Empire was the front line in Christianity's resistance to Islam. Despite considerable losses, Byzantium preserved its European lands, stopping the Arab advance. Constantinople seemed eternal to its inhabitants, who saw the Empire as part of God's plan laid at the foundation of the world. The Emperor was a religious and secular leader with full authority in church and state. The church celebrated his majesty and avoided words or actions that might question the autocratic ruler's power.

In the fifteenth century a new Islamic enemy, the Ottoman Turks, attacked the Empire, capturing Byzantium in 1453. Shortly after that, the Turks converted the city's great church, St. Sophia— which tradition taught stood over the navel of the earth—into a mosque. The Turkish advance continued into the Balkans and Greece and threatened Vienna. Eastern Catholics (those descendants of Greek-speaking Christianity who had remained in communion with the church at Constantinople, but not the church at Rome) resisted the invader, and their leaders made a temporary peace with Rome to recruit Western support. Charles V (1500–1558), Holy Roman Emperor and king of Spain, was the last Western ruler with a chance to expel the Turks. But just as the Turkish invasion kept Charles too busy to end Protestantism, so Protestantism kept him too occupied to destroy the Turks (see above, chapter 1). Ironically, the French allied themselves with the Turks, at least to a degree, hence weakening the Emperor's control of the sea.

The fall of Byzantium marked the beginning of modern Orthodoxy. Before the conquest, Orthodoxy was the soul of a culture that continued ancient Christian tradition. After the conquest of Constantinople, this changed. The orthodox churches became representatives of an oppressed minority that had to maintain its physical and cultural life against a hostile occupying power.

Turkish power was not absolute. Like other premodern rulers, the Sultan's government was unable to impose uniform policies on its conquered territories, because its communication, transportation, and bureaucratic techniques were primitive. Consequently Turkish control was strongest in Istanbul and Asia Minor and weaker toward their empire's fringe areas. This enabled the monasteries to maintain some degree of autonomy. The holy mountain Athos, the location of many monasteries, retained much of its power, and the monks may even have increased their influence, since the conquest made them symbols of independent national life.

The Koran counseled toleration for Christianity and Judaism since these were, like Islam, revealed religions. The Turks did not live up to this ideal. The government seized young men every year and forced them to convert before conscripting them into the Turkish army. The Sultan also forcibly recruited eunuchs for his personal government from among his Christian subjects. At times the Turkish dislike for the Orthodox produced violent persecution. Christian education suffered in the Turkish domains. The ancient Eastern Empire had sustained a substantial intellectual culture through state-supported monasteries, schools, and universities. The Turkish authorities closed these schools. Further, poverty and distance limited the number of those who might be educated in the West. Ironically, Protestants and Catholics pressured those Eastern Catholics to convert and stay in the West!

The Church Co-opted

To govern its vast territories, the Turkish government adopted the *millet* system, under which the Sultan appointed an ethnic group's religious leaders as state officials and held them responsible for the administration of the law. The Turks made the various Orthodox bishops the heads of the Christian *millets*.

The Turks believed that the patriarch of Constantinople was the most important Christian leader, analogous to the pope, and they negotiated with him whenever an issue concerned the whole Christian community. This practice, despite the equality of Eastern bishops, inspired others in authority to treat the bishop of Constantinople more like the bishop of Rome. Hence, other patriarchs often moved to Constantinople to influence him in order to secure governmental favors. The *millet* system involved the Orthodox deeply in political life. Wealthy Greek families saw the patriarchy as the key to their own dynastic fortunes and sought to control the office for their own private ends. The election of a new patriarch or other important bishop required the new church official to bribe prominent Turkish bureaucrats. The new patriarch was permitted to assume office only after the bureaucrats were satisfied with the amount. Since the merchants were the only source of contributions, the bishops became the voices of the upper classes.

The most important ecclesiastical offices became prizes in the competition between various ethnic groups. Both the Syrians and the Greeks, for example, coveted the patriarchate of Antioch. The two communities often engaged in an unfriendly competition that enriched the local Turkish officials. When Turkish power waned in the nineteenth century, national Orthodox churches became "autocephalous," or self-governing.

The Lure of the West

Both Catholics and Protestants saw the weakened condition of the Eastern churches as an opportunity to expand their influence. To win these churches to a new allegiance to Rome, the Roman Church appealed to the understanding of unity achieved at the Council of Ferrara-Florence (1438–45). Essentially, the Council agreed that union with Rome established a doctrinal and organization unity, while allowing a diversity of rites and customs. An Eastern church which united with Rome could nonetheless retain its ancient liturgy, its practice of baptism by immersion, communion in both kinds, and the marriage of priests. Under this arrangement many such Uniate churches joined Rome: the Chaldean (1551), the Albanians in Italy (1554) the Ruthenian (1596), the Armenian rite church in Poland (1635), the Armenians of Cilicia (1649), the Syrian Uniates (1661), the Rumanian Uniates (1697), the Melkite Uniates (1724), the Bulgarian Uniates (1839), and the Greek Uniates (1860).

The Protestant approach was more theological than institutional. In the patriarchate of Cyril Lucar (1572–1638), the Protestants almost persuaded the East to accept their perspective. In 1617, Lucar sent Metrophanes Critopoulos to England to study at Oxford, and he returned home through Switzerland, Germany, and Austria. In each country that Critopoules visited, he studied the university and ecclesiastical structures. Critopoulos became patriarch of Alexandria in 1636.

Meanwhile, Lucar found himself in a desperate struggle for power. Although the Turks removed him from his throne several times, the English and Dutch ambassadors pressured the Turks to restore him. In gratitude, Lucar sent Charles I a copy of the *Codex Alexandrinus*, a key early manuscript of the New Testament. In his *Confessio Fidei*, published in 1629, Lucar advocated a Calvinist reinterpretation of Eastern Orthodoxy. When the document became known following Lucar's execution by the Turks, a debate among Eastern Orthodox bishops ensued. Synods meeting in Constantinople (1638, 1642) and in Jerusalem (1672) condemned the *Confessio*.

Holy Russia

In 1228 the Mongols, a nomadic tribe from Asia, defeated the Russian princes at the battle of Kalha. Within the next ten years the Mongols subjected all Russia to their ultimate authority. During the long Mongol rule, Orthodoxy became the soul of Russian autonomy. The Russian princes, who believed that God punished them for their sins, began a long campaign to expel the invaders. Although the Mongols controlled much territory, the 1380 Battle of Kulikovo marked the beginning of their collapse. In 1480 Ivan III of Moscow refused to pay tribute to the Golden Horde and established himself as the ruler of all Russia, taking the title Czar. In 1473 Ivan III married Sophia Palailogos, a relative of the last Byzantine emperor.

Filofej von Paskov, a monk, expressed the implicit theology behind the marriage. When the first Rome had become schismatic, God moved the seat of empire to the New Rome or Constantinople. When that holy city fell to the infidel, God raised the Third Rome, Moscow, to protect and further the true faith. In 1589 Constantinople's patriarch, Jeremias II, recognized Moscow as a patriarchate, equal to such orthodox bishoprics as Alexandria or Antioch.

Russian belief in the Third Rome was part of a larger drive for an expanded empire. Just as English and later American Christians argued that the course of empire always moved west, so the Russians believed that God's new actions would occur in the East. In 1598, the Russians completed the conquest of Siberia, and in 1784 established a settlement on Kodiak Island near the Alaskan penninsula. As in the West, the sending of missionaries followed political expansion.

Monasticism was central to Russian Orthodoxy, and the whole church felt disruptions with the monastic community. One such disruption occurred in 1503 between the "possessors" and the "non-possessors." The non-possessors, led by St. Nil Storski (c.1493–1508), demanded that the monasteries interpret St. Basil's rule literally. In concrete terms, this meant that monasteries could not own estates or accept secular responsibilities. In contrast, St. Joseph of Volokalamsk (1439–1515), leader of the possessors, maintained that the monasteries needed their wealth to support hospitals, schools, and orphanages. Hence, the endowments were not possessions but a trust that God gave them for the poor. The Czars, who otherwise might have had to pay for these services, supported the possessors.

Under the Romanovs, church and state merged. Michael (1613–33) assumed power after the wars and the instability that followed Boris Godonov (1598–1605). Michael shared his power with his father, Philaret, the patriarch of Moscow. The union between the two was an important symbol.

The *Raskol*, or great separation, weakened the Romanovs' system of church-state cooperation. The Patriarch Nikon (1662–66) noted that the Russian liturgy, based on old Slavonic texts, differed from the service used in other orthodox churches. Nikon apparently did not consider that the Russian services might be older than the contemporary Greek forms. In any event, he ordered the Russian churches to conform to the more widespread practices. Led by the Archpriest Aukvakun and the monks of the great monastery of Solovski, many Russians refused to accept the changes. The state responded with intense persecution. The Romanovs exiled many Old Believers (as those who resisted the change were known) to new colonies in Siberia and passed severe laws that required dissenters to pay double taxes and to marry only within their sect. The Czars excluded Old Believers from all non-conscripted state service.

The original reasons for the *Raskol* were liturgical, but the question of the hierarchy divided the dissenters. Priests, ordained by bishops of the state church, served the main body of Old Believers until 1849 when the state consented to the consecration of Old Believer bishops. Other Old Believers, called "priestless," argued that the whole Russian church became heretical through Nikon's reforms. Therefore, no valid hierarchy existed in Russia. The "priestless" continued their Eucharist by diluting a supply of wine, bread, and holy oil.

Peter the Great (reigned 1696–1725), the fourth Romanov, wanted to remodel Russia on a Western model. As a young man, Peter traveled throughout Western Europe, often in disguise, studying economics and government. The West's agricultural and manufacturing wealth impressed the young Romanov. As part of his attempt to recreate Russia in the West's image, Peter moved his capital from Moscow to the new city of St. Petersburg.

Peter needed to make the church subject to his will to carry out his reforms. Working with his ecclesiastical advisor, Feofan Prokovitch

(1651–1738), Peter transformed the Russian church into a Western-styled state church. In the *Ecclesiastical Regulations*, Peter eliminated the patriarch and placed the church under a Holy Council headed by a royal official, responsible to the Czar. Peter's program of westernization required the Russian nobles, many of whom wore beards for religious reasons, to shave if they were to retain their status. The authorities forcibly shaved those who refused, although some fled east and joined the Old Believers.

The education of the clergy, an abiding problem of the Russian church, was essential to Peter's program of westernization. The clergy had made major contributions to literacy and technology in the West, and Russia could not enter the modern world without better trained ecclesiastical leaders. Yet the Russian church did not want to become westernized or to compromise its national character by adopting Western patterns.

Part of Peter's program of reform was the establishment of an academy for the training of priests at Kiev. He assigned the task to Peter Mogila (1596–1647), an ardent nationalist. Although Mogila wanted to make the school as Orthodox as possible, the best available texts were in Latin. To use them, Mogila had to admit more Western influence than he believed appropriate.

Czar Paul I (1796–1801) formalized the church's education of its own leaders by establishing a separate system of education for priests. The male children of the clergy, whom the state expected to follow in their fathers' footsteps, attended their own elementary schools. Once these were completed, the young men could take one of two paths. Prospective parish priests could either attended seminaries or, if the government destined them for ecclesiastical leadership, academies. Only one-third of those attending the elementary schools were ordained, and most seminary students found segregated education stifling.

One reason behind the separation of clerical and lay education was to protect Russia from Western rationalism and revolution. The Czars believed a theologically conservative church would support the government. In retrospect, their policy was ill-advised. The University of Moscow, established in 1755, did not have a faculty of theology, and church leaders lacked the intellectual resources to discuss modern philosophy or ethics.

The monks, who often were *startsi* or spirit-filled men, were the most influential Russian religious leaders. Modern Russian monasticism began when Peter Velichkovski (1722–94) returned from Mount Athos in Greece. Velichkovski summarized Greek monastic practices in his *Phi-*

lokratia which contained many important translations into Old Slavonic. Another important influence on Russian spirituality was Seraphim of Sarov (1739–1833), who also helped shape Russian spirituality. After a retreat to a hermitage, he became a spiritual counselor who urged ordinary men and women to live spiritually. Seraphim advocated the repetition of the Jesus prayer ("O Lord Jesus, be merciful to me, a sinner"). Seraphim's most noted successor was Amvrosli Grenkov (1812–92) who directed both Dostoyevsky and Tolstoy in their spiritual quests.

In the nineteenth century, the great monastery at Optima Pustyn was a center for religious retreats and personal spiritual direction. Optima was a series of small huts, each inhabited by a monk who spent the day in prayer and devotion. Lev Nagolkin [born Leonid] (1768–1841) was the best known Optima leader.

Since the state and its legally established religious and theological norms so dominated the hierarchy, the monks presented the more individual aspects of the Christian tradition. Yet Russian monasticism also had its dangers. For example, historians suspect that Rasputin (1872–1916), *startsi* to the last Romanov, Nicholas II (1894–1917), may have given advice that contributed to Russia's loss of the First World War.

The Russian Nineteenth Century

The Napoleonic Wars cast a shadow over nineteenth-century Russia. Alexander I (1801–25) was of two minds about the French dictator. He believed that Napoleon was an upstart who could do Europe little good. Yet Alexander had a grudging admiration for the man and his program, especially after Russia's 1807 defeat by the French army.

When Napoleon struck again in his 1812 invasion, the czar directed an orderly retreat, while the Russian army burned the supplies that Napoleon might have used to reprovision his army. The destruction of foodstuffs and other supplies made the French conquest of Moscow a hollow victory. Starving and without adequate munitions, Napoleon's grand army was forced to retreat from Russia with the czar in pursuit.

In the midst of the war, Alexander experienced a religious renewal. The czar's military advisors included many German Pietists (his mother was a German princess), and he was fond of mystical literature. In 1812 Alexander helped establish the Russian Bible Society, modeled on the British and Foreign Bible Society, to distribute the Bible in the various languages of his empire. The Society lasted until 1826 when Czar

Nicholas I (reigned 1825–55) abolished it. Nicholas feared that the Society might make the Russian church too Protestant.

Mysticism inspired the most interesting of Alexander's schemes: the Holy Alliance. The Alliance was an agreement between the czar, the emperor of Austria, and the king of Prussia to cooperate in maintaining peace. What the czar wanted was to create something like the medieval *corpus Christianum* in which Christian ideals informed chivalry and, theoretically, international relationships. A sinister subtext could be read between the lines of the Treaty's pious phrases, in that the czar and his allies believed that God want them to save "civilization" from the "liberalism" that inspired the French Revolution.

Alexander and his successors believed that the church was the primary source of social stability. Although Russian orthodox missions declined during the late eighteenth century, the czar's government sponsored missionary priests throughout the Eastern provinces. Eugenius Kasantseff, bishop of Tobolsk from 1826 to 1831, created a large missionary diocese near the boundary with Mongolia. Archimandrite Macarius later served the area. Macarius studied the languages and customs of the region and baptized more than seven hundred people. The dark side of Orthodox expansion was the persecution of Roman Catholics, Protestants, and, especially, Jews.

The role of the church was part of every Russian political debate. The Russian intelligentsia was composed of two factions. The westernizers wanted Russia modeled after England and France. They believed that the church was behind the times and needed further reformation based on Western practice. The various socialist leaders who became influential after 1850 were similar to the westernizers. Like their Western comrades, they saw the church as an organ of oppression. Although Russian socialists rejected God and the church, many found Jesus an inspiration for their movement.

The slavophiles (literally, lovers of the slavs) were nationalists who argued that Orthodoxy was part of the genius of the Russian soul. Alexey Khomiakov (1804–60), a skilled lay theologian, believed that the Russian church was the ideal expression of the gospel's assertion of the spiritual unity of all people and the organic expression of the Russian people's genius.

Novelists often communicated Russian spirituality better than philosophers or theologians. Such writers as Nikolay Vasilyevich Gogol (1809–52) and Fyodor Dostoyevsky (1821–81) made the struggle for a spiritual life primary in their writings. While deeply ambivalent about orthodox theology, both believed that sin and destruction struggled against God and life in all human experience. Both Gogol and Dostoyevsky believed that wounded Russia needed Christ to heal its soul.

Leo Tolstoy (1828–1910) represented another facet of the Russian soul. Unlike his contemporaries Gogol and Dostoyevski, Tolstoy lost his concern with sin and grace at the university. To him, Jesus was an ethical teacher who set forth the ideal of a god-filled humanity in the Sermon on the Mount. Tolstoy tried to attain that goal by refraining from anger, by teaching nonresistance to evil, and by advocating love as the guide to human relationships. Animals and nature were also to benefit from Christ-like behavior. Tolstoy's vision and style of life attracted much Western attention where some Christian intellectuals saw Christianity as a help in solving social problems.

Russia's 1905 defeat by the Japanese was a shock to Russia and also to Europe. Many Russians became convinced that Russia needed to modernize, and in 1905 Czar Nicholas II issued a proclamation establishing religious toleration. Russia had entered a period of reexamination.

The End of the Turkish Domination of the Balkans

By 1800 the Turks, although still in possession of a vast empire that reached from Greece to North Africa, were the "sick nation" in European politics. The Sultan's government had not modernized as fast as its western and northern rivals. The question was no longer whether the Turkish domination of the Balkans would end. Rather, people wondered whether Austria, Russia, or a series of small states, perhaps under the protection of a Great Power, would rule the area next. The tensions between the advocates of these different futures led to the 1854 Crimean War between Russia and England, France, and Sardinia.

A religious and national revival began in Greece during the latter part of the nineteenth century. In 1821, a revolution commenced that continued until 1830. Interest in Greek history was reviving at the time, and the revolt attracted attention in all European capitals. After the intervention of England, Russia, and France, the Turks conceded Greek independence.

The independence of the nation required a reorganization of the church. In 1833 the new Greek monarchy reorganized the church on the Rússian model, placing ecclesiastical authority in a Holy Synod. As a matter of course the government declared the church to be *autocephalous* (self-governing). The Patriarch of Constantinople continued to claim some authority over the church in Greece (and there was a short-lived schism among his followers), but the Greek church limited his authority to the Greek-speaking areas under Turkish control.

Despite its formal establishment the Greek Orthodox Church was poor. Many poorly educated priests worked long hours on small plots of land to earn their living. Although the church founded schools for prospective priests in 1837 and 1843, little was done to improve the conditions of the average minister.

As in Russia, holy men played an important role in Greek piety. Christophanes Panaghiotopoulos, a former hermit, was a strong advocate of the Orthodox Church, as was Apostolos Makrates, the layman who founded the Athenian School of the Logos in 1874. Eusebius Matthopoulos, a companion of Makrates, founded the *Zoë*, a band of theologians who published the journal of the same name.

Other Balkan states followed the Greek model when they became independent. Turkey granted Serbia self-rule in 1829, and in 1882 Serbia's government claimed full independence. Rumania (the ancient provinces of Wallachia and Moldavia) declared its Orthodox Church independent of Constantinople in 1859, and the Ecumenical Patriarch recognized this new church in 1873. The European powers recognized the full independence of Rumania in 1880. The Orthodox Church in Bulgaria gradually gained independence from the Ecumenical Patriarch. In 1870 the Turks allowed the region to direct its own ecclesiastical affairs, and in 1878 Turkey recognized Bulgaria as an independent monarchy.

CHAPTER FIFTEEN

IMMIGRANT CHURCHES IN THE UNITED STATES

The Dutch Reformed Church (the present-day Reformed Church in America) is among the oldest ethnic denominations in the United States. In the seventeenth century, when they controlled New York, the Dutch started their first congregations in that province and in New Jersey. During the eighteenth century, the Dutch Reformed became a more American denomination. Theodore Frelinghuysen, the New Jersey revivalist, led a party that formed an independent *Coetus* in 1755. While contemporaries justified the withdrawal by arguing about the revival, Americanization was an important (but often hidden) issue. Most churches that joined the new Union adopted the use of English in their services earlier than did those in the rival *Conferentie*. After the American Revolution, the Dutch Reformed became officially independent of the Classis (Presbytery) of Amsterdam that had formerly approved all the denomination's ministers.

In the 1840s a new wave of Dutch immigrants arrived on American shores. Potatoes were as important in Holland as in Ireland, and when the potato blight caused Dutch production to all but cease, many Hollanders were forced to leave. The new Dutch settlers moved to the Midwest where inexpensive land was available.

Although the Dutch Reformed labored to reach these new brothers and sisters, the older Dutch were separated from the new immigrants by theological and cultural differences. A conservative revival movement in Holland inspired some to leave the state church, and the seceders were well represented among the new Dutch immigrants. They established the American Christian Reformed Church in the 1870s.

The Lutherans

The word "Lutheran" refers to those European churches that subscribe to the Augsburg Confession. These include the state churches of the Scandinavian countries (including Norway, which became independent in the nineteenth century), many *Landeskirchen* (official state churches) in Germany, and free Lutheran churches in such cities as Amsterdam and London.

Lutherans were a major component of Pennsylvania's religious history. The General Synod, organized in 1820, succeeded Muhlenberg's ministerium and wanted to gather all Lutherans into common benevolences. Samuel Schmucker (1799–1873), professor of theology at Gettysburg Seminary, was the Synod's spokesperson. His *Elements of Popular Theology* (1834) was the first Lutheran systematic theology written in the new world.

Schmucker's American Lutheranism did not impress the German immigrants who came in the 1830s and 1840s. Many were from the more conservative areas in Germany, and their pastors often held a strongly confessional theology. In the 1860s the neo-conservatives, led by Charles Porterfield Krauth (1823–83), established their own organizations, including their own General Council.

Krauth was one of the most able theologians of his time. In his magnum opus, *The Conservative Reformation and Its Theology*, Krauth defended the thesis that Luther intended to reform the church, not destroy its deepest traditions. Lutheranism was a *via media* between Catholicism and Calvinism. Krauth wanted American Lutherans to retain their belief in the real presence of Christ in the Sacrament of the Altar and in baptismal regeneration. In many ways Krauth's argument was similar to that of the contemporary Oxford Movement in Anglicanism.

German missionary societies also formed some American Lutheran denominations. For example, missionaries sent by Wilhelm Loehe (1808–72) formed the Iowa Synod. Loehe was a romantic and a convinced confessionalist who hoped that the German Lutheran Churches would return to sixteenth-century theology. Like Krauth, Loehe advocated a strong doctrine of the real presence of Christ in the Sacrament of the Altar.

Loehe became interested in America in the 1840s (the potato famine years). Noting the large number of immigrants, Loehe published an influential essay, *Kirchliche Mitteilungen aus und über Nordamerika,* calling for missionaries to go to the New World. Once here, Loehe's men established a practical seminary that became an important Missouri Synod school, although his followers later split from that group.

The small pietist sect led by Martin Stephan (1777–1846) was the most complex branch of Lutheranism to enter America. Stephan, originally a Bohemian, organized his friends to fight rationalism in the Church of Saxony. When he received word that his dismissal from the church was imminent, he convinced more than six hundred of his followers to emigrate to America. The small group went to St. Louis, then a frontier boom town, and purchased land in Perry County, Missouri. Once there, the congregation caught Stephan in immorality and deposed him.

Stephan's successor was Carl F. W. Walther (1811–87) who convinced the small and dispirited sect that they had a valid ministry in the New World, organizing the Missouri Synod around Concordia Seminary in St. Louis and his journal, *Der Lutheraner*. The practical seminary, which trained men who lacked a classical education, aided in the establishment of many Missouri Synod congregations.

The Missouri Synod was a new type of Lutheranism in America; its adherents would preferred to say that they represented a recovery of "old time" Lutheranism. The church was rigorously confessionalist, and the ministers pledged their adherence to the full Book of Concord. At the same time the synod's pastors maintained the pietism that inspired the first immigrants. This combination of piety and confessionalism, conjoined with effective organization, enabled the synod to unite many other German immigrants under its banner. The parochial schools constructed by the new church, which emphasized German language and culture, were another source of the denomination's popularity.

Scandinavian Lutherans formed several synods and other denominational bodies. The largest was the Augustana synod formed by Swedish Lutherans in 1860. Its founders hoped to include all Scandinavian Lutherans in a single church. However, the Danish and Norwegian churches left this synod and formed their own synod which later divided into two churches. Those Norwegians influenced by the preaching of Hans Nielsen Hauge (1771–1826), the Norwegian Wesley, organized their own synod in 1866. Shortly after that, more confessional Norwegian Lutherans organized the Old Norwegian Synod. Other groups from Scandinavia organized their own Lutheran synods around other ethnic or theological concerns.

Catholic America

The Roman Catholic Church was numerically small in colonial America. At the end of the American Revolution, there were approximately 25,000 Catholics, most of whom lived in Maryland or Philadelphia. In colonial Maryland, "penal" laws imposed heavy penalties for the practice of the Catholic faith. The faithful were served by itinerant missionary priests, usually Jesuits, who carried portable altars in their saddlebags and heard confessions behind improvised screens. As long as the faith was practiced privately, individual Catholics were, despite the law's provisions, left in peace.

The pope suppressed the Jesuits in 1773, due to pressure from Catholic Portugal and France, leaving the American priests without supervision. Jesuit property had passed to a "Select Body of Clergy" which had continued to minister in Maryland. Shortly after the penal laws were repealed, these former Jesuits petitioned Rome for a more formal organization and elected John Carroll (1735–1815), the scion of an old Catholic family, as their superior in 1784. Five years later (1789) the pope granted the American clergy the right to elect their own bishop. The American priests again chose Carroll and Rome confirmed the appointment.

Carroll was an interesting blend of patriot and Catholic activist. Like other American Catholics at the time, Carroll strongly believed in the separation of church and state. He successfully petitioned to have removed from his consecration oath the promise to exterminate heretics, and frequently praised the American Constitution. One of his goals was to show his fellow Americans that no incongruity existed between Catholic faith and liberty.

Carroll was also an institution builder. In 1791 he summoned his first Council to regulate the American Church (some seven nationalities were present), and in 1808 became an archbishop or metropolitan. In that year the pope created new dioceses at Boston, New York, Philadelphia, and Bardstown, Kentucky.

In 1790 Carroll and the Society of St. Sulpice, a French order devoted to training Catholic priests, agreed to establish a seminary outside Baltimore. The new school, present-day St. Mary's, opened in 1791 under the leadership of Charles Francois Nagot. Carroll was also instrumental in the establishment of Georgetown Academy, later chartered as a liberal arts college.

Trusteeship

The most serious crisis in Carroll's reign and that of his successors Leonard Neale (1815–17) and Ambrose Marechal (1817–21) was "trusteeship." In accord with American law, lay Catholics incorporated their parishes under trustees. An incorporated congregation was a "legal person" in any court action that involved real estate or contracts. Incorporation also allowed individual church members to limit their fiscal responsibility for the debts of the church. These secular rights, however, raised many religious questions. Did the trustees' right to make contracts include the right to negotiate with a particular priest for his services? If so, did it include the right to set his stipend and the term of office?

Ordinarily, the issues would have been adjudicated over a long period in which the hierarchy, Rome, and the courts decided issues on a case-by-case basis. Bishop Carroll's original decision was to handle the issue in this way. But these were not ordinary times. Many American Catholic priests and bishops had come to America fleeing the French Revolution. After France adopted the Civil Constitution of the Clergy that called for the election of priests and bishops by those they served, many priests refused the new law. Subsequently the French government persecuted the Church. The émigrés were naturally suspicious of any system that brought priestly appointments under lay control.

Americans also had reason to distrust the trustee system. The United States was a missionary country that did not have enough priests to serve a rapidly growing Catholic population. Each bishop had to use the few priests available to maximum advantage. The trustee issue also involved ethnicity. One reason that parishioners wanted control over the appointment of their priests was to secure clergy from the "old country" who spoke their language. Many Catholics feared that the American Church might divide into ethnic churches, united only by their allegiance to Rome, if trusteeship continued.

The Hogan case illustrated the Catholic dilemma. William Hogan (1788–1848), a popular Catholic priest, was called by the trustees of St. Mary's in Philadelphia to serve their parish. In 1820 Hogan criticized the new bishop, Henry Conwell, who then revoked Hogan's faculties in the diocese. To support their controversial pastor, the trustees barred the bishop from the building which was also the cathedral church. Thereupon Conwell declared St. Mary's unsuitable for Catholic worship and excommunicated Hogan. Hogan later left the priesthood, married, and became an anti-Catholic lecturer.

Although Francis Kenrick, who became Bishop of Philadelphia in 1831, asserted his authority over St. Mary's, no particular church decision ended trusteeship. What happened was more mundane. Using their political influence, Catholics secured laws that permitted their bishops to serve as sole trustee of Catholic property. Over time, the bishops persuaded the trustees of churches organized earlier to surrender their property.

French and Irish Refugees

When French Catholics resisted the Civil Constitution of the Clergy, the Revolution entered an anticlerical phase. The state deprived priests loyal to Rome of their parishes. Sometimes the authorities ordered their arrest and trial before revolutionary tribunals. Following such *pro forma* procedures, the courts sentenced many to the guillotine. Many priests emigrated to America where they provided a pool of leadership for the new hierarchy, including Bishops Ambrose Maréchal (Baltimore), Benedict Flaget (Bardstown, Kentucky), Jean Dubois (New York), and Jean-Louis Lebrevre de Cheverus (Boston).

The French bishops faced a difficult situation. Irish and German immigrants were entering the United States in significant numbers, and some of their leaders resisted what they called a foreign hierarchy. Nonetheless the French bishops brought to their task administrative experience and knowledge of the larger Catholic world which they used to lay strong foundations for the church's future development. The French bishops also carefully selected the next generation of American Catholic leaders from among the newcomers and provided for an orderly transition to new leadership.

Ireland was an impoverished island where the average land holding was under an acre. The only crop that flourished was potatoes, and in 1845 the blight destroyed this means of subsistence. For many Irish, the choice was to starve or to leave. The Irish did not initially fare much better in America. Unlike the Germans, they lacked funds to invest in farmland and lived in the nation's largest cities and towns. Since the only jobs available to them paid poorly, the Irish section of town was often squalid, racked by poor housing, poor food, and disease.

To serve the Irish the Catholic Church had to develop a ministry suitable to a "religion of the dispossessed." Catholicism historically conducted a program of social service through its religious orders, and many orders established American branches to serve the Irish population. Catholic leaders taught a morality that resembled that of the evangelical churches: work hard, save, and follow a strict sexual ethic. American Catholic leaders also urged the temperate use (and occasionally, the renunciation) of alcohol and the duty to educate the next generation.

Parochial schools helped the Catholic Irish advance economically. Although the clergy saw the schools as counterweights to the heavily Protestant public schools, they served other social purposes as well. The nuns who taught in the schools insisted that the students perform on as high a level as possible, refusing to accept their students' poverty (which they often shared) as an excuse for poor performance. Further, the sisters presented good "role models" for their students and taught that the Catholic Church had helped create and preserve American political values.

American Anti-Catholicism

By mid-century a reaction against the new immigrants was spreading. Many employers had signs that read simply "No Irish Need Apply." The American, or "Know Nothing," party (before its union with the Republicans) participated in many elections. In 1854, these nativists (anti-immigrants) elected seventy-five members of Congress and controlled the Massachusetts House of Representatives. In the next year, the "Know Nothings" won other American elections and seemed ready to triumph in 1856.

Parents of British descent had reared their children to hate popery from their infancy. So deep was English Protestant antipathy to Rome that millennial theology taught that the fall of the pope was the first sign of the coming of the millennium. Further, most Protestants believed that Catholic obedience to the pope limited their national loyalty, since they thought that Catholics could not act contrary to official church teaching without excommunication. The Catholic Church's hostility to democracy in Europe added to these fears.

Protestant leaders fed these anxieties. Samuel F. B. Morse (1791–1872), the inventor of the telegraph and a skilled American painter, became an avid anti-Catholic when he was accosted in Rome for not paying proper respect to the pope. In his *Foreign Conspiracy Against the Liberties of the United States*, Morse set out to prove that the pope, the Jesuits, and the immigrants were involved in a conspiracy to make the United States a Catholic country by seizing the Midwest. The popular evangelical leader Lyman Beecher expressed similar views in his *A Plea for the West* (1834), a popular sermon which was often reprinted as a tract.

Simultaneously, some Protestant pastors published pornographic (and false) exposés of Catholic misdeeds. Rebecca Reed's *Six Months in A Convent* (1935) and Maria Monks' *Awful Disclosures of the Hotel Dieu Nunnery* (1836) focused on Protestant suspicions of Catholic celibacy. Both volumes graphically portrayed the supposed sexual sins of the Catholic clergy and implied that many nunneries were houses of ill-repute maintained for oversexed priests.

In antebellum America, mobs were an accepted form of political action. Although the more socially prominent citizens did not personally participate in the mobbing of unpopular persons, evidence exists that the mobs had the support and encouragement of "gentlemen of property and standing." In 1834 a mob in Boston burned the Ursuline Convent, and Bishop Hughes posted armed guards around his churches for their protection. Ten years later (1844) a Kennington, Pennsylvania mob burned two Catholic churches and many Irish homes. The Governor had to call out the militia to restore order, which the troops only accomplished with difficulty.

Catholic Defenses

One effect of Protestant hostility was to reinforce Catholic tendencies toward a ghetto mentality. But Protestant hostility was not the only factor encouraging Catholic separation from the larger culture. During the latter part of the nineteenth century, Catholics everywhere were concerned with building a uniquely Catholic civilization. Faithful members of the church established their own labor unions, professional societies, magazines, and newspapers. The ideal Catholic education moved entirely within the orb of the church as a student progressed from parochial schools to Catholic secondary schools to Catholic colleges.

Besides the construction of their own institutions, American Catholics took special pride in their converts from Protestantism. Mother Elizabeth Seton (1774–1821), the founder of the American Sisters of Charity and a convert from Episcopalianism, was the first American proclaimed a saint. Orestes Brownson (1803–76) was more influential. Brownson passed through a long spiritual search that had included universalism and unitarianism before he discovered Catholic Christianity. Romantic philosophy deeply influenced Brownson, who argued that societies were organic units that formed a common personality out of disparate elements. In his *The American Republic: Its Constitution, Tendencies, and Destiny* (1866), Brownson combined this social theory with his belief in American democracy. The result was one of the most intellectual American defenses of Catholicism.

Isaac Hecker (1819–99) was more acceptable to the hierarchy. Although Hecker became a Catholic through the influence of Brownson, his own religious experience filled him with missionary zeal. Shortly after his conversion he organized the Congregation of Missionary Priests of Saint Paul to reach out to Protestant America through tracts and publications. The order founded *The Catholic World* in 1865.

Catholic and American

From the time of Archbishop Carroll, some American Catholics insisted that there was no conflict between religious commitment and American ideals, including the constitutionally mandated separation of church and state. Bishop John England (1786–1842) of Charleston, South Carolina, was one of the most vocal advocates of Catholic Americanism. Before emigrating to America, Bishop England was a vocal advocate of religious voluntarism and the separation of church and state, and he continued these emphases in the New World. His *United States Catholic Miscellany*, an early Catholic newspaper, advocated the American system as the best support for Catholic values.

Bishop England's version of Catholicism was very popular among American Catholics of Irish descent. In the later half of the nineteenth-century this position was strongly advocated by James Gibbons (1834–1921), Archbishop of Baltimore; John Keane (1838–1928), Bishop of Richmond and later Rector of the Catholic University; and Denis O'Connell (1849–1927), Rector of the American College at Rome. The Catholic University, opened in Washington, District of Columbia, in 1889, symbolized the determination to devise a philosophy at once Catholic and American. Originally the school was for the graduate theological training of American clergy and religious, although it later provided both undergraduate and graduate education for lay Catholics.

Not all American Catholics favored this direction. In particular, German Catholic leaders feared that the religion and culture of their people might be lost if the Church became too closely related to American democracy. When Archbishop Francisco Satolli visited America to negotiate certain issues dividing the Germans and the Irish, the Germans convinced Satolli that their position had merit. Satolli reported to the Vatican that liberalism threatened the integrity of the American Catholic mission.

Satolli's words arrived at a crucial point in European Catholic history. French Catholics were engaged in a bitter battle with the Third Republic over the status of their church, and the German church had just passed through a protracted battle with the new kaiser. In this context, the American suggestion that the separation of church and state was the ideal solution to the church's problems was unwelcome. In *Longinqua Oceana* (1895), Leo XIII warned the American church that wherever the church was not persecuted, Catholics were to work toward obtaining the full blessings of cooperation with the secular government. In 1899, this encyclical was followed by *Testum benevolentiae* in which the pope demanded that the American church end its teaching of "Americanism."

The papal documents accused no specific individual of teaching the rejected positions, and Cardinal Gibbons' reply argued that the positions, as described in the documents, were not held by anyone. Nonetheless, the papal documents served their purpose. Catholic leaders in the United States quietly, but surely, retreated from their more advanced positions and moved closer to traditional Catholic thought.

Maturation

In 1908 the pope removed the American Catholic Church from the jurisdiction of the Congregation of the Propaganda and officially recognized it as self-governing. In one sense the change was cosmetic. The American Catholic hierarchy had been independent for some time, and church law was only confirming history. Although ethnic parishes and ethnic disagreements would continue in America for some time, these phenomena were slowly ending. Catholic immigrants were becoming part of the mainstream of American society. The First World War encouraged American Catholics of German descent to emphasize their American patriotism. Further, the restriction of immigration in the 1920s meant that an increasingly larger percentage of Catholic Americans were born in this country. The massive exodus from the cities after World War II also set the American Catholic minority less apart from other Americans it had been. When the nation elected John F. Kennedy president in 1960, the Catholic Church attained considerable social prestige.

CHAPTER SIXTEEN

THE FRENCH REVOLUTION AND THE NAPOLEONIC WARS

In the eighteenth century two significant changes occurred in European economics:

1. Great wealth was less associated with agricultural production and more with trade and manufacturing, and
2. The agricultural economy modernized and claimed a smaller percent of a nation's workers.

Consequently, the nobility lost much of its luster, and the established churches, largely financed by their land holdings, saw their endowments decline in comparison with other social sectors.

France had difficulty adjusting to these changes. In response to the French defeat in the French and Indian Wars, Louis XVI (1754–93) increased the size of his navy and improved his army's ordinance. To revenge French honor, Louis committed his forces to the American Revolution. Although France won this round with her hated enemy, the effort bankrupted the state and restricted its ability to respond to crises.

In 1788 and 1789, Louis XVI's administration had problems that would have taxed any government. The government was out of money, the army was weak, and the court was divided on basic policy. Further, the winters were unusually hard, and the crops, especially the spring wheat on which the common people depended, failed. France, traditionally a rich land, was hungry and angry. Louis had few resources to meet this crisis, and these were weakened by poor credit, declining revenues, and an ineffective (but innovative) administration. Further, the king's popularity was declining, and many subjects held his queen, Marie Antoinette, in contempt.

With the stage thus set, the events which led to the French Revolution moved with almost blinding speed. The financial crisis broke first. In 1789, Louis called the *Etats Général* to meet to enact new taxes. However when the assembly convened on May 5, 1789, it refused to organize into three separate bodies (nobles, clergy, and commons). On July 14, 1789, the Bastille, a Paris fortress-prison, fell to the Paris mob. Less than a month later, the National Assembly (as it now called itself) abolished all feudal privileges. By October, the mob forced the king and the assembly to move to Paris where the hungry people of Paris could watch them. The assembly next composed a constitution. The initial proposal was for a "limited" or "constitutional" monarchy similar to the English government. However, negotiations over this document were interrupted by the king's attempt in June 1791 to flee France, and his recapture by the revolutionary forces. The situation was out of control, and the revolutionaries—never united in their goals—began to fear foreign intervention. In April 1792, the new French government declared war on Austria, and a few months later the Paris Commune seized control of the city. In September the revolutionaries officially abolished the monarchy.

The king's execution in 1793 began a reign of terror during which the radicals persecuted their adversaries under the authority of a Committee of Public Safety. Supposedly the executions were war-measures, but few of those executed were traitors or spies. Finally, a coup d'etat on July 27, 1794, led to the execution of Maximilien Robespierre (1758–94), the radical leader, on the next day.

In 1795, a young military commander named Napoleon Bonaparte (1769–1821) began to win a string of brilliant victories that included major battles in Egypt and Italy. As a result, no government could rule without Napoleon's open or tacit support, and he gradually became the most powerful French leader. In 1799, Napoleon became the French dictator, and a year later officially became the "first consul." In 1804, he was crowned emperor.

Napoleon thrived on war, but his military opponents gradually improved their armies and their internal morale. The Peninsula War (1808) with Spain revealed his loss of relative military strength, and his 1812 decision to invade Russia with his Grand Army of 500,000 led to a disastrous retreat. Following Napoleon's defeat at Leipzig (October 1813), Prussian and Russian armies occupied Paris. Napoleon accepted exile at Elbe, a small Mediterranean island. He returned to power briefly in 1815, only to be defeated by Wellington at Waterloo in Belgium. The revolution was over.

The end of the Napoleonic Wars did not restore the old order completely. The metric system, introduced by the revolutionaries to standardize weights and measures, was a popular and a scientific success. Even more important, the French revision of Roman law—the Code of Napoleon—became standard in western Europe and was (outside English-speaking areas) a model for laws elsewhere.

Europeans also thought differently. While the European rulers banded together to restore the old order, especially in international relations, many people continued to see "equality, fraternity, and liberty" as political goals. Whenever the political situation deteriorated, the barricades returned as a solution for their woes. For good or ill, revolution was now a permanent component of European idealism, a secular millennialism promising a better future.

The Church and the Coming of Revolution

The church's role in the coming of the revolution has many facets. What the church failed to do had as much impact as what it actually did. Rationalism weakened the eighteenth-century church, and many political and social leaders abandoned faith in Christianity in favor of secular solutions to France's problems. Church leaders were often in accord with this trend, especially the higher clergy who shared the perspective of their noble relatives. Not even Frenchmen with traditional Catholic beliefs expected moral leadership from the church.

Yet the French Revolution was not an example of the power of the acids of modernity to corrode tradition. Few French people knew enough to follow the new thought, and many with intellectual skills had the most to lose from a decline in religious conviction. The *philosophes* did not talk in front of the servants. The more serious problem was that while the average *curé* or parish priest retained his people's respect, people identified the church with the monarchy. After all, the church legitimated the monarchy by preaching obedience to the state and praying for the king. When famine and political crisis struck, the people held all of the components of the Old Order—the church included—responsible for their problems.

The Revolutionary Government of the Church

Traditionally, the French paid their clergy through an elaborate system of taxes, including a tithe on agricultural products, and from the profits earned by church lands. Religious orders participated in the larger system. They often served churches or named the pastors, while collecting parish revenues. The revolutionaries wiped out this system in a few months. After the renunciation of feudal privileges, the government seized the church's lands and used them as collateral for the growing national debt. The lands were also used to back the revolutionary currency, the assignats, since gold was not available. At the same time, the law abolished monasticism and pensioned off the older monks and ordered younger monks to become parish priests or to enter secular life.

The revolutionaries had to find a new way to pay for the church. After an interim arrangement under which the states paid clerical salaries, the assembly adopted a new law and regulations for the church on July 12, 1790, called the Civil Constitution of the Clergy. In addition to providing salaries for clerics, the law had five provisions.

1. The number of dioceses was reduced from 135 to 85 and parish boundaries were redrawn.
2. All district residents could participate in the election of bishops and *curés*.
3. The papal veto on ecclesiastical appointments was terminated.
4. Clergy had to reside in their parishes or diocese to collect their salaries.
5. Every minister had to take an oath of alliance to the new government.

Most Catholic leaders rejected the new law. The oath was the most serious problem, and only seven bishops and approximately half the parish priests took it. The bishops issued a formal protest, *An Exposition of the Civil Constitution of the Clergy*, which argued that the form of religion in France had been changed without ecclesiastical consent. Further, the bishops appealed to Rome. Perhaps to gain time, Pope Pius VI delayed his response until March 10, 1791, when he condemned the Civil Constitution in the document *Quod aliquantum*. The revolutionaries proceeded with the scheduled ecclesiastical elections and appointed clergy to replace the non-jurors.

Civil war erupted in many parishes with the new civil priest and the old non-juring pastor contesting the church building and parishioners dividing their loyalty between the two incumbents. The revolutionary leaders believed that popular resistance to the Civil Constitution was a threat to their own power. Nonjuring priests and bishops became the targets of the Terror, and the revolutionaries executed many, while others emigrated.

The revolutionaries moved beyond persecution. The Assembly replaced the Christian calendar with a new system. Henceforth citizens were to date documents from the beginning of the revolution. More significantly, the government replaced the seven-day week with a ten-day system that bypassed the traditional Christian Sabbath. Patriotic holidays that reflected the new spirit of France replaced the church's round of feast and fast days. Finally, the Assembly declared that the worship of the Supreme Being was to be the national religion of France. To replace Catholicism's pageantry, the authorities held a festival in November 1793 in which a young woman was paraded through the streets and crowned as the Goddess of Reason in Notre Dame. Church attendance fell, while resistance to the new order, especially among provincial women, increased.

After the 1794 fall of Robespierre, persecution eased and church attendance increased. In 1795, the government issued a decree establishing religious freedom. Despite sporadic attempts to reconstitute the cult of reason, the church had survived the storm. Although the split between the Roman (Catholics) and the Civil (those loyal to the Civil Constitution) continued, Catholicism had not been destroyed.

Napoleon had his own plans for the church. In his dreams, Napoleon saw himself as the head of a united Europe that would recapture the grandeur of the ancient Roman Empire. The new order was to be based on universal citizenship, the reign of law, and a common market. To accomplish this dream Napoleon needed the tacit support of the Catholic Church. In 1799, Napoleon removed some of the restrictions on Catholicism in France and began negotiations with Pius VII (1742–1823) for a concordat (treaty) which was ratified in 1801. The document acknowledged that Catholicism was the religion of most French people, and Napoleon agreed to allow the bishops to appoint the parish clergy and to return all church buildings to religious use. In exchange for the church's renunciation of its claims to former ecclesiastical property, the state was to pay the salaries of clergy and bishops. *Mutatis mutandis*, the church conceded France's right to pass secular laws in such areas as marriage and divorce and agreed to respect the rights of the civil clergy. As in other Catholic countries, the church granted the head of the French state, Napoleon, the right to prohibit the publication of any Bull that might disturb the secular peace. In 1804, Pius VII crowned Napoleon Emperor.

Napoleon's later relationship with the church was stormy. Wherever his armies won a victory the dictator established "puppet" governments. In such traditionally Catholic areas as Germany's "priest's alley" (the powerful bishoprics along the Rhine), Napoleon stripped the bishops of their secular power, and arbitrarily reduced the number of Catholic universities in Germany to three (Freiburg, Münster, and Würzburg). He also abolished the Holy Roman Empire.

Napoleon followed similar policies in Spain, but his conflicts with the church were most serious in Italy. The dictator wanted Italy to be an example of enlightened French rule. Napoleon's Italian puppets passed ecclesiastical and secular laws modeled on those of France. In 1808, Napoleon invaded the Papal States. In turn, Rome became increasingly critical of Napoleon's Italian policies. When Napoleon annulled his marriage to Josephine in 1809, Pius VII refused to approve the divorce or to sanctify the dictator's subsequent marriage to Marie Louise of Austria. Further, the pope refused to perform certain ecclesiastical acts, hoping to inspire political resistance. In response, Napoleon arrested Pius VII and imprisoned him in France from 1809 until 1814.

Faith and Nationalism

To wage war on a Napoleonic scale, societies had to harness all their resources to warfare. In the first war with Austria, the French resorted to conscription and called young men to the colors, not to fight the government's war, but to fight for France. The tactic succeeded. French armies were almost invincible against more traditional royal forces. In large measure, France lost the Napoleonic Wars when her enemies adopted a similar nationalistic approach to war. Even as philosophical and critical a theologian as Friedrich Schleiermacher encouraged the idea of the "German" character. Other voices also demanded national renewal, including those of the philosopher Schelling and the poet Novalis. In Vienna, Napoleon's excesses so angered the composer Ludwig van Beethoven (1770–1827) that he scratched out Napoleon's name from the dedication of his Third Symphony ("Eroica," 1803). Beethoven's later "Wellington's Victory," a nationalistic potboiler, was among the most popular of the composer's works.

France did not create nationalism. European nationalism dated to the thirteenth and fourteenth centuries when France, Spain, and England became conscious of their national languages and characters. Unconsciously, Reformation leaders forged an alliance between religious affiliation and national thought. To be French was to be Catholic; to be Prussian was to be Protestant. Yet the Napoleonic wars did much to make nationalism a major theme of nineteenth century Christian history, and the union of religion and nationalism fired the post-Napoleonic revival. Theologians contrasted organic Christian societies with their presumably less just associative counterparts.

Church Reorganizations

Once Napoleon was defeated, the allies called the Congress of Vienna (1814–15) to restore the old European order. Under the leadership of Austria's Prince Metternich (1773–1859) and the wily French ambassador Talleyrand (1754–1838), the great powers redrew the European map. The victors allowed France to retain its traditional territory, hoping that this concession would stay the growth of renewed revolutionary sentiment. Consequently, the diplomats made most of their territorial adjustments in Germany. The largest German governments, especially Prussia and Bavaria, found themselves governing religiously diverse lands. The treaties obliged the new governments to treat all confessions impartially.

To unify their countries, German governments promoted union between the Protestant confessional bodies. The German states did not create a single type of church union. In some lands, the only union was a law that admitted all Protestants, regardless of confession, to the sacraments of their local congregation. In the larger governments, the tendency was to establish a common ecclesiastical bureaucracy, while allowing each specific congregation control over its liturgy and confession of faith. Only rarely did a German state, such as that of Rheinplatz, attempt a full confessional union based on a theological consensus.

In Prussia, the largest and most powerful North German state, the United Church was a response to the need for more efficient church administration. But the faith of King Frederick William III (1770–1840) also motivated the union. The king was Reformed, but his queen was Lutheran. That the royal family could not partake of the Lord's Supper together bothered Frederick William, who wanted his family to be a religious example for the nation. In 1816 a cabinet order established a common synodical form of government for both communions, and in 1817 a further cabinet order asked Lutheran and Reformed theologians to work toward closer cooperation. In this same year, Frederick William spoke frequently on the need for religious reform. The king stressed that he did not want the Lutherans to absorb the Reformed or vice versa. His hope was that a new church, based on the presence of the Holy Spirit, would find deeper truths behind the confessional bickering.

On Reformation Day, October 31, 1817—the three hundredth anniversary of the Ninety-Five Theses—the king held a common communion service with the Berlin clergy. The next day, Frederick William hosted a similar service for the court and the army leadership. The union was now a fact. However, Frederick William's program was not complete. In 1822, the king published an *Agenda* or liturgy for congregational use. Theologians from both the Lutheran and Reformed churches protested the new book, and public opinion forced the government to make the new order of worship optional.

Neo-Lutheranism

Many conservative Protestants bitterly opposed the new church unions. On October 31, 1817, Claus Harms (1788–1855), a talented theologian who had been converted by Schleiermacher's *Speeches*, republished Luther's Ninety-Five Theses with some theses of his own. Harms argued that the time had come for Lutherans to return to confessional purity and to maintain their own sacramental traditions. Other conservative pastors quickly joined Harms.

Only a handful of conservative Lutheran pastors separated from their state churches and formed independent ecclesiastical bodies; the majority remained within their churches and worked for theological change. The most important institutional center for the new Lutheranism was the University of Erlangen, in Bavaria, whose faculty included Adolph Harless (1806–79), Gerhard Thomasius (1803–75), and Johann Hoffmann (1810–77). In Saxony, Christopher Ludhard of Leipzig maintained a similar position, as did Berlin's F. J. Stahl (1802–61), the founder of the Conservative Party.

The neo-Lutheran theologians stressed four primary theological ideas. First, the Bible was objectively true in all that it taught. The Scriptures were the way in which the Holy Spirit transmitted faith in Christ across the generations. The more extreme confessionalists argued that the Holy Spirit was united to the biblical text in much the same way that the divine and human natures in Christ were united. Just as Christ was the Word incarnate, so the Bible was the Spirit inscriptured. Second, while the Scriptures transmitted saving faith, the church's confessions were the way God protected the biblical faith from misinterpretation. Thus, to hear the confessions was to hear the Scriptures and to bypass the confessions was to ignore them. Third, the so-called Catholic elements in Lutheranism—especially the doctrines of the real presence and baptismal regeneration—were essential Christian teachings that Lutherans could not surrender. Any union with the Reformed, consequently, was illegitimate. Fourth, sacramental and liturgical worship were essential to the Reformation heritage that the church had to maintain.

The neo-Lutheran movement slowed the rate of church union in Germany. When the state of Prussia expanded, treaties required the government to maintain the traditional faith of the new territories. Once Prussia achieved German unification in 1871, the stricter Lutherans resisted any attempt to form an empire-wide church and insisted that the various churches only enter an informal church federation. As late as the 1930s and 1940s, confessional Lutherans made it impossible for the German state churches to find a common theological position opposed to the Nazi state.

The Age of Ideology

The French Revolution began the age of ideology in European history. The ideals of the revolutionaries, especially the belief in democracy and human rights, became a permanent part of European thinking. The struggle to enact these ideas into law or to find an alternative to them dominated European political life for the next two hundred years. European liberalism was an element in successive French revolutions (1830, 1848, and 1870), the European-wide revolution of 1848, and the restructuring of European political life after each World War.

How Christianity and the new ideology related to each other was an important theological question. Outside of the United States, the majority opinion, among both Catholics and Protestants, was that Christianity was a conservative force in society that spoke for tradition over modernity. In 1868 Pope Pius IX provided the classic exposition of this position in his Syllabus of Errors. In that document, the pope said flatly that the church could not reconcile its message with such modern, liberal ideas as the freedom of the press or religious freedom. Protestant thinkers were seldom as extreme, but the widespread exaltation of the union of "Throne and Altar" expressed a similar sentiment.

The other side of the church's conservatism was the rise of a strong European anticlerical tradition. Karl Marx's observation that the criticism of society began with the criticism of religion was valid for nineteenth-century Europe. In almost all Catholic countries many males ceased to attend church, and a similar phenomenon (although not as marked) occurred among Protestant men as well. Equally significant, most proposals for social change in Europe came to include a stringent demand that the state disestablish the church and abolish its privileges.

Although most theologians who tried to adjust the church's thought to the modern world were politically conservative, a handful of liberal theologians and pastors had another view of the relationship between religion and modern political life. Friedrich Schleiermacher, the great German theologian, believed that religious freedom and the separation of church and state were natural rights. Schleiermacher and his followers believed that the church's primary influence on public life was through the shaping of ethical individuals and moral communities.

Richard Rothe (1799–1867), author of an influential *Theological Ethics*, carried the argument one step further. Rothe believed that a modern government might assume many traditional roles of the established churches and thus free the churches for their religious work.

CHAPTER SEVENTEEN

EUROPE AWAKENED

Despite the territorial readjustments resulting from the Napoleonic Wars, Germany remained more a geographic or linguistic designation than a nation. The continued political division of Germany shaped the German *Landeskirchen*. While some progress toward Protestant church unity was made in the larger states such as Prussia, the various *Landeskirchen* retained their separate identities.

In Prussia, many military conscripts experienced religious rebirth through various ecclesiastical exercises, including the blessings of flags and the regimental singing of chorals. The Prussian motto "God With Us," inscribed on every soldier's belt buckle, reflected the belief that military service was a sacred duty. Many Prussian ministers, further, became more self-confident through chaplaincy service.

The revival in Berlin, Prussia's capital, was particularly significant. After the French overran the University of Halle, Frederick William III resolved to create a new, more modern university, based on the Berlin Academy of Arts and Sciences. Planned by Wilhelm von Humboldt (1767–1835) and Friedrich Schleiermacher, Berlin rapidly became the leading German university. While the new school continued to see intellectual formation (*Bildung*) as its primary goal, it was also dedicated to the newer research ideal, pioneered at Göttingen.

Baron Hans Ernst von Kottwitz (1757–1843) was responsible for much of the awakening in Berlin. As a young man, he toured Europe and studied contemporary religious organizations, including the Free Masons and Jesuits. After Kottwitz returned to Germany, the Moravians converted him. The new Christian resolved to devote his life to benevolences, especially educating the poor and inspiring others to take up Christian service. His disciples included the Swiss educator Johann Pestalozzi (1746–1827). In Berlin, Kottwitz formed many prayer circles, usually involving university intellectuals. The Baron's prayer partners included theologians August Neander, Ernst Hengstenberg, and August Tholuck.

August Neander (1789–1850), whose original name was David Mendel, became a Christian in 1806 after reading Schleiermacher's *Speeches on Religion* and later taught church history at Berlin. In his studies, Neander maintained that the history of the church was the story of the unfolding of the Holy Spirit in time. Neander's best-known work was *The Planting and Training of the Church by the Apostles*, among the first histories to make Christian missions a major theme.

The Berlin revival touched Friedrich August Tholuck (1799–1877) while he was a student at the university. Tholuck began a long teaching career at Halle in 1826. To many Anglo-Saxon scholars, including Edward Pusey, the Oxford theologian, and Charles Hodge, the American Presbyterian, Tholuck symbolized the best in German Protestantism. They depended on him for their knowledge of German scholarship. Tholuck was the first German scholar interested in Wesley, and he published much on Wesleyan theology. In addition, Tholuck was among the founders of the British and Foreign Bible Society, the most important nineteenth-century organization for the distribution of the Scriptures, and an active member of the Berlin Bible Society.

Friedrich Wilhelm Krummacher (1796–1868) conducted revivals in the area around Frankfurt. In 1847 the consistory called Krummacher to the pastorate of Trinity Church in Berlin where his preaching continued to be well-received. Krummacher's careful biblical style of preaching was an important model for many young German pastors. He deeply impressed such coworkers as Ernst von Hengstenberg, professor of theology at Berlin and editor of the influential *Evangelical Church News*.

Christian Kraft (1784–1845), Professor of Practical Theology at Erlangen, used his classes to teach the importance of faith and prayer. One of the first Protestant theologians to offer a course in missions, Kraft was a founder of modern missiology. Under the leadership of Adolf von Harless (1806–1878), the Erlangen faculty also probed the meaning of the historic Lutheran confessions. Their theme was Christ's humiliation in the incarnation and his continued presence with us in Scripture and the sacraments.

Wilhelm Loehe fused the new confessional theology with a passion for Christian activity. Following study at Erlangen and Berlin, the church authorities expelled Loehe from two Bavarian parishes because of his vigorous preaching, finally exiling him to the small village of Neuendettelsau. Loehe decided to make this place of isolation a model Christian community. Neuendettelsau came to house several institutions devoted to Christian social service, including a training center for deaconesses. Concerned with the German diaspora, Loehe established a training school for Lutheran missionaries and dispatched workers to America and Australia.

Although Loehe believed in the Lutheran confessions, he held an almost Catholic doctrine of the Church that emphasized private confession, frequent communion, and formal liturgical celebration. At times his belief in the Catholic substrata of Lutheran faith involved him in controversy. Once the church government tried the embattled pastor for his refusal to remarry a couple with a valid state divorce.

While the pastor of Neuendettelsau yearned for the (supposed) social and religious solidarity of the Middle Ages, the modern problem of authority was his real concern. For Loehe, the church's authority was complete within the religious realm, and the state had to respect the church's actions. Such purity seemed impossible in Bavaria where the official Bavarian government included both Reformed and Lutheran ministers. In the 1850s, Loehe threatened to leave the official church if the Bavarian state did not support a purer Lutheranism.

In Württemberg, the awakening was primarily a reinvigoration of the older Pietist tradition of Bengel and Hahn. Ludwig Hofacker (1798–1828) began a renewal movement in his small parish at Rielingshausen. Thousands attended his services and many more read his books, especially his *Preaching For Every Sunday, Festival, and Feastday*. Unfortunately, Hofacker's ministry was cut short by a heat stroke, suffered in 1820, that forced him to rest for long periods. His brother Wilhelm conducted a successful, but less strenuous, ministry in Stuttgart.

Württemberger Pietism supported the Basel complex of Christian institutions. These institutions had their headquarters in Basel, because Switzerland's laws permitted the voluntary societies to be incorporated. The earliest Basel organization was the German Christian Association, founded by Johann August Ulsperger (1728–1806), to aid those in need. In 1815 missionary enthusiasts established the Basel Missionary School, and in 1822 they created the Basel Missionary Society.

The German awakening was similar to other awakening movements, including American revivalism. While the awakeners wanted to return to orthodoxy after the long reign of rationalism, they also wanted to affirm the old theology in a new way. The awakeners believed that people should experience faith, since individuals needed a personal experience of Christ to resist modern doubt. They formed voluntary societies to take action against evil, including poverty and drunkenness, and used newspapers, journals, books, and sermons to popularize their causes.

The German awakening inspired interest in missions. Besides the societies that supplied pastors for Germans living in North and South America, German churches had active ministries in Africa, India, China, and Indonesia.

Switzerland

In the eighteenth century, the state church in French-speaking Switzerland drifted toward a theological position similar to American Unitarianism. The Genevan church was particularly affected by this malaise. In 1805 it published a rationalistic version of the Bible, and, shortly after that, replaced Calvin's catechism with a more modern statement of faith.

Robert Haldane (1764–1842), the evangelist who founded the Scottish Congregational movement, traveled to Geneva in 1816. Once there, he organized a series of meetings with students in his apartment. Three of his converts—Henry Malan (1787–1864), François Gaussen (1790–1863), and Jean D'Aubigne (1794–1872)— became active evangelists. When the Venerable Company of Pastors opposed their revival as schismatic, the revived organized their own congregations. To supply these churches with pastors, the Evangelical Society of Geneva formed the Evangelical Theological Seminary of Geneva in 1832.

In Vaud, the revival also met stern official resistance. The government forbade conventicles in 1824, and in 1839 declared that the Helvetic Confession was no longer binding. Alexandre Vinet (1797–1847), known as the Swiss Schleiermacher, tried to mediate between the evangelicals and the rationalists. Vinet believed that since real faith was a matter of the heart, not the head, no dogma ever completely expressed Christianity. Yet, like other liberal evangelicals, he feared that a church without a formal confession might lose Christ's centrality. In 1847, after an agonizing self-examination, Vinet joined the Free Church of Vaud and left the state church. Vinet's writings profoundly influenced many American Christians, especially, his *Pastoral Theology* (English translation 1853).

Controversy between rationalism and evangelicalism was also important in the German canons. The church historian Karl Rudolph Hagenbach (1801–74) and his followers labored to keep the church in Basel on a middle course, yet were ultimately unsuccessful. A strong party in the state church wanted to remove the Apostle's Creed from the worship of the church. An equally strong party, the Evangelical

Church Union, defended the traditional ritual. Christoph Johannes Riggenbach (1818–70), a capable confessional theologian, led the Evangelical Church Union which established its own theological school.

Some of the nastiest debates occurred in Zürich. In 1839 the university called David Strauss (1808–74) whose *Life of Jesus Critically Examined* (1835–36), argued that the Gospel accounts were largely "mythical," and that modern theology needed Hegelian philosophy to find the truth in the ancient stories. Strauss's appointment provoked a strong reaction from the voting population, and the city council dismissed him.

In 1850 the University of Zürich appointed Alois Biedermann (1818–90), another radical Hegelian, to the chair of theology. While Biedermann often used orthodox language, his theology stripped Christianity of much supernatural content. For example, Biedermann believed that the Christian teaching of immortality was a symbolic expression of the fullness of our present earthly life. Although the same people opposed Biedermann as had earlier opposed Strauss, Biedermann remained at the University throughout his career.

Zürich was also the scene of a lively debate over the Apostle's Creed. In 1837 conservatives formed an evangelical union to defend traditional worship practices. Later, the city council passed a law (in 1868) that allowed two forms of the service, one with the creed and one without.

Scandinavia

The nineteenth century was a period of modernization and economic development in Scandinavia. Norway broke away from Denmark in 1814 and became an independent government under the Swedish crown. Denmark itself sought to maintain its independence and to integrate its economy into the North Sea market. Sweden became an industrial state, a major source of European iron ore.

Hans Nielson Hauge (1771–1824) led a Methodist-styled revival in Norway, with his followers becoming numerous enough to sponsor their own independent theological faculty. Gisle Johnson (1822–94), a professor at the University of Christiana, led "Bible Hours" (lay groups) and helped create voluntary organizations. Carl Paul Caspari (1814–93) taught Old Testament at Christiana and gave the revival a biblical dimension.

In 1808 Swedish awakeners formed an Evangelical Society in Stockholm, modeled on the London Tract Society. In northern Sweden, the followers of Lars Levi Laetadius (1800–1861) formed the enthusiastic "New Readers." The New Readers had semi-pentecostal forms of worship that included prayer with upraised arms. Despite these particularities, the New Readers remained in the established church. In South Sweden George Scott (1804–74), a Scottish evangelist, preached in Stockholm from 1830 to 1868. Scott converted Rosénius, the founder of the journal *The Pietist*. When the government expelled Scott, Rosénius took over the mission. While Rosénius did not want to leave the established church, his followers believed that step necessary. These separatists later became the Swedish Baptists, the Swedish Methodists, and the Swedish Covenant Mission.

Swedes consumed large quantities of hard liquor during this period. After Dr. Peter Wieselgren (1800–1897) witnessed the execution of a young man for the drunken murder of his wife, he resolved to work to prevent such tragedies. Under Wieselgren's leadership, many Swedes pledged to avoid spirituous liquors, and in 1854 Sweden experimented with the prohibition of brandy.

Scotland

Although Edinburgh was not a provincial capital after the creation of Great Britain in 1707, it was a brilliant city inhabited by many leading contemporary philosophers. The church there, however, was split into two factions: the Moderates and the Evangelicals. The two parties disagreed on almost every issue: the value of Calvinism, the value of ritual in worship, and tolerance for the pleasures of the upper classes. These issues fused in the question of church government. The Evangelicals believed that patronage (an individual or family's ownership of the right of appointment to a church) was inconsistent with Scripture. The Moderates agreed that the practice was not biblical but believed that the custom was a harmless accommodation to Scottish tradition.

Although only minor schisms occurred in the eighteenth century, the nineteenth-century argument was more divisive. The 1834 General Assembly of the Scottish church passed legislation that granted individual parishes the right to reject any candidate for the pulpit. In 1842 the General Assembly claimed the right to reject decisions of the Court of Sessions and Parliament, if those conflicted with church teaching. The government vetoed the measure with the result that more that four hundred churchmen, led by Thomas Chalmers, seceded from the Established Church to form the Free Church of Scotland.

The Free Church had to construct its own institutions. Independent congregations were established and money was collected for new theological colleges in Edinburgh, Aberdeen, and Glasgow. New College,

Edinburgh, became a leading center for the study of Reformed theology. In addition, the Free Church established home and foreign mission societies. Since the Free Church depended on converts, its leaders were evangelistic.

Scotland experienced a major debate over J. McLeod Campbell's doctrine of the atonement. In his view, the Bible taught that the cross expressed God's love for all people and did not represent divine satisfaction for sin. In 1831 the General Assembly heard Campbell's last appeal and upheld his deposition from the ministry.

England

The nineteenth century was the British century. England possessed the strongest economy in the world, and her navy commanded an empire on which the sun never set. The Anglican family of churches included churches on every continent.

When Victoria became queen in 1837, English public life was openly religious. Both William Gladstone (1809–1898), a four-time prime minister, and his famous rival Benjamin Disraeli (1804–81), the scion of a wealthy Jewish family baptized in 1817, publicly supported faith and conventional morality. The Victorians prized family life and moral stability, and literature maintained a high moral tone.

England hosted many worldwide Christian voluntary societies. The British and Foreign Bible Society (the largest nineteenth-century organization for the distribution of the Scriptures), the Sunday school, the Young Men's Christian Association (Y.M.C.A.), and many missionary societies began in England. The headquarters of these movements was in London, which seemed to function as the capital of worldwide Protestantism, analogous to Catholic Rome.

John Venn (1759–1813) continued the work of his father Henry as the rector of Clapham, near London. His parishioners included Charles Grant (1746–1832), Lord Teignmouth (1758–1834), Granville Sharp (1735–1813), and William Wilberforce (1759–1833). Charles Simeon (1759–1836), a Clapham convert and later vicar of Holy Trinity Church, Cambridge, converted many university men who subsequently entered Christian service, often as missionaries. The Clapham Sect secured the laws that ended first the slave trade and then slavery itself (1833) in the British Empire.

Half of those who regularly attended church were members of the free churches (non-conformity). In response to their growing political power, Parliament removed the disabilities that barred non-conformists from public life. The law that opened the ancient universities of Cambridge and Oxford to the dissenters was the potent symbol of these former outsiders' integration into the establishment.

Crisis in Albion

Yet British religion was not as healthy as it appeared. In an age of reform, the Church of England was the least reformed part of English life. Clerical education was at a low ebb; ministers continued to practice pluralism (holding more than one church office or appointment at a time); and many pastors were inept and often unconcerned. Further, the parish structure of the Church of England followed ancient agricultural patterns, resulting in disproportionally few congregations in the new industrial cities. Despite an 1817 parliamentary grant of one million pounds for the construction of new churches, the government did little to remedy the situation. One bright spot was Bishop Charles Bloomfield of London's (1786–1857) consecration of two hundred new churches in his diocese. Since the government did not vote him sufficient subsidies, the bishop raised private funds to finance the new construction.

The Irish Temporalities Act (1833), an eminently reasonable law, marked the beginning of a serious Anglo-Catholic revival. Like the Church of Wales, the established Church of Ireland was an Anglican disaster. The Church had lands, wealth, and benefices; it only lacked members, devotion, and purpose. While the new bill could not attack all these problems, it did reduce the number of bishoprics and used the income to supplement the financial support of the clergy. However, since Parliament adopted the law without the formal consent of the Irish church, many Irish bishops protested it as an invasion of their rights.

John Keble (1792–1866), a young Oxford don, addressed Anglicans worried about the Irish Act in his sermon "National Apostasy," preached on July 14, 1833. According to Keble, the real sin was erastianism, the belief that the state ought to control the church. Keble's sermon was not delivered in a vacuum. The high church party at Oxford included Richard Froude (1803–36) and the former evangelical John Henry Newman (1801–90). These men summoned a meeting of high church leaders at Hadleigh that marked the beginning of a decided campaign to save the church.

Newman, Keble, and other high church theologians, including Oxford's Regius Professor of Hebrew, Edward Pusey (1800–1882), published a series of articles, entitled *The Tracts For the Times*, intended to defend the high church position. Newman and his fellow writers began from the premise that growth and development characterized all social and cultural entities. The Christian faith required centuries to mature fully, and Scripture was not clear until Tradition clarified its meaning. Such ancient landmarks of the faith as apostolic succession, baptismal regeneration, and the Real Presence of Christ grew from biblical seeds. However, what made the experience of the church different was that God's Holy Spirit was the inner principle of its growth.

The Church of England was a particularly important manifestation of this process, they argued. Oxford Movement theologians believed that the Church of England was a *via media* between Roman Catholicism and Protestantism. Like Rome, the English Church held firmly to the ancient creeds, to the ministry of bishops, deacons, and priests (elders), and to a doctrine of the Real Presence of Christ in the Eucharist. However, the Tractarians also believed that the Catholic church had been corrupted during the Middle Ages, and that the Church of England had reformed its doctrine and life in the sixteenth century on the basis of Scripture.

Yet this ideal of a *via media* proved unstable. The Protestant side of the doctrine seemed to demand that the faithful subject all ecclesiastical life to the Bible, while the Catholic side apparently led to the belief that the Roman Church was a true church of God. Newman attempted in *Tract 90* to show that the Thirty-nine Articles and the Council of Trent taught a common Catholic soteriology, an attempt at lessening the tension which instead only heightened it. If Newman's argument was valid, then the schism between the two churches had no justification. The Oxford Movement divided into those who (like Newman) followed their Catholic convictions to Rome and those who remained with Canterbury.

The Oxford Movement was close to the ritualist movement which wanted to return to more Catholic liturgical practices. Ritualists introduced presence lights, vestments, chanting, auricular confession, and holy water into the English liturgy. Since Ritualism was controversial, bishops often assigned ritualistic priests the poorer parishes. Opponents also charged clergy in the church courts. The controversy grew so intense that the crown appointed the Ritual Commission in 1867 to reconcile the differences. The commission's four reports argued that the Church of England should follow only those practices that prevailed in the Church of England since the Reformation. Bishops were to discipline those clergy that departed from these instructions, especially in such areas as the wearing of eucharistic vestments.

Anglo-Catholicism contributed to a broader renewal of Christian worship, one which has had lasting consequences. During the twentieth century many churches have reformed their worship practices on more patristic lines. Among Roman Catholics, this renewed interest in liturgics led to the first major revision of the Latin Rite since the sixteenth-century Council of Trent. Lutherans have also moved toward new services that recapture more of the ancient pattern of worship. Even among Congregationalists and Baptists, the use of worship aids such as litanies, candles, robed choirs, and the lectionary is now commonplace.

CHAPTER EIGHTEEN

THE REVOLUTION IN BIBLICAL STUDIES

In the nineteenth century, a new style of biblical interpretation, the historical-critical method, largely replaced older forms of study among scholars. The Greek root of the word "critical" means to discern, judge, or separate. Since the late medieval period, scholars have used the term to designate those studies that analyzed a text. For example a critical commentary discusses a text's history, meaning and grammar, explains any geographical, historical or literary references, and notes the use of literary genres.

Nineteenth-century historical criticism was part of the professionalization of historiography. While in the eighteenth century amateurs still wrote most history, in the nineteenth century history became a profession. Such noted scholars as the Germans Leopold von Ranke (1795–1886) and Barthold Niebuhr (1776–1831) developed new historical standards that stressed the need to read historical sources as witnesses to their own times.

Meanwhile, literary scholars were unraveling the authorship of ancient masterpieces. For example, scholars learned that the Homeric poems were compiled from more ancient poems that were refined over centuries. Similar conclusions were reached about other materials. The brothers Grimm collected and analyzed the traditional German peasant stories. Their comprehensive research showed that these stories, despite their medieval trappings, originated in Asia before the German migration west.

The Enlightenment also provided an impetus for the new biblical studies. During the eighteenth century European thinkers struggled with the implications of modern science (especially physics) for Christian faith. The historicity of the miracles of the Bible was widely debated. What was the character of those biblical events that contradicted the ordinary rules of science? Could modern people accept these stories as actual historical events? The eighteenth-century Christological debates also inspired some to study the Gospels more closely.

Enlightenment scholars identified many of the issues that would occupy their nineteenth-century successors. Hugo Grotius (1583–1645) argued that Solomon did not write the book of Ecclesiastes and maintained that the book of Job reflected post-exilic conditions. The most radical of Grotius' conclusions was that Joshua was written much later than the events the book describes.

Grotius's compatriot Baruch Spinoza (1632–77) applied similar analysis to the Pentateuch in his *Tractatus Theologico-politicus* and his *Ethica ordina geometrico*. Spinoza's primary philosophical point was that divine causality and natural causality were identical, and hence that God was the *natura naturans* (the most natural part of nature). This conclusion led Spinoza to critique the tradition that Moses wrote the Pentateuch. On both literary and philosophical grounds, Spinoza decided, the author or authors of the first five books of the Bible must have lived after the Exodus.

Catholic apologetics provided the motive for Richard Simon's (1638–1707) historical-critical studies. Simon hoped to establish that the Scriptures evolved through a process of historical transmission and interpretation analogous to the development of Catholic tradition. In his *Historie critique de Vieux Testament*, Simon argued that the Pentateuch as we have it was the result of a long historical process that began with Moses and continued throughout Israel's history.

These early studies informed the work of J. G. Eichhorn (1742–1827), Professor of Old Testament at the University of Jena. In his *Introduction to the Old Testament* (three volumes, 1780–83), Eichhorn argued that several diverse sources existed for the Pentateuch. Since the divine names alternated in the book of Genesis, Eichhorn suggested that these different divine names reflected diverse sources. Further, he noted that the distinctions between the legal code in Deuteronomy and the more priestly code in Leviticus pointed to a different historical context for these works.

During his lifetime, Herman Reimarus (1694–1768) withheld publication of his *Apology for the Rational Worshipers of God* which attacked the veracity of the Church's claims about Christ. Released after his death, the work was typical of eighteenth-century Deism, although it also presented some advanced critical analyses of the Gospels. In particular

Reimarus distinguished between the Gospel of John, which he regarded as late, and the earlier synoptic accounts.

From Eichhorn to Gunkel

In the early nineteenth century Old Testament studies made important technical progress. Wilhelm Gesenius (1786–1842), professor of Hebrew at the University of Halle, conducted extensive investigations into the historical linguistics of the Hebrew language. He published the results of his studies in his *Hebrew and Chaldean Dictionary* (1810–12) and in his *Hebrew Grammar* (1813). Every major nineteenth-century work of Old Testament scholarship was indebted to Genesius's meticulous examination of the development of Hebrew words.

Much research after Eichhorn and Gesenius answered particular questions about this or that aspect of the Old Testament text, an effort that seems to have reached its critical mass by the 1860s. Although Wilhelm De Wette (1780–1849) made many fruitful suggestions that later scholars would follow, de Wette's work did not have much initial impact since he often lacked a convincing rationale for his conclusions. In contrast, Julius Wellhausen (1844–1918), Professor of Semitics at Marburg and later at Göttingen, summarized the century's research. In 1878 Wellhausen published his *History of Israel*, revised two years later as the *Prolegomena To The Old Testament*. Abraham Kuen and Karl Graf reached many similar conclusions at the same time.

Wellhausen linked the literary history of the Pentateuch with the cultic history of Israel's religion. For example, if the description of a sacrifice reflected Second Temple practice, then the account was probably post-exilic. When literary and cultic history were paralleled, the historian could date the earliest strata of the Pentateuch in the time of the early kings, the next strata in the time of Josiah's reform, and the last (including the final production of the books) in the post-exilic period.

Other Old Testament scholars quickly accepted Wellhausen's conclusions. In Scotland, William Robertson Smith, a professor in the Free Church University at Glasgow, published an article on the Pentateuch in the *Encyclopedia Britannica* of 1880 that presented Wellhausen's arguments. Although the controversy over the piece cost Smith his chair, the battle showed the widespread British acceptance of the newer critical directions. Charles Brigg's *Biblical Study*, published at roughly the same time, represented a similar triumph in the United States.

The next stage in the investigation was associated with Hermann Gunkel (1862–1932) and the history of religions. To understand the prehistory of the biblical text, Gunkel turned to the history of folklore where scholars interpreted the development of a unit of tradition by studying the literary forms used in its transmission (form criticism). Gunkel also interpreted the religion of Israel in relation to Canaanite and other ancient Semitic religions.

The New Testament

Progress in the study of the New Testament text was rapid. In his 1737 edition of the New Testament, Johann Bengel (1687–1752) set forth many principles of textual study, for example the idea that the most difficult reading of a particular passage was likely the oldest. Johann Griesbach (1745–1812) published the first critical edition of the New Testament that did not start with the *textus receptus* (the "standard" edition of the Greek text, based on relatively few, mostly older manuscripts). Griesbach's edition was repeatedly updated when new texts became available by Constantin Tischendorf (1815–74), himself the discoverer of *Codex Sinaiticus*, a text probably transcribed in Egypt in the fourth century. Tischendorf reissued his edition of the New Testament frequently between 1841 and 1869. In England conservative biblical scholars, Brooke Westcott (1825–1901) and Fenton Hort (1828–92), published a critical edition of the New Testament in 1881.

Friedrich Schleiermacher (1768–1834), often called the father of modern theology, was an important early New Testament critic. In his lectures on the introduction to the New Testament and on the life of Jesus, Schleiermacher argued that the synoptic Gospels were compilations of stories and sayings that had been transmitted orally. Only the Gospel of John, he believed, contained a unified account. For Schleiermacher, this established John's historicity.

In contrast, F. C. Baur (1792–1860) of Tübingen began his studies by examining the Hellenistic world in which Christianity originated. Baur began with the relationship between Paul's letters and the Book of Acts, noting that either the first chapters of Galatians were rewritten by someone other than Paul or that Acts was written considerably later. Since no evidence supported the former supposition, Baur concluded that Acts was a second-century document. Baur later concluded that Paul only wrote the four primary Pauline epistles, Romans, 1 and 2 Corinthians, and Galatians. Like Acts, the other letters attributed to Paul reflected the second-century church's theology.

In 1835–36, David F. Strauss's (1808–74) two volume *Life of Christ, Critically Examined* appeared. Although the book's literary criticism was derived from Griesbach, Strauss's contribution lay in his understanding of the role of myth in ancient societies. Strauss averred that the disciples and their followers used myth to interpret the Gospels in much the same way that a nineteenth-century scholar used scientific method. In that sense, myth was the language of religion. The historian should not ignore this mythology or explain it away. Instead, Strauss argued that the modern scholar must interpret myth philosophically.

Nineteenth-century New Testament study concluded that Mark was the oldest of the Gospels and was used by the other two synoptic writers as a source for their work. Burnett Streeter (1874–1937) popularized this interpretation in English-speaking countries. Streeter's picture of the development of the Gospels was chaste. During the earliest period, the sayings and stories of Jesus circulated orally. Perhaps during the reign of Nero, the author of the Second Gospel wrote Mark's gospel. Next, the authors of the First and Third Gospels used Mark's chronological framework to order their own work and departed from that order only when they wished to make a specific theological point. In addition, the authors of the First and Third Gospels had a collection of the sayings of Jesus, often called Q (from the German *Quelle*, "source") that they included in their narratives. These authors also had their own sources that informed materials that appear only in the First and Third Gospels.

Adolf von Harnack (1852–1930), the historian and polymath, popularized the new biblical studies and provided scholars with a sense of the New Testament's larger historical context. Harnack believed that the development of Christian thought was entwined with the geographic expansion of the church. Whenever Christianity entered a new area, the church's leaders, consciously or unconsciously, reinterpreted their message to make it intelligible to their hearers. As the historian moved from Jesus to the Council of Nicea, he or she could see that the earliest Hebraic teachings of the church were replaced by philosophic formulas—a process Harnack called "Hellenization."

In the early twentieth century scholars often spoke of the "assured results" of scholarship. In retrospect, their boasts were premature. Twentieth-century biblical critics have reopened many questions that nineteenth-century scholars believed they had settled. Further, scholars have devised new approaches to the biblical materials, including rhetorical and social criticism. Nonetheless, the nineteenth-century achievement was significant. The method that nineteenth-century critics pioneered is now used by most Christian schools preparing ministers and theologians.

The Controversy over Biblical Studies

Many found the new scholarship disturbing, because they believed that it eroded confidence in Scripture. Some demanded that churches prohibit the new studies wherever possible. The Catholic Church went furthest in this direction. Reaffirming the Council of Trent's doctrine of biblical inerrancy, the popes required all Catholic seminary teachers to take an oath that they would not teach the new biblical studies.

The professionalization of scholarship complicated the debate over the new biblical studies. In earlier times, a basic liberal education enabled a person to participate in almost any discussion. However, during the nineteenth century the various fields of intellectual inquiry became separate academic disciplines, each with their own methods and literature. Very few people had the time or training to review the literature to learn the details of the arguments.

Particularly in England and the United States, popular opinion connected the historical interpretation of the Bible with Charles Darwin (1809–82) and the new biology. In the 1830s and the 1840s geologists recognized that the Earth was far older than had been supposed. Further, their studies showed that many once flourishing forms of life were now extinct. Even a conservative dating of fossils (petrified remains) showed that many animals had existed millions of years before the appearance of human beings.

Darwin studied these findings before he began his voyage on the *Beagle* (1831–36). As he subsequently studied exotic wildlife in the South Seas, Darwin saw that living things had changed in this isolated environment. Darwin found an important clue to why this was the case in the writings of Thomas Malthus (1766–1834), a social economist, who argued that all things being equal, human population increased faster than the means of human subsistence. Widespread starvation would result unless wars, famines, or diseases culled the human population. Applying this insight to all life, Darwin concluded in his 1859 *Origin of Species* that all living organisms struggled for existence with all other organisms and, at the same time, tended to increase until they exhausted available food. Those most fitted (best adapted) to their environment would survive and produce new offspring; the less fit might die without issue. Over time, Darwin reasoned, variations in a given population might result in a new species. Naturally, this meant that all presently existing forms of life had evolved from earlier life.

This new teaching appeared to strike at the very heart of Christian faith. Traditional Christian theology taught that God created humankind perfect, and that humans fell from grace and became tainted by original sin soon afterwards. Christ redeemed humans by reversing this primordial fall. In contrast, Darwin's theory seemed to leave no place for either fall or regeneration. If anything, modern humans were biologically more developed than their ancestors. Further, the theory seemed to threaten the popular argument for the existence of God from design, since evolution moved by chance, not conscious plan.

In the popular mind, the new science and the new biblical criticism reached similar conclusions. Many theologians searching for a way to discuss biblical criticism found the new science a useful ally. They believed that the biblical message itself developed from very primitive religious insights until it reached the heights of the ethical monotheism taught by the Hebrew prophets and Jesus. More conservative thinkers often became more suspicious of biblical criticism because evolution and criticism reinforced each other.

The 1860 debates between Thomas Huxley (1825–95), Darwin's pugnacious associate and an agnostic, and Bishop Samuel Wilberforce (1805–73) convinced many that evolution was supported by the best evidence. The well-read Huxley destroyed the bishop's argument in a cross-examination that showed that Wilberforce was ill-informed about the new science.

The subject of the new science and criticism was more thoughtfully discussed in *Essays and Reviews* (1860), a collection of essays by such thoughtful commentators as Frederick Temple and Benjamin Jowett. According to the essayists, the new science and biblical study aided faith. The cosmology of Genesis, the authors argued, was part of the ancient understanding of the world that moderns had already abandoned. Hence, the church ought publicly to abandon efforts to reconcile Genesis and modern cosmology. Bishop Samuel Wilberforce condemned *Essays and Reviews*, and 11,000 clergymen proclaimed their allegiance to the older interpretation of the Bible. The protests made the book—a dry, scholarly volume—a best-seller.

A second collection of essays, *Lux Mundi*, appeared in 1889, edited by Charles Gore (1853–1931), Canon of Westminster and the leading Anglo-Catholic theologian of his day. *Lux Mundi's* authors argued that the new biblical criticism gave us a more human view of the Scriptures, one that enabled the interpreter to recognize the incarnational character of God's work. According to the authors, the Holy Spirit inspired people within history, rather than affecting history from outside.

Charles Haddon Spurgeon (1834–92), pastor of the Metropolitan Temple in London and England's foremost evangelical preacher, believed that the new views of the Bible would sap the churches' energies. Like a train that was gaining speed as it moved down a hillside, the churches were rapidly moving toward disaster. Unless someone applied the brakes soon, the whole enterprise would derail. When the Baptist Union refused to heed Spurgeon's warnings, the evangelist and his congregation withdrew.

In Holland, Abraham Kuyper (1837–1920), a founder of the Free University of Amsterdam (1880), and Herman Bavinck (1854–1921) revised the traditional Reformed doctrine of Scripture. In their view, the Holy Spirit inspired the Bible from within history rather than superintending its writings from above. While both Kuyper and Bavinck remained ultraconservative, their doctrine enabled their followers to incorporate some new criticism in their exegesis. James Orr (1844–1913), a Scottish theologian who was influential in conservative circles, held a similar doctrine.

The Bible as a Popular Book

Biblical criticism was only a small part of the nineteenth century's fascination with the Bible. As technology reduced the cost of the Scriptures, the Bible became more available. Ordinary Christians read the Bible at home, often following plans that enabled a person to read the whole book in a year. Although the Sunday schools often used such helps as quarterlies and teacher's guides, their primary text was the Scriptures. Members of nineteenth-century congregations often read silently while their pastors read the Bible aloud to the church.

One nineteenth-century Protestant goal was to distribute the Bible to every person who wished to read it. In 1804, nonconformists and members of the Church of England joined to form the British and Foreign Bible Society. The Society's goal was to publish inexpensive Bibles for use at home and by foreign missionaries. Other Bible societies followed, including the Netherlands's Bible Society, the Royal Württemberg Bible Company, and the American Bible Society.

Since Bible society leaders believed that individuals should interpret God's Word for themselves, the Bible societies published the Bible without note or comment—a position that caused much controversy. For example, high church Anglicans believed that the Society should publish the Bible with the Apocrypha. In turn, Baptists argued that the Greek word *baptizein* should be translated as "immerse," rather than simply "baptize," especially in versions of the Bible sent to non-western lands.

Nineteenth-century missionaries, supported by the Bible Societies, translated the Bible into all the major languages of the world. For instance, the Societies published the original translations of William Carey, Robert Morrison, and Henry Martyn. By the end of the nineteenth century, translators had begun their work on the various African languages and dialects. In 1934, L. L. Legters and W. Camerson Townsend (1896–1982) formed the Wyclif Bible Translators. The Wyclif translators wanted to provide the Bible to the world's less numerous peoples, including the Central American Indians. In 1804, the Bible was available in 72 tongues; in 1850, 567; and in 1968, 1,392. In the 1990s, experts estimated that over one-half of the world's peoples had access to the Bible in their own language.

Revisions of the Bible

During the nineteenth century interest in the revision of the standard European Bibles grew. In part this new interest came from advances in biblical scholarship. Clearly, the newer readings of the biblical texts needed to be incorporated into the text that ordinary Christians used. But changes in the reading of the biblical text were not the only motive. European languages had changed significantly since the sixteenth century. Many passages, once clear, were now confusing.

English evangelicals, within and without the Church, were the primary advocates of revision. In 1725, John Wesley—an avid Greek scholar—published a revision of the New Testament for his societies' use. In 1870, the convocation of Canterbury authorized a committee to revise the King James Version. The Oxford and Cambridge University Presses published the New Testament portion of this revised translation in 1881 and the whole Bible in 1885.

The English Revised Version, as the revision was known, dissatisfied the American scholars who had worked with the English committee because they believed that the published version did not follow the newer scholarship closely enough. Their minority report encouraged many unauthorized, and often inaccurate, editions, and in 1901 the Americans published their own revision.

Few church members found the new editions satisfactory. In 1937, the International Council of Religious Education, which inherited the copyright to the American revised edition, appointed a new committee. Although the Second World War interfered with the work, the Federal

Council of Churches published the New Testament in 1946, followed by the whole Bible in 1952. Known as the Revised Standard Version, it was the most successful of the recent editions. In 1990, the Council published a revision of the Revised Standard (the New Revised Standard Version) that sought to restate many passages in more gender-inclusive language. In Britain the Church of Scotland called for a completely new translation in 1946. The New Testament appeared in 1961, and the whole Bible in 1971 as the New English Bible.

Churches and societies have done similar translation work. The theological faculty of the University of Leyden, for example, prepared a new Dutch translation that was published in 1901, and a committee of German scholars published a revised edition of the Luther Bible in 1892. This latter work was revised again in 1912.

The new translations of the Bible had some unanticipated consequences. The earlier Reformation translations had provided a bond that linked Christians together. Believers heard the same Bible from the pulpit, studied it at home, and carried it to church. Serious Christians often memorized important portions of the text, and regular church attenders recognized the most popular passages. The loss of this uniformity contributed to the apparent decline in biblical literacy among church members. It would be ironic, if the nineteenth-century drive to make the Bible readily available to all, ended with the Bible known by fewer people.

CHAPTER NINETEEN

NEW THEOLOGICAL BEGINNINGS

Gotthold Ephraim Lessing (1729–81) was a professional writer who earned his living by his keen eye for intellectual fashion. Like his contemporary, Samuel Johnson in England, Lessing was the master of the memorable witticism, the clever remark, and the epigram. Lessing began thinking seriously about history while he was librarian at the Duke of Brunswick's castle at Wolfenbüttel. In the duke's collection, Lessing "found" the notes of H. S. Reimarus subjecting the Gospels to critical analysis. Lessing published some of Reimarus's work as the *Wolfenbüttel Fragments* (1774–78) which quickly landed him in a literary debate with some of Germany's leading pastors. For Lessing, the debate was fun and, since religious polemic sells books, profitable.

Lessing's literary duels posed the problem of history and faith clearly. In a famous *bon mot*, Lessing asked how accidental truths of history might become the eternal truths of reason and *vice versa*. This, he continued, was the "big ugly ditch" that he could not cross. Lessing's aphorism raised two questions. First was the issue of *certainty*. An axiom of historical study is that the veracity of any account of the past is no stronger than the evidence on which that narrative is based. Yet the evidence is never perfect or complete. Second, Lessing's aphorism also pointed to the difficulty of translating one age's assumptions into the language of another. In the *Education of the Human Race* (1780), he argued that every historical period finds the truth needed for its own cultural life. The problem (here he used the provocative image of a "primer" or schoolbook), was that every age needed to advance beyond earlier periods. Should an advanced student still read elementary texts? Should modern Europeans tie their culture to the first Christian century?

Lessing offered no solution to the problems that he posed, and he probably had none. The power and influence of religion impressed Lessing, but he knew that vitality was no evidence of the truth or falsity

of specific claims or propositions. In a parable, Lessing compared religion to other unprovable beliefs. Did the truth or falsity of belief in the
power of snails' blood to improve crops contribute anything to the fruits
produced by the peasant's labor? According to Lessing, the wise man
eats the fruits, savors their juices, and never gives the ancient supersti-
tion another thought.

Kant and the End of "Rational Religion"

Immanuel Kant (1724–1804) was a philosophy professor at the University of Königsberg in East Prussia. Although Kant never left his own
province, he read in every area from physics to history. His writings
included significant essays on the culture of China, astronomy, and
physics.

Kant's central concern was epistemology, or the philosophy of
knowledge. Whether human beings can know anything was not, for
him, the epistemologist's primary concern. Rather, epistemology dealt
with the limits of what we know and how we understand those limits.
In his early years, the philosophy of Christian Wolff (1679–1754) satisfied
Kant. Wolff's basic argument, illustrated primarily through mathematics, was that the world and human beings are rational, and that therefore
logical analysis of reality should lead us to the truth.

Kant's reading of Hume destroyed his confidence in Wolff's system.
Hume had dissolved the apparent link between reason and experience
by demanding that philosophers offer empirical evidence of their inher-
ent connection. Since no one could produce such evidence, Hume
concluded scientific thought was basically a rational habit, a conclusion
which Kant did not fully accept, believing that science had a firmer
foundation than Hume supposed.

In the *Critique of Pure Reason*, Kant took Hume's conclusions in a
different direction. He argued that logical structures—including space,
time, and causation—were the products of the mind itself. The proofs
of the existence of God, one of the purest applications of logic, were a
case in point. When the critical mind examined these proofs the arguments were inconclusive. In other words, much traditional metaphysics
was only reason reflecting on itself.

However, when we join logic to our apprehension of the world,
humans discern a rational pattern or order in nature that other human
observers can validate. Thus, science is a synthesis of thought and
apprehension that thinkers can use to predict successive natural states.

Since Kant had already proved that moral and religious statements were not scientific, he needed either to show that they had an independent basis or abandon them as meaningless. In his *Critique of Practical Reason* (1790), he argued that religion and ethics were founded on human moral experience. Through what he called the "categorical imperative," Kant believed that we know that we ought to do certain things, and that we cannot ignore these duties without experiencing guilt. He then asked, "What must be true about the world for this moral experience to be meaningful?" Kant suggested that reason could postulate (claim as reasonable without empirical proof) that God existed, that human life was not limited to its earthly duration, and that a system of rewards and punishments encouraged virtue over vice.

Later, in *Religion Within the Boundaries of Reason Alone*, Kant argued that human beings surround these moral postulates with symbols that enabled people to live uprightly, even after they had departed from the good. The figure of Christ thus functioned for Kant as the most important of these, because it promised forgiveness of moral fault.

Kant's works pointed to four conclusions that were—despite many variations—basic to nineteenth-century theology.

1. All claims to knowledge are assertions that relate the knower or subject and the known or object. Pure "facts" do not exist anywhere, since all knowledge is relational (synthetic).
2. Although knowledge depends on reason, the thinker needs to distinguish between the operation of reason and knowledge. Knowledge comes from the rational interpretation of the world and not from reason or experience by themselves.
3. Religious propositions are incapable of formal proof or disproof, and, therefore, are not statements about the world or logic. The task for philosophy, consequently, is to discover how religious affirmations function in life.
4. Kant suggested that religious statements were postulates from our moral experience. If the categorical imperative is to be valid, humans must affirm certain propositions about the world.

The Romantic Movement

While Kant was continuing the work of the Enlightenment, younger intellectuals were embracing romanticism. Although some romantics yearned for the intellectual security of the medieval world, most strongly supported science and technology. In Central and Eastern Europe the romantics often were in the forefront of those demanding the modernization of human life.

Yet the romantics believed that science had not answered all of humankind's questions. In particular they argued that people often confused questions of meaning with matters of fact. Since romantics believed that history was the record of the unfolding of the human spirit, they believed every past contributed to our present self-understanding. Thus, J. G. Herder (1744–1803) argued in his *Elements of Hebrew Poetry* that the ancient Hebrews gave present-day people insights into the nature of poetry.

The unique and particular fascinated the romantics. In a sense, the reigning romantic metaphor was art, with the self as the ultimate work of art. Just as every artist created unique works, so every person differed from every other. The romantic fascination with the individual might express itself through outlandish dress, such as the bright yellow coats popular at this period, or through a style of life.

At least in theory, romantics hoped that their involvement with the particular would "mediate" the whole universe. Many romantics became passionate Roman Catholics because they believed that the mass was an ideal expression of the way in which the finite bore the infinite. Others sought the infinite through the particularities of nature.

Philosophically, romantic philosophers often combined motifs from Kant and Plato. Such thinkers as Friedrich Heinrich Jacobi (1743–1819) in Germany and Samuel Taylor Coleridge (1772–1834) in England followed Kant in distinguishing between science and intuition or reason. But where Kant had confined real knowledge to science, the romantic philosophers believed reason (intuition) actually penetrated reality's outer hull.

Very few pure romantics existed. Romanticism was as much a mood or style as it was a coherent philosophic or literary movement. In a sense, romanticism's diversity reflected the movement's individualism. If each person is unique, human beings should have different philosophies, arts, and literatures.

Further, many romantics felt little need to avoid contradiction. Although Georg W. F. Hegel (1770–1831) and Søren Kierkegaard (1813–55) differed on many matters, they agreed that truth came from the dialectical clash of ideas. For Hegel, contradiction forced the mind to redefine the problem; for Kierkegaard, dialectic forced the self to decision. For both, the clash of ideas was more important than the ideas themselves.

Friedrich Daniel Ernst Schleiermacher

Schleiermacher (1768–1834) was the scion of a long line of Reformed pastors. Although his father, Gottlieb, an army chaplain, began his career as a neologian or rationalist, he was converted in 1778 by the Moravians. Gottlieb might have resigned his commission, but he elected to continue his career and conform outwardly to the official theology. However, the older Schleiermacher wanted his children to share his newly found faith, and he sent them to strict Moravian schools. In those institutions the younger Schleiermacher experienced the range of pietist religious emotions. Later, Friedrich called himself "a Moravian of a higher order."

The young Schleiermacher found the atmosphere of Moravianism confining. After developing doubts about the substitutionary atonement and the historicity of some biblical narratives, Schleiermacher entered the University of Halle where he immersed himself in modern philosophy. Schleiermacher took his first theological exam in 1790 and his second in 1794. Ironically, he received a "satisfactory" in dogmatics on both tests.

In 1796 Schleiermacher was appointed the chaplain of the Clarité hospital in Berlin, where the young pastor joined Berlin's romantic young intellectuals. As Schleiermacher went from one discussion to another, he became progressively more interested in addressing his companions, many of whom rejected Christianity totally. In his 1799 *On Religion: Speeches to Its Cultural Despisers*, he did so.

Schleiermacher couched *On Religion* in the elevated language favored by the Berlin romantics, complete with the self-conscious use of unusual words, inverted phraseology, and pathos. Although the style renders Schleiermacher's apologetic less accessible to twentieth-century readers, his contemporaries believed it added grace to the author's appeal.

On Religion is an apologetic argument. The author hopes to lead the reader from initial unbelief to a full confession of faith. Thus the argument is not complete when Schleiermacher identifies religion with feeling, or after he has shown that a historical community shapes human emotions. The argument proceeds until the readers learn that Christ is the source of their most elevated ideals.

Schleiermacher began the *Speeches* with a discussion of the self as it relates to the world. How is it, he asks, that we are aware of ourselves at all? The answer is that self-consciousness is a feeling or an awareness that is a response to the world around us. But this particular feeling is not tied, as so many emotions are, to specific circumstances. For example, our consciousness of the world is not like our happiness when others acknowledge our birthday or when we take pride in our nation. In that sense, this feeling is not related to any particular finite reality. Thus it must be an awareness of the Infinite itself; that is, of "God."

Once the reader concedes this point, Schleiermacher has already won his argument. For the only remaining task is to demonstrate that this awareness must necessarily be present in us only in historical forms. Clearly, these forms include communal and historical human relationships. For Europeans, their source must be the general consciousness or the spirit of the church. Yet, the church is not self-explanatory either. Since this community shapes our own awareness, then we must ask, "what has shaped the church?" When one allows for the church's imperfections, the secret of its inner life can only be Jesus' awareness of God. The question for us is how we incorporate Jesus' awareness of God into our own lives.

The *Speeches* were a bare outline of a theological position. Like Calvin, Schleiermacher spent much of the rest of his professional life developing the implications of his early thought. His translation of Plato was an important part of his maturation. Plato's dialogues gave Schleiermacher a deeper appreciation of the role of dialectics in philosophy and of the need to make a clearer separation between God and the world.

Schleiermacher's career developed in an orderly manner. The *Speeches'* success contributed to his 1804 call to teach at the University of Halle. After Napoleon occupied that city, Schleiermacher moved to Berlin where he helped plan the king's new university. In 1807 Schleiermacher became pastor of the Trinity Church, the most prestigious Reformed church in the capital, and in 1810 the Prussian government formally appointed him Professor of Theology at the University of Berlin. He would hold both positions until his death in 1834.

In 1821 Schleiermacher published *The Christian Faith*, his *magnum opus*. This new dogmatics began an attempt to understand Christianity as a religion or a modification of the human experience of dependence. But there were many religions, and Schleiermacher wanted to show what made Christianity unique.

After a careful analysis, Schleiermacher concluded that Christianity was a moral (teleological) monotheism that relates everything to the redemption accomplished by Jesus of Nazareth. Theological statements that are far from this center, such as belief in angels or demons, are not necessary to the inner core of Christian belief and can be discarded.

As Schleiermacher understood Christian existence, the believer moves continually between experiencing God and forgetting God. However, forgetting God is not the same as our experience of sin. Paradoxically, the more believers increase their awareness of Christ, the more they feel their own sinfulness, an experience which is itself an experience of grace.

Schleiermacher discussed his understanding of Jesus from the standpoint of Christ's human experience. Christ differed from other people by his intense consciousness of God's presence within him. This experience of oneness with God was so abiding that neither Jesus nor his disciples could distinguish Christ's own consciousness from his awareness of God or *vice versa*. Through faith in Christ, Christians come to share Jesus's own God-consciousness.

Schleiermacher was a theologian's theologian whose works primarily influenced the church's educated elite, and his impact on such leaders, both among his contemporaries and future theologians, was considerable. Schleiermacher's influence can be seen in five observations.

1. Schleiermacher's separation of religious and metaphysical language was foundational for much later theology. Since the publication of his work, theologians have sought to understand the religious use of symbol, the specifically religious elements in any understanding of the world, and the uniquely Christian elements in Christian theology. For many theologians, this separation enabled them to accept Christian doctrine while also affirming modern science.

2. Schleiermacher offered an important alternative to rationalism. Whereas the rationalist sought to remove all elements from faith that conflicted with science, Schleiermacher suggested that reinterpretation was more fruitful. Theologians needed to be sure that they understood what the affirmations meant before they engaged in radical criticism. In other words, Schleiermacher focused the modern theological task on hermeneutics.

3. Schleiermacher's work proved that a theologian's method influenced that thinker's interpretation of doctrine. Like workers in the other "spiritual sciences," theologians had to self-consciously decide how their discipline knew and understood truth.

4. Schleiermacher noted that the most serious problem for modern people was the relationship between faith and

culture and suggested that theologians thoroughly explore this issue.

5. Schleiermacher insisted that theologians understand and use the newer approaches in history and science, particularly historical criticism, where these were appropriate to their task. Since true Christianity was the vivid experience of the presence of Christ, no intellectual conclusion could threaten faith.

Georg W. F. Hegel

Georg W. F. Hegel (1770–1831), professor of philosophy at the University of Berlin, was a seminal thinker who sought to complete Kant's revolution. Beginning with the premise that whatever is, is rational, Hegel argued that human beings could understand the development of their own thought. To know anything is to think historically. Thus, each age finds truths that it transmits to the next generation which, in turn, modifies these truths, and passes these modifications onward. The goal of this process is for the human mind to understand everything that existed.

Hegel believed that the human spirit moved through clearly discernable stages. At the end of each stage, human thought reached a new level of insight. Each new beginning then moved toward the next breakthrough. Hegel believed that art and politics followed a similar progressive development. Thus, religious ideas evolved until religion reached its most complete fulfillment. Once that occurred (as Hegel believed that it had in the Christian doctrine of the incarnation), the mind began to examine religion for its rational content and to transform that content into its own categories. Thus, Hegel could affirm that it was precisely because Christianity was the absolute religion that philosophy had to transform faith into philosophy.

Hegel's view of intellectual progress meant that he had to find a positive meaning for error. The very fact that humankind moved toward truth meant that people had to begin their intellectual quest with less than truth. Hegel's answer to this dilemma was brilliant. Reaching back to Plato's understanding of learning as dialogue, Hegel asserted that philosophy moved dialectically, or as follows: First, an idea (or *thesis*) would arise, perhaps out of the human struggle with existence. Second, another thinker (or even another historical circumstance) would suggest another idea (*antithesis*). Naturally, the two ideas would interact with one another as people debated them back and forth. The result would be a third idea, not identical to the other two, that would then form the beginning point for a new development (a *synthesis*). In other words, Hegel shifted intellectual attention away from specific conclusions to the process by which those conclusions were reached.

One might call Hegel's discovery historical relativism, if the term is carefully defined. The position that every truth is relative to its own time is, of course, a logical contradiction. Like the assertion "all Cretans are liars, said the Cretan," a pure relativism collapses once one thinks seriously about its structure. What Hegel did when he posited the Absolute as the goal of the intellectual process was to anchor relativism. While truth is the goal of all thought, any given proposition or idea is only part of the process by which people learn the nature of things. Final truth will exist only when the search for truth ends.

Hegel's intellectual star arose during a crucial period in German intellectual history. The governments of the various German states, frightened by the rise of democratic sentiment, restricted enrollment in the universities to suppress dissent. Many first-rate minds were unable to find academic employment and became independent intellectuals, often in exile in Paris or London.

The "Young Hegelians" included Ludwig Feuerbach (1804–74) and Karl Marx (1818–83), both of whom developed Hegel's insights in novel ways. In *The Essence of Christianity*, Feuerbach set out to explain why Christian faith was so psychologically attractive to humankind. What happened, Feuerbach argued, was that human beings had mentally separated themselves from their own nature as free beings. This alienation (a technical term in Hegel's philosophy) was so fundamental that people had to seek to overcome it. They did so, Feuerbach said, by attributing all good to God, while living their own lives in misery. Once people recognized that they had forged their own chains, the argument continued, they could end this alienation and take responsibility for their own lives.

Karl Marx began his own philosophical work by attempting to extend Hegel's understanding of the dialectic to economics. As Marx carried out this project (and its significance for modern economic theory has been profound), he concluded that he needed to "stand Hegel on his head." Such spiritual abstractions as truth and freedom did not determine human life. Rather, the fundamental force in human history was economic production. Therefore, one could understand human experience as a struggle over wealth and the means of its creation. This struggle would eventuate in a final revolution that replaced private property with socialism.

Marx believed that Christianity had been a negative factor in European development. Consequently, he believed that it was necessary to provide an intellectual critique of Christianity to clear away an impediment to social change. Marx's argument was simplicity itself. Since the economic order does not provide most humankind with a humane standard of living, people seek compensation for their deprivation. Christian faith enabled them to do this by providing assurances that their present misery was only an antechamber to the greater glory to come. Since people believed that their future was better than their past, they would not take responsibility for their own lives. In a telling metaphor, Marx called faith the flowers woven into the chains that bind humanity. Once the flowers were removed, people could see the chains for what they were.

CHAPTER TWENTY

INDUSTRIAL LIFE
AND EUROPEAN FAITH

In the nineteenth century, European industrial production increased rapidly, and Europe experienced the "Industrial Revolution." Although "revolutions" usually have a beginning, a middle, and an end, industrialization was a process in which one step led to another without apparent end. The decision to build a railroad from Manchester to London made the towns between excellent sites for factories. In turn, these factories encouraged the shipment of raw materials via London and Liverpool.

The new wealth resulted as much from transportation advances as factory production. In 1800, goods were transported by animal or wind power; in 1900, most of Europe, the Americas, and Asia were crisscrossed by railroads. At sea, ships were powered by steam. Few parts of the world were more than two weeks distant from any other. In a related development, the telegraph and the undersea cable enabled information to travel almost instantaneously over extended distances.

At the beginning of the nineteenth century, Europeans lived in the late medieval world of privilege where the primary sources of wealth were commerce and land. A hundred years later this order had eroded. The middle classes expanded to include professionals, managers, bureaucrats, and engineers. What united these occupations was their use of specialized knowledge as a way to wealth and prosperity. The makeup of the wealthiest European class also changed. Although the landed nobility still existed, entrepreneurs and capitalists now held the greatest economic power, and wise nobles invested their surplus in stocks and bonds. The composition of the lower classes also changed. Although peasants continued to be numerous and often poor, the industrial worker replaced the peasant as the base of the social pyramid.

Changes in Parish and Ministry

In the early Middle Ages, the church divided Europe into jurisdictions or parishes. In theory, a parish was the area that the priest could circumnavigate in a day. In the towns, parishes often reflected traditional patterns of settlement. The wealthiest town and city parishes were near the center of the town with the poorer parishes in outlying areas.

When Europe industrialized, the shift of population to the cities overwhelmed these traditional structures. Parishes were no longer located where the majority of people lived. In 1800, Berlin had a population of 800,000 and only 25,000 seats at worship services. In Hamburg, some parishes had as many as 20,000 communicants. England, where religious competition complicated the picture, followed a similar pattern.

Finding the resources to build new churches was not easy. The traditional patrons of the church, the nobility and the old merchant class, were unable to meet the demand for new buildings, and often lacked the wealth to construct the type of churches needed in the cities. Although governments were a traditional source of ecclesiastical patronage, they faced serious financial problems, and their costs were rising geometrically. Most western governments adopted expensive programs of universal public education and, toward the end of the century, provided other social services. Military expenses increased exponentially, with every military invention costing more than the older technology.

Hence, the construction of new churches was left to voluntary effort. In 1818, Joshua Watson established the Church Building Society in England to build new churches and to seek parliamentary grants. The Ecclesiological Society, founded by John Mason Neale in 1845, took a lead in the restoration and reconstruction of churches. Neale's Society favored a neo-gothic architecture with a split chancel, stained glass, and organs. Although Christians established similar organizations in other western European countries, the churches did not keep up with the increase in the urban population.

The clergy, especially in Protestant Europe, were educated in the traditional foundations of European culture: classical languages, Scripture, philosophy, and theology. The purpose of this liberal education was to enable the minister to join the provincial elite that governed the European countryside. At the same time, liberal education also enabled ministers to transmit European culture to the next generation. Ironically, the high German standards of theological education may have made the nineteenth-century Protestant ministry less effective. Since the knowledge needed for the state examination was traditional, few ministers took any courses apart from their theological specialities, and fewer had any knowledge of science or technology.

New Forms of Ministry

The irrelevance of much traditional parish ministry led to experimentation with new forms of Christian outreach and service. Since it was difficult, if not impossible, to convince the traditional church authorities to sponsor experiments, voluntary societies paid for most new ministries. Often these agencies were continuations of earlier pietist societies or modeled on contemporary foreign missionary societies. Many believed that Europe itself was a missionary field in as much need of conversion as any exotic land. William Booth (1829–1912), the founder of the Salvation Army, entitled his most influential pamphlet *In Darkest England and the Way Out*.

The most important German home missions agency was the Inner Mission created by Johann Hinrich Wichern (1808–81). Wichern studied theology at Göttingen and at Berlin, where he reflected on the doctrine of the Holy Spirit with Schleiermacher and Neander. For Wichern, the Spirit was the presence of Christ turning the Church toward God's will.

Completing his studies, Wichern returned to his native Hamburg, a principal center of industrialization in western Germany with an active port and railhead. Wichern became involved in the revival movement (*Erweckungsbewegung*) in the city and began a society devoted to religious visitation. Soon, however, Wichern was drawn to the port area where large numbers of youths lived without supervision. His first outreach to this group was the establishment of a Sunday school for boys, and then an orphanage, *Rauhe Haus*, which placed children in a family-like atmosphere where they lived with a single counselor, often a theological student or ministerial graduate.

Wichern was interested in educational reform, and in 1842 he founded a training school for his workers. While he was establishing this institution, Wichern conceived the idea of a total mission to Germany aimed at the "Christian and social rebirth" of the people. In 1844 Wichern founded *Die Fliegenden Blätter aus dem Rauhen Hause* to popularize his views. The journal soon became the voice for many German Christian charities.

Wichern believed that the Revolution of 1848 was a divine judgment on the European states for their economic sins. At the 1848 Church Congress (*Kirchentag*), he called for the church to promote works of love in addition to works of faith. In a pamphlet summarizing his views, *The Inner Mission of the German Evangelical Church: An Address to the German Nation*, Wichern explained that the church had to regenerate all three of the orders of creation: family, church, and state. The only way that Christians could do this, he argued, was when they confessed Christ as Lord of all of life.

In 1849 representatives of the various Protestant churches formed the Central Committee of the Inner Mission to coordinate homeland ministries. The new organization hoped to serve wherever there was need. The Inner Mission inspired work directed toward boys, girls, and youth, including Sunday school. Wichern and the Inner Mission also helped to secure new laws, leading in the legal battles for legislation protecting Sunday. Since the Inner Mission provided chaplains for prisons, the organization became involved in prison reform. In 1857 the Prussian government invited Wichern to reform the Prussian prison system.

After taking charge of a small home for epileptics near Bielefeld, Friedrich von Bodelschwingh (1831–1910) quickly made the hospital a center for various Christian ministries: a home for deaconesses, a training school for male nurses, a worker's colony, and a seminary for young men planning to enter social ministries.

The historian Neander had stressed the role of the deacon and the deaconess in the early church, and nineteenth-century German churches wanted to restore this ancient office. Wichern recruited *Felddiakonen* ("army-" or "field-deacons") to serve the troops in the wars of German liberation. But it was the English Quaker Elizabeth Fry who inspired Theodore Flieder (1800–1864) to establish the first deaconess house at Kaiserwert. The sisters quickly became proficient nurses. As their skills and medical knowledge increased, nursing became a profession that did more than comfort the sick. In addition the deaconesses did social work, ministered to prostitutes, taught in church schools, and conducted retreats.

The organization of the Red Cross was another Christian response to the changing European social order. In 1859, Henri Dunant (1828–1910) witnessed the terrible battle at Solferino and resolved to find a way to alleviate soldiers' sufferings. After four years of speaking and writing, Dunant organized a sixteen-nation conference that established the International Red Cross. Dunant's work also led to the Geneva Convention in 1864 which adopted an agreement binding the signatories to agreed-upon laws of war, especially the humane treatment of prisoners.

English Philanthropy

The English experience with social missions differed from that of the continent. Since John Wesley's day, evangelicals had preached to the poor, and the Primitive Methodists and other radical Wesleyan sects conducted a vigorous nineteenth-century mission to the workers. Further, England had a long history of philanthropy and social reform. After the Restoration, dissenters made organized charity a mark of English social life. Philanthropists founded trusts to build schools, to establish and maintain hospitals, and to alleviate suffering.

These organizations also became part of the very complex English system of social class. For example, a membership on the board of governors of a charity was a mark of high social status. The most prestigious charities had the patronage of a member of the royal family and the landed gentry.

English Christians used Parliament to effect needed changes in social life. The Clapham Sect's crusade against slavery is the best-known of these movements. Christians also led in political campaigns to limit the hours that children could work, to establish common schools, to promote public health, and to improve housing. To be a Christian was often to be a reformer.

Elizabeth Fry (1780–1845) and John Gurney (1788–1847) led the drive for reform of criminal law and of prisons. Although the English crime rate was one of the highest in Europe, English legal penalties for crime were more severe than on the continent. Despite England's legal traditions, few poor men received a fair trial, and the criminal code mandated the death penalty for many petty offenses. The prisons were barbaric alternatives for those who escaped the noose.

Industrialization did not cause prostitution, but it did create conditions that encouraged its growth. The temptation to become a buyer or seller in the sexual marketplace was a part of urban life. Young men and women, fresh from the countryside, entered a highly competitive urban world where employment was either unavailable or the pay was too low to cover the cost of living. Poorer people delayed marriage or postponed it indefinitely. In some working-class communities, many women worked as prostitutes before marriage.

The Magdalene Societies provided shelter for homeless women and placed former prostitutes in "suitable" jobs to enable them to avoid their disreputable trade in the future. Christians also crusaded to make prostitution illegal. Josephine Elizabeth Butler (1828–1906) led a successful effort to repeal the Contagious Diseases Act which provided for the medical inspection of prostitutes by the police. These activists believed that such laws virtually licensed the trade. In time, they secured Parliamentary acts prohibiting prostitution completely.

The Young Men's Christian Association was another approach to the problems of urban industrial society. George Williams (1821–1905) formed the organization in 1844 with two objectives. First, he wanted to win young urban males for Christ. Second, he wanted to provide a place where Christian fellowship and healthful activities might serve as an alternative to urban immorality. The Y.M.C.A. popularized sports and sports competition for men between thirteen and thirty. By 1900 the "Y" had branches in all Protestant countries and the British possessions, including India and Hong Kong.

The well-being of children was another cause that English Christians favored. All British denominations maintained orphanages. Often factories employed children for fourteen or more hours each day with little or no provision for food, water, or sanitation. Benjamin Waugh (1839–1908) was one of the reformers who worked to bring these conditions to the attention of Parliament. Over the course of the century, new legislation first regulated working conditions for children and finally restricted employment to those fourteen years and older.

Urban evangelization was another Protestant crusade. Many pastors attempted to turn their urban parishes into "institutional churches." The institutional church was a local parish that provided night schools, meeting places, clubs, nursing care, sewing rooms, and charity for a poor neighborhood. The members of these churches rarely were able to support them from the congregation's own revenues and had to raise outside funds to pay for their work.

David Naismith (1799–1839) established the first City Mission in his native Glasgow. The City Mission was similar to the institutional church. City Missions reached out to the poorer sections of a city with the Gospel and, also, provided needed social services. Evangelicals in other cities copied the Glasgow mission.

Although primarily appealing to the upper classes, the Settlement House movement was similar to the drive to establish City Missions. The problems of the poor in England's large cities long interested Samuel Barnett (1844–1913), who helped establish the first Settlement House, Toynbee Hall, in 1863. The Settlement House was a place where men and women (usually university students) could live (or settle) in a poor neighborhood and provide social and religious services. Barnett hoped that the training would provide students with a firsthand experience of poverty that would make them reformers.

William Booth was an independent Wesleyan evangelist who left the Methodist New Connection in 1861. Booth organized his followers along the model of an army, complete with officers, soldiers, uniforms, and discipline. The mission of the Salvation Army (as it came to be known) was to reach those whom society ignored, especially the unemployed and alcoholics. Besides preaching, Booth wanted the Army to help these people meet their basic physical needs, including the desiderata of warm food and shelter. The Salvation Army spread throughout the English-speaking world, and many prominent people, including King Edward VII, who served as a patron, supported its work.

Christianity and Socialism

Socialism was a radical response to the new industrial society. The first socialists were such idealists as Charles Fourier, Robert Owen, and the Comte de Saint-Simon who dreamed of a society in which cooperation replaced competition. The profits of industry would meet everyone's needs equally. Karl Marx and Friedrich Engels attempted to put socialism on a "scientific" basis. In 1859 Marx published *Das Kapital* in which he argued that the foundation of history was the conflict between social classes. Sooner or later, Marx believed, this class conflict would lead to a socialist revolution, the dictatorship of the proletariat, and, finally, a classless society.

From 1860 to 1914, workers and their supporters formed socialist parties in all European states. With the broadening of the franchise, the socialists became one of the largest parties in the various national legislatures.

Many sincere Christians feared that socialism was the first step on the road to anarchy and that any concession to the workers was an invitation to social unrest. Other Christians recognized an affinity between socialism's idealism and the Gospel. Samuel Taylor Coleridge (1772–1834) inspired many of the later attempts to create a Christian Socialism. Coleridge's theology combined German romantic philosophy with Christianity to argue that Christ and society were spiritually one. John Frederick Denison Maurice (1805–72), a follower of Coleridge, began his career as an instructor at London's King's College, but ran afoul of the authorities with his 1853 *Theological Essays*. In this controversial work Maurice argued that damnation did not mean that God would endlessly deprive a person of all communion with God. A year later the College authorities dismissed Maurice from his teaching position. At this time Maurice became acquainted with John Ludlow

(1821–1911) and Charles Kingsley (1819–75). They established the Working Man's College in 1854, and in 1866 Maurice summarized their ideals in *Social Morality*. The work argued that human solidarity, not individualism, was the obligatory foundation for contemporary ethics.

The Christian Socialist Society led by John Clifford (1836–1923), an English Baptist, took a similar position. The majority of the society's members were nonconformists. Clifford's group demanded the nationalization of natural resources, production, and distribution, especially the railroads. The Christian Socialists joined the coalition that formed the Labour party in 1900 (originally called the Labour Representation Committee and renamed in 1906).

In 1889, Anglo-Catholics interested in social reform formed the Christian Social Union under the leadership of Brooke Foss Westcott and Henry Holland Scott. The Social Union stood for cooperation between classes and concrete actions to aid working people. Both labor and capital recognized Westcott's ability as a mediator in labor disputes, particularly when, in 1892, he negotiated a settlement of the coal strike that was disrupting English industry.

German Christian Socialism

After a series of well-orchestrated Prussian wars against Denmark, Austria, and France, the smaller German states had no alternative but to join a greater German confederation under the Prussian monarchy. The resultant government had some features characteristic of the western democracies and others of the Russian autocracy. The German middle class was primarily composed of state employees.

Otto von Bismarck (1815–98), Germany's Iron Chancellor, was violently opposed to the Socialists during the early years of his government (1862–83). However, in 1883 Bismarck began a program of social reform to solve the most serious social problems. Under his leadership, Germany adopted laws that regulated child labor, set a maximum work week, and set standards for industrial safety. In addition Germany created a system of social insurance that provided compensation for illness, unemployment, and old age.

Friedrich Naumann (1860–1919) was deeply influenced by his service in the Inner Mission and his contact with the Social Democrats. However, the Socialists' failure to root their movement in religious prepositions deeply disturbed Naumann. Through his journal *Die Hilfe* and in his frequent contributions to Martin Rade's *Christliche Welt*,

Naumann attempted to prove the relevance of Christian ideas to social changes.

Johann Christoph Blumhardt (1805–80) created a novel expression of Christian Socialism. The case of a young woman, Gottlieben Dittus, who appeared to have serious mental problems, confronted Blumhardt in his early ministry. No doctor could help her. After Blumhardt and Gottlieben prayed together for two years, Dittus's sister cried out, "Jesus is Victor!" and Gottlieben was healed. A revival followed in the small parish of Möttingen, and the local *classis* (Blumhardt was a Reformed pastor) became increasingly critical of Blumhardt's enthusiasm. Blumhardt withdrew from the Reformed Church and established a retreat center at Bad Böll devoted to pastoral care, Christian recreation, and prayer. His son, Christoph Friedrich (1842–1919) followed him in this ministry and served for a season as a Social Democratic delegate to the Württemberg *Landstag*.

The Blumhardts based their theology on the simple affirmation that "Jesus is Victor." Since Christ had claimed all reality, including the social life of humankind, Jesus would bring all corporate life under God's dominion. Christians had to learn to allow Christ to work thorough them.

Although the Blumhardts were not technical theologians, their ideas inspired many later Christian leaders, especially in Switzerland. Hermann Kutter (1869–1931) and Leonhard Ragaz (1868–1945) were the leading Swiss Christian Socialists. Kutter's social theology, like the theology of the Blumhardts, was based on the conviction that God could provide the solution to all human problems. What the churches needed was an open recognition of the divine sovereignty in the midst of human distress. Kutter developed this perspective in his classic studies *You Must, Righteousness,* and *We Pastors.*

Leonhard Ragaz's theology was a form of Ritschlean liberalism. In his *The Gospel and The Present Social Situation*, Ragaz argued that Jesus' central message was the coming of the Kingdom of God. Ragaz believed that the Kingdom was already present in Jesus' life and that each generation discovered more of its reality in their obedience to the Lord's teachings. If the church would consistently apply those teachings to the present industrial situation, Ragaz argued, Christians would experience a new apprehension of the Gospel. Ragaz's life was a testimony to his ideals. Ragaz was a voice for righteousness and justice, and the champion of every form of Christian social service, including agricultural cooperatives, settlement houses, and folk schools.

European Christian Socialism became far less influential after the First World War. To many who lived on the other side of that tragic event, the early social prophets seemed too optimistic about humankind and about the possibility of social regeneration. Yet to say that Christian Socialism was only a temporary flowering of Christian concern is not completely accurate. After their witness, European Protestantism found it difficult to withdraw from the political arena. By the 1960s, a new and more radical form of Christian Socialism, the theology of liberation, won some acceptance among both European Protestants and Catholics.

CHAPTER TWENTY-ONE

POST-CIVIL WAR AMERICA

The latter part of the nineteenth century in the United States has been designated "the Third Great Awakening." However, little new was introduced in this revival. Most churches continued earlier practices or followed contemporary European examples. As the churches grew numerically, they adopted contemporary bureaucratic or business forms of organization. Denominational distinctiveness waned, and for many denominations good will and cooperation with other churches was normative.

Women increasingly entered positions of religious leadership. On the mission fields, unmarried women were a crucial component of the work force. Missionary women did more than evangelize other women. They staffed missionary schools, provided nurses for the hospitals, did the routine tasks of administration, and occasionally preached. At home, the women's missionary societies, which provided women with a place in the new church bureaucracies, were the backbone of most denominations' missionary financing.

The social ministries that originated in England were also popular in the United States. For example, the Young Men's Christian Association spread to almost all of the nation's campuses and major cities. Most Northern cities had city missions, and colleges and seminaries participated in the Settlement house movement. As in England, Christians worked to enact laws to protect the family. In addition, states passed laws protecting public decency, prohibiting pornography, and banning the sale of birth control devices.

Under the leadership of the Anti-Saloon League, public opinion turned against the manufacture, sale, and use of alcohol. After a major women's campaign in the upper Midwest picketed bars and occasionally physically destroyed bar-owner's stocks, the Women's Christian

Temperance Union was organized to work for prohibition and other reforms. Frances Willard (1839–98), the W.C.T.U. president and an enthusiastic Methodist, led the organization to campaign for other women's issues. Willard popularized the belief, for instance, that women's suffrage was crucial to prohibition, because more women would vote against alcohol than men. Many states were dry before the nation adopted the Eighteenth Amendment that prohibited the manufacture or sale of alcoholic beverages.

Dwight L. Moody (1837–99), a Chicago businessman, built a successful Sunday school in the slums, gathered a "free" (no pew rent) church, and developed the Young Men's Christian Association. When the 1871 fire destroyed his evangelistic empire, Moody went to London to raise funds. On this trip he discovered his talents as a revivalist and preacher. Returning to the United States, Moody launched a series of city campaigns that combined an appeal for salvation through Christ with an awareness of contemporary social ills.

In 1888 the great evangelist invited the leaders of college Y.M.C.A.s to a conference at his Mount Hermon School in Northfield, Massachusetts, where Arthur Pierson (1837–1911), a missionary enthusiast, challenged them to volunteer for foreign service. One hundred students responded by organizing the Student Volunteer Movement (S.V.M.), pledged to the "evangelization of the world in this generation."

Although the Southern churches accepted some evangelical emphases, particularly prohibition, these churches tended to stand apart from the main developments among American evangelicals. Southern particularism stemmed from the churches' decision to preserve the memory of the Grand Old Cause. Since defeat was intolerable, Southerners found ways to deny that it happened. As far as possible, life had to remain as it was before the Civil War. Thus, the churches refurbished their arguments justifying slavery to support racial segregation and called for "states' rights."

Intellectual Ferment

After Darwin, many educated Americans experienced a spiritual crisis that destroyed their childhood faith. American theologians were divided over how to handle this crisis. The more liberal sought to adjust inherited teachings to new conditions, while the more conservative sought ways to hold the line. Conflict between the two perspectives was common, with some national denominations conducting widely publicized heresy trials.

The most significant American theologian in the middle decades of the nineteenth century was Horace Bushnell (1802–76). As a young man, Bushnell studied at Yale College where he took the full course in the Divinity Department. Without conscious decision, Bushnell discarded the traditional doctrines of original sin, the substitutionary atonement, and conversion. Shortly after graduation, the young minister entered a serious depression. He was delivered from his spiritual doldrums by reading the English romantic Samuel Taylor Coleridge (1772–1834) who taught that the Bible should be read as a literary and not a scientific document. As literature, Coleridge maintained, the Bible informed our conscience and provided an existential understanding of the problems of human life.

In *God Was in Christ* (1848), Bushnell analyzed the nature of human language, which he believed began when people learned to use first simple names and then verbs and then expanded both by analogy or simile to include the non-material or spiritual aspects of life. If this is the case, he argued, then the more abstract and spiritual language might be, the less precise it was. Given the nature of words, two theologians might appear to maintain contradictory points of views while affirming the same spiritual reality.

Bushnell argued against a division of life into sacred and the secular in *Nature and the Supernatural* (1858). For Bushnell, God and humankind existed on a spiritual continuum, and both shaped and reshaped the natural world. For example, when we manufacture a chair, we make something that did not exist apart from human will. Similarly, God affects the world through God's spiritual power. For Bushnell, the debate over literal miracles largely misses the point since the only difference between what we call a miracle and God's ordinary work is our description of the divine activity.

Although Bushnell had no close disciples, his thought inspired many New England pastors, including Theodore Munger, Newman Smyth, Philips Brooks, and George Gordon. At one point this Bushnellian theology, called Progressive Orthodoxy, was the dominant theology at Andover Seminary.

Although Washington Gladden (1836–1918), a follower of Bushnell, was not an original thinker, he spoke to ordinary people's theological concerns in such books as *Burning Questions in Theology* (1886), *Who Wrote the Bible* (1897), and *How Much is Left of the Old Doctrines*. In clear language, Gladden discussed such hot issues as the new biblical criticism, the contemporary understanding of the person and work of Jesus, and organized labor. His *The Christian Pastor and the Working Church* (1908) pointed to a new style of ministry among those who now had to administer a complex social organization, providing different services to its members and community. Gladden believed that the clergy should renounce their traditional authority and serve their congregations as counselors or friends who might help people apply faith to their daily lives.

The Bushnellian tradition was only one variety of religious liberalism. In the late nineteenth century, the thought of Albrecht Ritschl (1822–89) and his school attracted many American seminary professors. Ritschl began his career as a member of the Tübingen School of F. C. Baur, but later rejected its Hegelian basis in favor of the neo-Kantian philosophy of Hermann Lotze (1817–81). Lotze followed Kant in insisting that religious statements were not metaphysical affirmations but were rather "value judgments" that described ideas, things, or actions in terms of their ethical meaning.

Ritschl's *The Christian Doctrine of Justification and Reconciliation* argued that we can best understand Christianity as an ellipse with two foci: forgiveness of sins and reconciliation. For Ritschl, Christian experience moves back and forth between forgiveness from God and reconciliation with one's neighbor. When a person is forgiven, he or she can then accept others as God's children; and this love for the neighbor, in turn, leads to a closer relationship with God.

Many creative German theologians, including Wilhelm Herrmann (1846–1922), Adolf von Harnack (1851–1930), and Ernst Troeltsch (1865–1923) shared Ritschl's basic theological orientation. On a less theoretical level, Martin Rade (1857–1940), the editor of the *Christliche Welt*, made Ritschl's thought into a practical theology that informed the local pastor's struggle with social issues.

Ritschlian theology had three attractions. First, Ritschl's separation of value and fact enabled theologians to separate religious and scientific affirmations. This separation was particularly valuable in a period when many people, both ministers and laity, feared the effects of the teaching of evolution and biblical criticism on Christian faith.

Second, Ritschlianism provided a definition of Christianity that was open to historical investigation. For the members of this school, what distinguished Christianity from other religions (the essence of Christianity) was its focus on Jesus of Nazareth. While Ritschlians did not claim that we know everything about the historical Jesus, they maintained that historical research could discern the outlines of Jesus' message and, perhaps, give us some insight into his personality.

Third, Ritschlian theology offered a way for Christians to think constructively about the social order. Ritschl's thought suggested that every religious doctrine had two applications: one individual, the other social.

The leading American Ritschlians were William Adams Brown (1865–1943), Walter Rauschenbusch (1861–1918), and Harry Emerson Fosdick (1878–1969). Brown, a student of Harnack at Berlin, believed (as did many American Protestants) that the American churches were losing their moral influence on society because of their divisions. Working with such agencies as the Federal Council of Churches and the various world missionary organizations, Brown provided theological justification for "federative Protestantism." In his view, individual churches could express their theological distinctives as strongly as they liked. But they also had a moral obligation to cooperate with people who thought differently. Further, the Christian churches needed a common witness, especially on national and international matters, to be heard.

Walter Rauschenbusch, the son of a German immigrant, served as a Baptist pastor in New York's Hell's Kitchen after graduation from seminary. A progressive loss of hearing lead him to change careers. After advanced study in Germany, Rochester Seminary appointed him Professor of Church History in their German department. In *Christianity and the Social Crisis* (1907), *Christianizing the Social Order* (1912) and *A Theology for the Social Gospel* (1917), Rauschenbusch argued that Christians had to work for social justice.

For Rauschenbusch, the failure of the churches to address social issues was a theological problem. Although revivalism had encouraged theological individualism, Rauchenbusch argued, industrialization should encourage Americans to think more corporately. When modern readers opened the Bible, he hoped, they would rediscover the prophetic demand for justice and Jesus' teachings about the Kingdom of God.

Harry Emerson Fosdick was a national figure whose radio broadcasts from New York's prestigious Riverside Church addressed contemporary religious issues. Fosdick's contribution to American theological thought was his belief that religion had an important role in mental health. The New York pastor believed the church should use psychological insights to interpret the Bible and his own preaching demonstrated how this could be done.

A closely related version of evangelical liberalism was the personalism of Bordon Parker Bowne (1847–1910). Like the American Ritschlians, Bowne was a neo-Kantian in philosophy who spoke about value judgments as the basis for religion. However, Bowne went beyond other American liberals in asserting that all knowledge comes through the knower's personality. Our knowledge of physics or biology is as personal as our knowledge of history or philosophy or of religion. According to Bowne, people apprehended God through their individual self-consciousnesses. Therefore, every person's experience of God and of moral value differs from that of others.

Princeton Seminary was the home of one of the few lasting schools of American theological thought. Archibald Alexander (1772–1851), Charles Hodge (1797–1878), A. A. Hodge (1823–1886), B. B. Warfield (1851–1921), and J. Gresham Machen (1881–1937) were a series of teachers and students. Each new disciple took up the work of his teacher and carried it forward. Although the immediate issues changed, the two consistent themes of the Princeton school were the rational defense of Christianity and the inspiration of the Scriptures.

For the Princetonians, Christianity was a doctrinal or teaching religion. To be a Christian meant that a person accepted certain affirmations about God, humankind, and the world as true. While Princetonians were personally pious, they did not equate their piety with Christianity. Further, Princetonians refused to argue about the religious feelings or Christian character of their opponents. Instead, they asked only one question: was a disputed teaching in accord with the teachings of the Bible? If a doctrine failed this test, it should be rejected, no matter how Christian its advocates might feel or act.

J. Gresham Machen's *Christianity and Liberalism* (1924) was the logical outcome of this argument. In this well-argued volume, Machen admitted that he admired the ethics and activism of contemporary liberals. But Christianity was a doctrinal religion, and contemporary liberals denied so many basic Christian affirmations that they had become unbelievers.

The Princetonians were also noted for their doctrine of inspiration. They believed that God so inspired the Bible in the original autographs that its teachings were infallible and inerrant. Inspiration also meant that the Scriptures were also free from contradiction or logical absurdity. However, the Princetonians were not literalists. They considered it axiomatic that the Bible contained different literary genres which communicated faith differently.

The Princetonians did not believe that they taught any new doctrines, since their theology only re-stated what (according to them) Reformed Christians had always believed. What was unusual about their position was the context in which they taught it. At a time when other American and European theologians were searching for alternate ways to do theology, the Princetonians held to a course set in the seventeenth-century.

Premillennial dispensationalism was a popular late nineteenth-century American theology. John Nelson Darby (1800–1882), a priest of the Church of Ireland, believed that rather than acting out of convictions formed by the gospel, his church settled every issue in accord with general English policy. As the founders of the Oxford Movement said of the Church of England, Darby maintained that his church had fallen into apostasy. However, instead of attempting to reform the situation, Darby resigned his position and joined a small sect, the Plymouth Brethren.

Most of Darby's theology was commonplace. For example, his division of biblical history into seven dispensations or covenants could already be found in most Puritan handbooks. What was unique, however, was Darby's eschatology. Traditionally, many Protestants believed that Christ would not return until after a sequence of events foretold in Daniel and Revelation had happened. Darby added two events to this prophetic calendar. First, Darby argued that shortly after Christ's death, the church entered the "Great Apostasy," and that God, consequently, had suspended the predicted course of events. Second, Darby inserted the Rapture into the prophetic calendar. Not itself the Second Coming of Christ, the Rapture was instead a preparatory gathering of the church in the heavens which had no necessary precedents and, hence, might occur at any moment. Once the Rapture had occurred the prophetic calendar would resume and the events predicted in Revelation and Daniel would follow.

To maintain this eschatology, Darby and his followers modified other Christian teachings. The most controversial was their insistence that God intended the church to obey Jesus's teachings literally only in the end-time when Christ reigned as the earthly king of the Jews. Another was Darby's demotion of the church. Since all denominations were part of the Great Apostasy, no church had the true means of grace. Hence the dispensationalists considered existing churches only as agencies for evangelism. In effect, the church "happened" when people responded to a Darbyite invitation.

Dispensationalists argued that Christians should take the Bible literally, especially its prophetic passages. Hence, dispensational interpretation frequently compared one passage with another, tracing a theme or a word through the Bible and drawing conclusions about its meaning in the different prophetic periods.

Dispensationalism spread in the American churches through different means. Perhaps because it seemed to encourage evangelism, Dwight L. Moody and other evangelists accepted the system and adapted it for their own purposes. Traditionally, evangelists pleaded with sinners on the grounds that while the day of one's death was uncertain, the fact of one's death was not. Consequently, one needed to make peace with God. The new evangelists, perhaps because modern medicine made death seem less imminent, used the Rapture instead of death in their appeals. Since the date of the Rapture was unknown, one should prepare for its inevitability. One did not want Jesus to find one playing cards, drinking, or the like when the Rapture occurred.

Although dispensationalism appeared complex, it was a remarkably easy theology to teach. By 1900, dispensationalism was the mainstay of most conservative Bible schools in the United States. In part this was the work of R. A. Torrey (1856–1928), the president of The Chicago Training Institute (Moody Bible Institute) and later, the Bible Institute of Los Angeles. But other factors also played a role. Many Bible school teachers were graduates of Dallas Theological Seminary, where Lewis Sperry Chafer (1871–1952), Dallas's Professor of Theology, provided many materials for the Bible school movement, including his 1948 *Systematic Theology.*

Many Christians learned dispensationalism from such popular biblical aids as C. I. Schofield's (1843–1921) *Schofield Reference Bible*, first published in 1909 by Oxford Press. Schofield's edition was easy to use, thoroughly cross-referenced, and provided many resources that Sunday school teachers found of use in interpreting Scripture.

By 1870 many mainstream Methodists had lost their interest in personal holiness, an emphasis which nonetheless many other American Wesleyans wished to maintain. Phoebe Palmer (1807–74), a popular lay evangelist, began her renewal of the Holiness movement in 1845. She understood the Bible to teach three things about holiness:

1. People should consecrate themselves wholly to God;
2. God has promised to keep for Godself anything that we sanctify to God; and
3. Christians should bear witness to their own sanctification.

Although Palmer apparently believed that sanctification and justification might occur simultaneously, she tended to interpret holiness as a "second blessing;" that is, an emotional experience similar to conversion and separated from that event by some time.

Daniel Warner (1842–1925) experienced entire sanctification in 1878 and became an evangelist for the holiness message. In 1881, Warner renounced sectarian church membership, including denominational membership and licenses to preach, and gathered those who shared similar beliefs. Although the new Church of God which would arise from Warner's movement eventually organized its ministry, it continued to believe that the true church (church universal) had no need of organization.

Phineas F. Bresee (1838–1916) had a similar experience. Bresee was a successful Methodist pastor in Iowa who experienced a personal financial disaster which led him to move west to begin anew. Once there, Bresee became the pastor of Los Angeles' First Methodist Church. In 1895, perhaps inspired by the number of his church members who had experienced entire sanctification, he joined J. P. Widney in forming the Church of the Nazarene. The Nazarenes stressed simplicity in daily life and committed themselves to a ministry among the poor.

The Holiness movement helped create twentieth-century Pentecostalism. Many historians date the beginnings of Pentecostalism from January 1, 1901 when Agnes Ozmen (1870–1937) spoke in tongues in a meeting at Charles Parham's Bible Institute in Topeka, Kansas. Parham popularized the account of this meeting, and later converted a young preacher, William J. Seymour (1870–1922), in Houston, Texas. In April 1906, Seymour preached an interracial revival in Los Angeles that became so large that the revival moved to a building on Azuza Street. What Pentecostals added to holiness doctrine was the belief that all of the Holy Spirit's gifts (casting-out demons, speaking in tongues, and divine healing) were presently available to anyone who is totally consecrated to Christ.

The Keswick movement promoted a similarly immediate experience of the divine and emphasis on personal holiness. William E. Boardman (1810–86), a student of Charles Finney and Asa Mahan at Oberlin, developed much of the Keswick movement's theology. In his book, *The Higher Christian Life*, Boardman argued that every Christian could experience victory over their sinful nature. While some passages in the book suggest the more Wesleyan concept of a second blessing, Boardman carefully argued that sanctification was an inward experience that did not occur in a moment. Rather the individual had to pass through a long struggle to master his or her sinful nature before they won victory. Once the believer attained that victory, Boardman argued, the Christian had to watch, since sinful human nature could take control again. Similar teachings were common at the Conferences organized by Canon T. D. Harford-Battersley in his parish in Keswick in England.

CHAPTER TWENTY-TWO

ROMAN REACTION

From Napoleon to the Second Vatican Council, the Roman Catholic Church devoted much of its energy to opposing the modern world and its values, hoping to return to a simpler time. Many Catholic thinkers believed that the nineteenth century's spiritual poverty was the consequence of a secularization process that began with Renaissance individualism and became more humanistic as time passed. The church's message to a world living without God was to call Europe back to its roots in the great Catholic synthesis, especially as illustrated by St. Thomas's theology.

The Catholic leadership's intense conservatism had mixed effects on its membership. Many Catholics lived in two worlds. On Sunday parishioners participated in a medieval society with its pageantry, prayer, and processions; on weekdays they worked in the modern culture of industries, offices, and schools. The church attempted to bridge the two worlds with numerous Catholic organizations—labor unions, professional associations, learned societies, youth organizations, and political parties—but the problem refused to vanish.

In some traditionally Catholic countries such as France and Italy, the church lost many male members who associated Rome with political suppression. Often these men sought religious satisfaction in other organizations, especially, their unions and, despite vigorous church condemnation, the Masonic movement.

Ironically, the Catholic Church often benefited from the modern ideologies that it opposed so strongly. The church sponsored nationalism in some areas such as Ireland, where Protestantism was associated with foreign rule. In the United States, the separation of church and state permitted Catholicism to develop without legal interference from the Protestant majority.

Roman Centralization

The eighteenth-century Catholic Church was a federation of semi-independent churches under Roman primacy. The historical trend of this period of the church's life was toward greater political control. In Austria, Emperor Joseph II (1741–90) enacted a series of reforms that included toleration, diocesan control of the monasteries, and restrictions on the papacy. Taken together, Joseph's laws made the Austrian Church almost as independent as the French or Spanish Church. The 1773 suppression of the Jesuits further increased the power of the state.

Similar tendencies guided the bishops on the "priests' alley," the independent ecclesiastical principalities along the Rhine River. Johann Hontheim (1701–93), Archbishop of Trier, in his *The Ecclesiastical State and the Legitimate Power of the Pope* argued (1763) for a state church system similar to the one in France. The great error of the Middle Ages, Febronius (Hontheim's alias) argued, was the belief that the pope was the church's administrator, when he was only a symbol of the church's agreement in faith and morals.

Governments did not protect the church during the French Revolution when many priests, monks, and nuns were martyred. This inspired a new style of church life, "ultramontanism," which urged Catholics to refer all matters "beyond the mountains" to Rome. In politics, ultramontanism meant concordat diplomacy. A concordat was a formal treaty between the church, represented by the Vatican, and a government that regulated such matters as education, marriage law, divorce, the appointment of priests, and the election of bishops. These treaties often provided mutual benefits. In exchange for legal protection, for instance, the pope often allowed a government to veto episcopal nominations.

Religiously, ultramontanists placed the pope at the center of much popular devotion. Catholics often displayed pictures of the reigning pope in their homes, and items blessed by the pope, especially rosaries, became commonplace. The popes officially approved popular Catholic piety's accentuated supernaturalism by stressing the supernatural character of the mass, increasing indulgences and jubilee years, and canonizing local saints. Rome also sponsored devotion to the Sacred Hearts of Jesus and Mary. Pius IX (1792–1878) placed the church under the protection of the Sacred Heart and later his successor, Leo XIII (1810–1903), placed the whole world under the Sacred Heart's care. In 1942, Pius XII (1886–1958) also placed the world under the protection of the Sacred Heart of Mary.

Ultramontanists also stressed Marian devotions and, to commemorate Mary's appearance to Catherine Laboure, Pius VIII approved the wearing of miraculous medals in 1830. In 1854, Pius IX issued the bull *Ineffabilis Deus* that proclaimed the doctrine of the Immaculate Conception of Mary. The dogma taught that God so ordered providence that Mary was conceived without taint of original sin. Shortly thereafter in 1858, a noted appearance of Mary occurred at Lourdes, France, when Mary was said to have appeared to Bernadette Soubirous (1844–79), a young French peasant, as the "Immaculate Conception." Almost a century later in 1950, Pius XII issued *Munificicentissimus Deus*, proclaiming that God had assumed Mary's body and soul into heavenly glory at the end of her earthly life.

The ultramontanists wanted to establish administrative and personal ties between the clergy and the pope. The Vatican established national seminaries, such as the American College in Rome, and the pope personally ordained their graduates. National hierarchies made every effort to send the best students to these schools, called "bishop factories," because the popes so often selected bishops from their graduates. Further, the popes rewarded faithful priests with the title "monsignor," which designated its bearer as a priest of the diocese of Rome.

The papacy also took the lead in the direction and promotion of Catholic missions. In 1800, the once great Catholic missionary force numbered only three hundred missionary priests, because Catholic governments had relaxed their financial support of missionary work. To remedy this situation, Rome organized new missionary orders and strengthened missionary societies. Leo XIII, a missionary-minded pope, established regular hierarchies in India, North Africa, and Japan. By 1900 the Catholic Church again had the largest Christian missionary force, and the number of Catholics in Asia and Africa was rapidly growing. In the reign of Pius XII the church adopted the policy of replacing colonial bishops with indigenous leaders wherever possible.

The consolidation of missionary work was part of a larger program of administrative centralization. Modern transportation, especially the railroad and steamship, made it possible for Rome to oversee matters previously in local hands. Pius IX frequently summoned the bishops to Rome, and he required *ad limina* pilgrimages. Originally, an *ad limina* was a visit to the graves of Peter and Paul during which bishops renewed their vows. The new visits were more administrative. During a bishop's Roman stay, he had to visit the pope, reaffirm his loyalty to the Holy See, and make a full report on his diocese. The process implied that the pope supervised the bishops and could act to correct problems in their dioceses.

Likewise, the popes expanded their claims to universal authority during this period. In 1868, Pius IX summoned the bishops to an ecumenical council in Rome, the First Vatican Council. As the council debated an elaborate constitution on the faith and several disciplinary matters, the papacy worked to pass *Pastor Aeternus* which recognized the pope's immediate episcopal authority over the whole church. The bull meant that Rome legitimately governed, not only guided, the worldwide Catholic Church.

The council also defined papal infallibility. The new dogma was simple: whenever the pope spoke *ex cathedra* (that is, whenever the pope spoke as the universal pastor and teacher of the church), his teachings on faith and ethics were irreformable and infallible. Bishops from Germany, England, and the United States argued against the doctrine in the council, and the church's best-known theologians, including J. J. I. von Döllinger (1799–1890), maintained that the doctrine had no foundation in Scripture or tradition. Although a small schism occurred, almost all accepted the new teaching after the council ended.

Political Catholicism

The Catholic Church often clashed with different European governments in the nineteenth century. In part these disputes grew out of economic and social changes. Taxation was necessary to pay for universal, compulsory schooling. The church wanted some voice in these state systems or state subsidies for its own. The number of interreligious marriages increased, creating debates over the religious education of the children.

Catholicism was also theologically opposed to much of modernity. The Syllabus of Errors, which appeared in 1864, summarized much of papal teaching about the modern world. The Syllabus's eighty concise paragraphs covered every major issue debated in the nineteenth century: rationalism, the modern, bureaucratic state, freedom of the press, religious liberty, the religious rights of immigrants, civil marriage, and divorce. The final paragraph of the Syllabus summarized the whole document when it stated it was an error to believe that the pope "can and should reconcile himself to and agree with progress, liberalism, and modern civilization." The Syllabus appalled the more democratic governments of western Europe, and the church lost much governmental support in those countries.

Italy and the Papal States

After the defeat of Napoleon, the Congress of Vienna restored papal government in central Italy. In 1861, a new Kingdom of Italy under the leadership of Savoy united most of the peninsula, including many areas formerly under papal control. However, the pope continued to govern Rome where the French army maintained his regime. When France withdrew its troops in 1870 due to the Franco-Prussian war, the Italian government took Rome without opposition.

The Italian government attempted to negotiate a settlement with the papacy. Under the Law of Guarantees, Italy granted the pope civil honors equal to the king, guaranteed his right to communicate with bishops throughout the world, allowed him to maintain his own diplomats and to make treaties, and promised substantial compensation for his lost revenues. Although accepting some of the law's benefits, the popes refused to negotiate until 1929 when the pope entered into a concordat with the Mussolini government. In the interim, the official position was that the pope was a prisoner in the Vatican. To compensate for its financial losses, the papacy increased its revenues raised outside Italy. Tragically, the popes prohibited lay Catholics from taking part in Italian politics.

France

The political life of nineteenth-century France was marked by the bitter rivalry between republicans and monarchists. Religion was often at the center of their battle, since both sides agreed that the church was essential to the maintenance of the old order. To support the church was often to support monarchy; to oppose it was as often to support republicanism.

The Abbé Felicité de Lamennais (1782–1854) attempted to reconcile Catholicism with modern republican France. When Louis Philippe—the citizen king—assumed control of France in 1830, Lamennais, a former ultramontanist, became the advocate of a "free church in a free state." Together with some companions, Lamennais founded the controversial journal *L'Avenir* (*The Future*) to advocate religious liberty in France. Accused of heresy, Lamennais went to Rome in 1831 to plead his case before Pope Gregory XVI, a reactionary pope whose opposition to modernity included the prohibition of railroads in the papal states. In 1834, Gregory issued *Mirari vos*, explicitly condemning Lamennais' views. Although Lamennais outwardly conformed, the radical priest continued to advocate the separation of church and state. The pope subsequently condemned him by name in *Singulari nos*. After that, Lamennais left the church.

The defeat of Napoleon III (1818–73) by the Prussians in 1870 led to the establishment of the unstable Third Republic. Many observers expected a monarchist coup, led by General Georges Boulanger (1837–97), to end the new democracy. However, Boulanger apparently lost his nerve and, accused of treason, fled France and committed suicide. The trial of Captain Alfred Dreyfus (1859–1935) was another royalist embarrassment. When the French found secret documents in the German embassy, the army accused Dreyfus, a Jew, of treason. He was quickly court-martialed and sent to Devil's Island. Later, the army found evidence that implicated Major Ferdinand Esterhazy, a Catholic royalist. When Esterhazy's court martial cleared him, Emile Zola, a famous novelist, accused the court of taking orders from the high command. In the ensuing public debate, royalists, Catholics, and nationalists supported Dreyfus's conviction, while democrats and socialists opposed it. Dreyfus' eventual acquittal harmed the church's reputation.

The disestablishment of the Catholic Church was related to these political controversies. At first, the Third Republic only expelled the Jesuits and taxed other religious orders. Then, the state removed all fees for attending the public schools—making Catholic education comparatively more expensive—and suspended religious instruction in the public schools. But as political tempers rose, the state's actions became harsher. In 1901, the French government passed the Associations Act that required legislative approval before a new religious congregation could be formed. A 1904 law prohibited members of religious orders from teaching in Catholic schools after 1914, and in 1905, the government disestablished Catholicism.

Germany

Nineteenth-century German political history revolved around national unification. After the Revolution of 1848, Prussia assumed the leadership of the "small Germany party" that wanted to exclude Austria from a future German government. Led by the Iron Chancellor, Otto von Bismarck, the Prussians fought a series of small wars against Denmark, Austria, and France. These wars made Prussia the dominant power in northern Germany. In 1871, fresh from victory over France, Prussia and the remaining princes formed the German Empire, a confederation of semi-independent states under a strong monarchy and weak parliament. Germany had become a modern, industrial state, managed by an educated and effective bureaucracy.

The Prussian state had serious problems with the Vatican before the *Kulturkampf* (struggle for civilization) of the 1870s. Prussian marriage laws required parents to rear the children of religiously mixed families in the faith of the parent of the same sex. Thus the law required the parents to rear a boy in the father's faith, a girl in the mother's. In 1830, Pius VIII issued an encyclical that strongly condemned mixed marriages and prohibited priests from conducting the wedding, unless the couple signed a binding agreement that they would raise their children as Catholics. Prussian pressure forced the church not to enforce its rule, but Archbishop Droste-Vischering (1773–1845) made opposition to mixed marriages a personal crusade. In 1835 the Prussians imprisoned Droste-Vischering, beginning a four-year struggle between the government and the church. The battle ended in a compromise. Prussia released the archbishop from prison, but the church agreed that a coadjutor would administer his diocese.

The papal actions that provoked the 1870s conflict with Germany were the Syllabus of Errors and the decrees of the First Vatican Council. In 1872, the German government placed elementary education under state control and expelled the more ultramontanist religious orders, including the Jesuits, the Redemptorists, and the Lazarists. The next year the Reichstag (Parliament) adopted the Falk Laws that required all Catholic priests to receive a university education and pass a state examination before they could begin their ministry. In addition, Prussia demanded that all religious instruction be in German and that Prussian civil law govern all marriages and divorces.

In turn, the church refused to appoint new priests or bishops, and church leaders encouraged the formation of the Center Party to protect their interests. This battle went back and forth until 1879 when Bismarck and the church, now headed by Leo XIII, reached an unofficial compromise. Bismarck relinquished his demand that the church educate all priests in universities and allowed church elementary schools more freedom. The church also retreated. The law requiring civil marriage remained in effect and state educational standards remained supreme.

Leo XIII and the Great Encyclicals

Leo XIII was the most complex representative of modern Catholic conservatism. In some ways, this important pope faced toward both past and future. Publicly, Leo continued to support the antimodernism of the Syllabus of Errors and the First Vatican Council. Thus he condemned Freemasons and socialists in his encyclicals *Quod apostolici muneris* (1878) and *Humanum genus* (1884), and frequently repeated the traditional Catholic teaching on mixed marriages.

Yet Leo XIII believed that the church had to find an accommodation with the modern secular state. As early as 1881, the pope had given democracy a qualified approval in his encyclical *Diuternum illud*. Later, in *Immortale Dei* (1885), Leo argued that Christians could cooperate with any form of government, including republicanism. The only restriction was that such cooperation must not surrender the Catholic claim to authority. In his 1888 encyclical *Libertas praestantissimum*, Leo contended that Catholics might work with non-Christians and Protestants to secure the common good.

France provided a special case for Leo XIII's policies. The growing radicalism of the French Republic disturbed Leo, and he sought to find some way for church and state to cooperate. In *Inter innumeras sollicitudines*, he urged French Catholics to accept the Republic and cooperate with established authority. The encyclical did help many French Catholics to be good citizens of their nation and loyal members of their church.

The most significant of Leo's encyclicals was *Rerum novarum*, in which the pope frankly acknowledged the serious economic and social problems that Europe's industrialization created for working people. While the pope did not question private property or encourage socialism, he did urge Christians to secure a just wage for workers and to participate in non-socialist labor organizations. *Rerum novarum* was ambiguous. Socially active Catholics could use the document to legitimate progressive political action. Yet other Catholics saw in it a legitimation for a government based on the vertical organization of social classes. Leo himself may not have been clear about the implications of his position.

Intellectual Conservatism

Nineteenth-century Catholics blamed the problems of the modern world on the Enlightenment. As Catholic apologists understood European intellectual history, the Enlightenment weakened legitimate authority and replaced it with an almost unbounded individualism. In this new world, people dared to do and to think as they pleased.

One consequence of this argument was an emphasis on papal infallibility. In the midst of the vagaries of modern thought, one authority always taught the truth. Another consequence was an attempt to define the parameters of Catholic thought. In 1878, Leo XIII issued *Aeterni Patris,* declaring that St. Thomas was the eternal teacher of the church and urging Catholic intellectuals to demonstrate that Thomas's system was still valid in the modern world. The encyclical reinforced an already lively Thomistic movement among Catholic philosophers.

The intellectual wall that Leo XIII hoped to construct around Catholic theology did not completely hold. By 1890 a flourishing Catholic modernist movement existed that included such able scholars as Alfred Loisy (1857–1940), Louis Duchesne (1843–1922), and George Tyrrell (1861–1909). Although the modernists addressed many questions, including biological evolution and Kantianism, their primary interest was Scripture and tradition. They argued that Scripture and tradition both developed in analogous ways. The Pentateuch began with some material from Moses' time and added new strata over centuries. In a similar way, dogma began in the Synoptic Gospels and was reformulated at Nicea. The modernists believed that a developmental understanding of religion favored Catholicism over Protestantism, since Catholicism always respected tradition.

Rome did not agree. In 1893, Leo XIII issued *Providentissimus Deus* in which the pope emphatically reaffirmed Catholic belief in the infallibility and inerrancy of the Scriptures. In 1902, the pope established the Papal Biblical Commission to monitor Catholic biblical studies and to decide which scholarly conclusions were heretical and which were not. In 1907, Pius X issued the decree *Lamentabili save* and the companion encyclical *Pascendi dominici gregis.* In these documents the pope listed sixty-five modernist errors and defined modernism as the sum of all past heresies. In 1910, Pius issued a *motu proprio* that imposed an anti-modernist oath on all seminary professors that was extended in 1931 to all professors in Catholic universities.

Whatever the popes might have wished, the new biblical scholarship did not vanish. In 1943, Rome allowed Catholic biblical scholars to participate in moderate historical studies, although the church retained the right to allow or disallow any particular result. However, Catholic scholars were to be careful to refer explicitly to the official teachings of the church in their published writings. By 1960, Catholic biblical scholarship had matured sufficiently to make important contributions to the Second Vatican Council.

CHAPTER TWENTY-THREE

THE FIRST WORLD WAR AND THE END OF THE CHRISTIAN ERA

From 1914 to 1919 the European great powers engaged in a wasteful modern war. After a brilliant attack that moved the German army almost to Paris, the western front stabilized, with both sides fighting defensively from elaborate trenches. In the east the Russians had the initial advantage, but the Germans, led by Paul von Hindenburg (1847–1934) and Erich Ludendorff (1865–1937), counterattacked. Their goal was to force Russia out of the war and to free German forces for a final drive in the west. Russia's situation became desperate, and after the czar abdicated, the new Communist government made peace. But victory came too late to aid the German effort in the west. The United States entered the war in 1917, reinforcing the Allied forces in the west and participating in a new offensive. Reluctantly, the German commanders informed the kaiser that further resistance was futile. Shortly thereafter the kaiser abdicated, a republic was formed, Germany surrendered, and on November 11, 1919, the fighting officially ended.

The war ended on a deceptively moral note. The American President Woodrow Wilson (1856–1924) promised a just peace that would make the "world safe for democracy." Wilson's specific proposals were the Fourteen Points, which included the self-determination of nations, the freedom of the seas, and an international organization to deter future aggression. However, the diplomacy of David Lloyd-George (1862–1945) and Georges Clemenceau (1841–1929) defeated the less experienced American, who surrendered his position on many specific proposals in order to save his League of Nations. Ironically, the American Senate rejected both the Treaty and the League.

The Treaty of Versailles, deliberately signed in the very place where Bismarck proclaimed the German Empire, was harsh and punitive. The allies forced Germany to accept sole guilt for the war, to pay potentially ruinous reparations, to surrender its surface and submarine navy, and to limit its army to 100,000 men. The allies also allowed various ethnic groups to create small states from the former Austro-Hungarian empire.

In retrospect the First World War was a turning point in Christian history. Throughout the nineteenth century, progressive Christians believed that Christianity was the heart of western civilization. After the war that belief seemed dated. Christianity failed to prevent or limit hostilities, and not even that most Christian leader, Woodrow Wilson, could secure a just peace.

The end of the war was also the end of the Victorian era. Sexual practices changed. In Protestant countries, opposition to birth control declined or ceased, and divorce became more socially acceptable and easier to obtain. While Catholic countries continued these prohibitions longer, many Catholics were dissatisfied with them. The temperance movement receded. Although alcohol-free restaurants in Europe continued, they were not the wave of the future. In America, the only major nation with prohibition, the consumption of alcoholic beverages declined and then increased despite the law.

Decline of the Christian Empires

European life and culture lost prestige in the larger world. In such areas as China, where prewar Christianity made great strides among educated young people, the church ceased to represent hope. While some Christians, such as Chiang Kai-shek (1886?–1975), continued in important political roles, many Chinese looked elsewhere. The Communists grew in numbers and military power.

Japan began to preach a message of Asia for the Asians. By 1920, Japan's military leaders believed that their nation's role in the Pacific was analogous to England's in the Atlantic. The Japanese leadership wanted to establish an economic co-prosperity sphere in the Pacific to replace the various European colonial empires. To support this goal, the government revived Shinto—an ancient Japanese religion of nature and land—and increased its opposition to Christian expansion.

In 1915, Mohandas Gandhi (1869–1948) began a movement for Indian independence that had profound religious roots. The Mahatma ("great-souled one") renounced western dress in favor of Hindu simplicity. Gandhi urged his followers to renounce violence and to adopt a policy of *santyagraha* or nonviolent resistance that he believed was the most effective way for oppressed people to effect social change.

The other world religions also experienced a post-war rebirth. Both Eastern and Western scholars began to study classical Buddhist writings with new appreciation. Not only were national Buddhist movements strengthened, but Buddhism began to have adherents in Europe and America.

At the same time, Muslim residents of the European empires demanded cultural and political independence. The Muslim missionary drive, always a strong competitor of Christianity, continued as Islam expanded in sub-Saharan Africa.

The American Religious Depression

The United States was less affected by the war than other western nations. The success of the Men and Religion Forward Movement, a cooperative attempt to reach males for the church, illustrated the advantages of cooperation between denominations. In 1918, the largest denominations launched the Interchurch World Movement to concentrate the financial resources of the evangelical churches on theological education, world missions, and social change. As dreams increased, the leaders set a financial goal of one billion dollars. While individual churches raised significant sums, the general drive failed. John D. Rockefeller (1839–1937), America's leading Protestant philanthropist, had to pay the national organization's debts. The Interchurch World Movement's failure began a difficult decade. Church attendance, membership, and giving declined, and the denominations experienced serious financial difficulties.

In part, the churches's wounds were self-inflicted. The churches blessed the war and used their prestige to further the military effort. However, when Americans learned more about the struggle, the discovery that munitions manufacturers had deliberately created war hysteria disillusioned Americans. They might sacrifice life for freedom, but never for the munitions makers' 10 percent.

Nobel prize-winning novelist Sinclair Lewis (1885–1951) exposed the emptiness of many American lives. In *Main Street* (1920), *Babbitt* (1922), and *Dodsworth* (1929), Lewis ridiculed the hypocrisy of middle-class Americans. Lewis's most savage attack, however, was *Elmer Gantry* (1927), the story of a successful minister unable to resist sexual temptation or find meaningful faith. H. L. Mencken (1880–1956), a popular American newspaper columnist, took every opportunity to poke fun at the churches and their leaders.

Modernists and Fundamentalists

The religious depression of the 1920s formed the backdrop for a bitter American religious quarrel, the fundamentalist-modernist controversy. Although historians often speak of the struggle as if two theological parties existed, the participants held many different theological opinions and represented many different social classes. For example, when Billy Sunday mocked the holders of advanced degrees, Sunday spoke for America's anti-intellectuals. This was a different group than those middle-class Americans represented by such conservative scholars as Augustus Strong (1836–1921) or J. Gresham Machen (1881–1937).

The fundamentalist-modernist controversy was at least two different conflicts. Ecclesiastically, the battle was between those who affirmed the freedom of ministers and, especially, theological teachers to interpret their churches' historic standards, and those who believed in a more strict adherence to confessional orthodoxy. Politically, the contest was between those who believed that the public schools ought to reflect American opinion and those who believed the schools should teach modern science. Class, gender, and other divisions lay behind these factions.

An easily overlooked debate in Chicago marked the hardening of the lines. When America entered the World War, Shailer Mathews (1863–1941) and Shirley Jackson Case (1872–1947), professors at the University of Chicago's Divinity School, wrote a series of articles attacking premillennial dispensationalism. They charged that dispensationalism weakened present patriotism by claiming that Christ's Kingdom was wholly future. The Moody Institute teachers, led by A. C. Gaebelein (1861–1945), in turn claimed that all liberal theology was a German import. Billy Sunday, whose popularity was waning, joined in, asserting that liberalism and treason were synonymous terms.

The Chicago debate merged with a Baptist debate over foreign missionaries's theology. Augustus Strong's 1916 *A Tour of the Missions* claimed that social work had almost completely replaced evangelism in China. As this debate raged, Harry Emerson Fosdick (1878–1969), a Baptist serving the First Presbyterian Church of New York, preached a 1922 sermon entitled "Shall the Fundamentalists Win?" The sermon identified three issues in the Baptist debate: the inerrancy of Scripture, the historicity of the Virgin Birth, and the literal Second Coming. The sermon did not calm the waters. Curtis Lee Laws (1868–1946), A. C. Dixon (1854–1925), and William Bell Riley (1861–1947) continued the battle.

Fosdick's sermon also renewed the debate among Presbyterians. In the midst of the 1890s heresy trials, the Presbyterian Church (U.S.A.) adopted the five-point Portland Declaration in 1892 to end theological debate. The document was ritualistically reapproved every four years until 1923. After the attack on Fosdick, Presbyterian liberals met at Auburn Seminary in 1924 and issued the Auburn Declaration, sharply distinguishing between religion and theology. In 1925, when the New York Presbytery was charged with refusing to require acceptance of the five points of the Portland Declaration, the motion failed. The conservatives had lost the battle. In 1927 the General Assembly declared that the five points were no longer essential for ordination. More important, Joseph Ross Stevenson, President of Princeton Theological Seminary, reorganized that school to make it more theologically inclusive. In 1929 Machen and his allies withdrew and founded Westminster Seminary.

Why did the conservatives, who had dominated Presbyterianism since the 1890s, lose? In part, the liberal argument that an American church needed to practice tolerance was effective. Few Presbyterians wanted to belong to a denomination that prohibited many scholarly and respected members from teaching or preaching. Equally important, many Presbyterians believed that the controversy might destroy the denomination's financial structure. Robert Eliot Speer (1867–1947), the lay secretary of the Presbyterian Board of Foreign Missions, organized denominational loyalists in favor of greater toleration.

Concurrent with these ecclesiastical battles, a noisy debate broke out over evolution in the nation's public schools. William Jennings Bryan (1860–1925) was a three-time Democratic candidate for president, a former secretary of state, and a popular Bible teacher. After the World War, Bryan noted a decline in American moral standards and wondered why. In "The Menace of Darwinism," Byran presented his answer: evolution weakened Americans' belief in God and, subsequently, their moral character. Bryan's conclusion convinced other confused Americans. State legislators introduced bills, particularly in the South, to outlaw the teaching of the theory. Local school boards usually ignored the laws.

Tennessee, however, was different. When the state passed an anti-evolution bill in 1925, the American Civil Liberties Union urged John T. Scopes, a young biology teacher in Dayton, to publicly break the law. Scopes did so and was charged. Next, the American Civil Liberties Union (A.C.L.U.) arranged a defense team that included the noted American criminal lawyer, Clarence Darrow. The state countered by accepting the unpaid services of William Jennings Bryan for the prosecution. The trial itself took place in a circus atmosphere. Vendors sold souvenirs, exhibitors showed monkeys and other oddities, and assorted evangelists hawked salvation on street corners. Correspondents representing the major newspapers wired stories that detailed the insanity.

Since the Tennessee law had declared the biblical account of creation normative, Darrow convinced Bryan to appear as an expert on the Bible. Once on the stand, Darrow destroyed the Great Commoner with questions about the literal meaning of the biblical text. Darrow's tactics were legally extraneous to the issues before the court, and the trial ended with Scopes' conviction. But Darrow won in the court of public opinion. The press, convinced that Bryan had made a fool of himself, declared the fundamentalists defeatedwith the result that the anti-evolution crusade went into a swift decline.

German Protestantism

Historically, the various Lutheran and Reformed state churches of Germany were closely related to their *Land's* ruling prince, who also served as the "highest bishop." Congregations remembered their royal family every week in prayer. The establishment of the Republic ended these relationships. Further, the churches faced an unknown financial situation. Under the kaiser, they were "public corporations" with the right to tax their members for their own maintenance. In addition, the governments supported the churches with gifts and subsidies. Since the Social Democratic Party had historically campaigned on the slogan that religion was a private matter, these privileges seemed threatened by that party's power in the post-war government.

Despite Socialist rhetoric, however, the new constitutions (the Reich and the various German states) favored the churches. Although the federal constitution explicitly abolished the state churches and prohibited religious discrimination, the same document allowed the churches to keep almost all of their privileges, including their status as public corporations. The *Landen* (states) also continued their subsidies.

The churches retained their privileges for two reasons. First, the Socialists needed the Roman Catholic Center Party's support to secure passage of any constitution. Throughout the 1920s, the Center Party participated in every German government and often named the Chancellor. Second, the German people were more supportive of their churches than the Socialists supposed. A 1919 *Reichstag* discussion of a law eliminating religious instruction in public schools led to a petition signed by one-fourth of the German electorate. Whatever ideology demanded, the political message was clear, and the Social Democrats heard it.

The abolition of the various German monarchies required the churches to formulate new patterns of government. In each of the twenty-eight separate *Landeskirchen,* a similar debate occurred. On the one hand, a conservative faction wanted to continue clerical control. On the other, a more liberal faction, usually headed by representatives of the Ritschlian school, favored a more democratic polity. Although some compromises were made, the conservatives won the major battles. The new church constitutions created an elaborate system of councils and synods that gave the ministers the preponderance of power. In the South, Lutherans broke with tradition and appointed bishops.

The *Landeskirchen* formed a church federation, similar to the Federal Council of Churches in the United States, to coordinate their ministries. The federation scheduled the Church Congresses, meetings of clerical and lay leaders, to discuss theological issues. The Church Congresses also passed resolutions on national issues.

The popularity of the "political theology" taught by Emanuel Hirsch and Paul Althaus showed the churches' conservatism. The argument was simple. The Western civilization's crisis resulted from the Enlightenment's exchange of the collective wisdom of the people (*Volk*) for the private judgment of individuals. Consequently, Western inner turmoil would only end when the West returned to the wisdom of the people (*Volk*). Just as Luther overcame the medieval problem of guilt through justification by faith, modern theologians had to overcome military defeat through national regeneration.

A significant revival of interest in worship also occurred in the 1920s. Sixteenth-century Lutheran worship in Germany was much closer to medieval patterns than the worship services of the twentieth century. What the liturgical reformers wanted was to return to that older pattern and to reinstate many elements of medieval worship, especially the wearing of eucharistic garments and more frequent communion services.

An issue raised by the defeat was the future of German missions abroad. In the nineteenth century, German Protestants and Catholics avidly supported missions and sent many committed women and men to Africa and Asia. German scholars also pioneered in the scholarly study of missionary work. When the war broke out, the British and French arrested German missionaries and either deported or imprisoned them. Although the Allies permitted American Lutherans to staff some stations, most missions were closed forcibly. When the war ended, the Allied governments—who added Germany's and Turkey's possessions to their own Empires—grudgingly allowed a few missionaries to return. But most missions were closed by the colonial officials. German church leaders debated whether they should refrain from participation in the ecumenical movement to protest these policies. Nevertheless, the German churches became involved in the Protestant ecumenical movement in the 1920s, and in 1923 the various Evangelical (Lutheran) *Landeskirchen* helped establish the Lutheran World Federation. German churches also participated in the various meetings that led to the formation of the World Council of Churches (see below, chapter 26).

The Churches in England

Despite the rapidly advancing secularization of the universities, British students often joined various student organizations. The World's Student Christian Federation (a union of student Christian movements in Europe, North America, Asia, and Africa founded in 1895) enrolled many students. The much smaller Inter-Varsity Christian Fellowship worked among science and engineering students and recruited students for missionary work outside England.

During the 1920s English theology assumed a philosophical form interested in showing the compatibility of Christianity with modern scientific thought. John Wood Oman (1860–1939) approached the problem in *The Natural and the Supernatural* (1931) by rooting all religion in the human experience of the Sacred which was self-authenticating. Thus, religion was similar to natural science which also did not seek to validate its foundational experiences. It followed, however, that just as all scientific statements are revisable, so religious statements are equally provisional.

Archbishop William Temple (1881–1944) took another approach in his *Nature, Man, and God* (1934). Temple applied categories from Alfred North Whitehead's philosophy to Christian theology and concluded that God continually participated in the development of nature and history. Therefore, God's creation (and perhaps God's own nature) will be complete only when nature and humanity reach their final consummation.

Roman Catholicism Between the Wars

Under Benedict XV (1854–1922), the Catholic Church attempted to be neutral in the First World War. Although Benedict's public statements called for the restoration of peace, he appears to have privately favored the Central Powers. The 1915 secret Treaty of London, signed at the request of Italy, excluded the pope from any peace conference after the war.

Benedict practiced an active papal diplomacy, one which was continued by his successor Pius XI, who became pope in 1922. Benedict sent representatives to the new nations of Eastern Europe and worked hard to secure diplomatic relations with various governments. In his reign, the number of diplomats assigned to the Vatican increased from 14 to 27. Benedict believed that the best way to secure Christian rights in Europe was through the negotiation of concordats (treaties) with the various states. Benedict's successors, Pius XI (1857–1939) and Pius XII (Eugenio Pacelli, secretary of state from 1930), continued this emphasis and negotiated treaties with Italy and Spain.

Rome recognized that the World War altered the relationship between Europe and the rest of the world. In 1919 the pope promulgated *Maximum illud*. This encyclical called for the development of indigenous priesthoods throughout the world. Pius XI completed that demand in his 1926 *Rerum ecclesiae* which called for national hierarchies in all missionary countries. To prove the Vatican commitment to this policy, Pius XI consecrated six Chinese bishops.

In the 1920s some Catholic leaders expressed a deepened appreciation for the Christian vocation of the laity. The phrase, Catholic Action, was a literal translation of the name of a specific Italian organization, the *Azione Cattolica*. Pius XI's 1922 encyclical, *Ubi arcano Dei*, defined Catholic Action as the participation of the laity in the apostolate of the hierarchy. "Catholic Action" included youth work, the building of Christian marriages, Christian education, and the establishment of Christian voluntary organizations.

A new liturgical movement wanted to recover the older, patristic forms of Roman worship. Lead by Benedictine scholars at Solesmes (France) and Maria Laach (Germany), they believed that the congregation should participate in the sacrifice at the altar. The reformers distributed missals with the traditional lay responses highlighted and taught people to use them. Wherever permitted, the reformers urged priests to use the vernacular.

Interest in worship paralleled a rejuvenated interest in the Eucharist. The church held international conferences on the Eucharist at Amsterdam (1924), Chicago (1926), Sidney (1928), Carthago (1930), Dublin (1932), Buenos Aires (1933), Manila (1936), and Budapest (1938).

While the theology that supported these conferences was still that of the Council of Trent, the hierarchy was responding to other theological trends as well. Johann Adam Möhler (1796–1838) in his *The Unity of the Church* (1825) taught that the church was the mystical body of Christ. Within the church, Christ formed the basis of worship, doctrine, and unity. Karl Adam (1876–1966), a Catholic theologian popular with educated lay people, developed this theme in his *Essence of Catholicism* (first edition, 1924). Although the fresh wind of Vatican II was still a breeze, new theologies were developing.

CHAPTER TWENTY-FOUR

THE THEOLOGICAL RENAISSANCE

Despite the problems of the post-World War I churches, a widespread theological renaissance occurred in the 1920s and 1930s that both revived traditional Christian teachings and initiated new theological directions. History was an important inspiration for theology. In the 1920s an impressive group of church historians, including Karl Holl, Ernest Wolf, Gerhard Ritter, Heinrich Bornkamm, and Franz Lau, looked at Luther anew. The Luther they found was a confused young intellectual torn between order and chaos whose every step was accompanied by anxiety. For this Luther the fall of the medieval Catholic Church was not a glorious event, but humanity's entry into radical freedom and uncertainty.

Søren Kierkegaard (1813–55), a Danish philosopher and theologian, was also rediscovered in the 1920s. Kierkegaard saw Christianity as a radical alternative to ordinary human life. God called the Christian to risk everything in a decision that lacked any external support. In a famous metaphor, Kierkegaard compared the decision for faith to discovering that one was suspended over forty thousand fathoms of water. In another simile, Kierkegaard spoke of life as a series of three disconnected stages. The first two stages ended in despair, and the individual had to decide whether to make a leap of faith to the next stage or remain without hope. Abraham best exemplified such faith, since he was ready to sacrifice Isaac on God's command.

In England and America, Puritan life and thought was reexamined. William Haller's reconstruction of early English Puritanism revealed a band of intellectuals struggling with a radically changing social order. Perry Miller's attempts to understand the colonial Puritans had similar results. The Puritans, as characterized by Miller in *The New England Mind: The Seventeenth Century*, were intellectuals, isolated and rejected by the establishment, who refused to surrender their own understanding.

Miller's studies of Puritanism were only part of an American reappropriation of the nation's religious tradition. In 1927 the University of Chicago appointed William Warren Sweet (1881–1959) Professor of American Church History, the first person to hold such a position. The new professor's research showed that religion inspired many creative aspects of American life.

Theologian H. Richard Niebuhr's (1894–1962) *Social Sources of Denominationalism* (1929) analyzed Protestant diversity and found that the differences between American religious groups were primarily social, rather than theological, distinctions. Later, Niebuhr saw this book as one-sided. In the *Kingdom of God in America* (1937), Niebuhr showed how American religious thinkers transformed the nation. For Niebuhr, Protestantism was one of the great formers of the American soul.

Karl Barth

Karl Barth (1886–1968) was the most important German theologian since Schleiermacher. Barth began his career as a student of the great liberal theologians Adolf von Harnack and Wilhelm Herrmann (1851–1913). In 1911 Barth was appointed pastor in the village of Safenwil, Switzerland. While serving there, Barth faced two interrelated crises. The first was what he ought to preach. Barth's parishioners did not respond to his polite liberalism, and many people in his village joined a local Pietist church. The second crisis was more profound. When the European powers went to war, the leading German theologians strongly supported the kaiser's military policy. Their apparent rejection of principle troubled the young idealist.

In despair, Barth turned to the Bible. Setting aside his previous interpretations, Barth tried to read the Bible as if God addressed it directly to Barth himself. Concentrating his attention on Romans, Barth published a commentary on that epistle in 1919. To Barth's surprise, his commentary was an immediate success. The message that Barth found in Romans was that God was "wholly other" than humankind. God's Word struck history like a meteor that hit the earth's surface, burned, and left only a hole where it landed. The human condition was crisis— sin and anxiety— and all religious statements involved both a "yes" and a "no." In 1921, Barth accepted a new chair in Reformed Theology at Göttingen. His later refusal to swear an oath of obedience to Hitler forced him to return to Switzerland where he taught at the University of Basel.

In his early writings, Barth referred to his theology either as a theology of crisis or as a dialectical theology. Both terms were ambiguous. The crisis was the moment of decision caused by God's contact with humankind that awakened humankind to their finitude and limitation. Barth's understanding of "dialectical theology" was more complicated. In a Platonic dialogue, no participant has all the truth. Instead, truth lies in the whole conversation when both "yes" and "no" are heard together. For Barth, every theological statement was both a "yes" and a "no."

Shortly after Barth published the first volume of a proposed systematic theology, *The Doctrine of the Word of God: A Prolegomenon to a Christian Dogmatics*, the young theologian entered another period of theological turmoil. While studying the works of the medieval Augustinian, Anselm of Canterbury, Barth discovered that his theology was as anthropocentric as that of his liberal teachers. The old liberals used Kant to interpret the Gospel, and Barth had used Kierkegaard in a similar way. Barth recalled the *Christian Dogmatics* and developed a new theological method.

In 1932 the first volume of Barth's *Church Dogmatics* appeared, and subsequent volumes followed until the project was interrupted by his death. Rather than use the logical and didactic structure of traditional scholastic theology, each volume (and part-volume) of the *Dogmatics* surveys faith from the perspective of a single doctrine. Moreover, in each new volume, Barth revised his earlier ideas. The changing configuration of the *Dogmatics* highlighted the one constant in Barth's new theological direction: Jesus Christ. For Barth, all theological questions led directly to Christ, God's Word Incarnate.

Barth wanted his readers to understand his work in the light of Scripture, and many footnotes in the text are long exegetical analyses of important biblical passages. Yet Barth's doctrine of Scripture was complex. On the one hand he accepted the right of modern critical scholars to read the text from their own perspective. Viewed from their standpoint, the Old Testament could be accurately described as a collection of the religious writings of a small band of Semitic people. Similarly, the New Testament was the compilation of some documents from a first-century religious community. The theologian was concerned, however, with the Scripture as the bearer of revelation. The Bible became the Word of God when it was preached in the church.

Similar to the theological perspective of Barth was the chastened liberalism of Emil Brunner (1889–1966). Like his predecessors, Brunner continued the theological dialogue with social science and believed that theology could learn much from other disciplines. For Brunner, God is the absolute subject, the One who is utterly beyond space and time. Human beings who approach God as God is in Godself find themselves speechless: God is too Holy for human eyes. Brunner, deeply influenced by the Jewish philosopher Martin Buber (1878–1965), believed that all religion was a personal relationship—an "I–Thou" relationship—with God. The Gospel is that this Holy God enters our history and establishes such a relationship with us.

For Brunner, God's presence with us here and now is revelation. In contrast, the Bible contains the history of past encounters with God. By comparing our meeting with God with Scripture, the theologian can determine whether our faith is the same as the faith of the ancient church.

Brunner's theology represented a mediating position. Conservative theologians found that Brunner's works enabled them to move, quietly but surely, out of an intellectual ghetto. In particular, many conservatives believed that Brunner's theology enabled them to accept modern biblical criticism without compromising their belief in the transcendence of God. Liberals also found Brunner helpful with their dilemmas. The liberals found sin and alienation relevant to the 1930s and 1940s, if someone could explain those topics without compromising liberal confidence in historical-critical analysis.

Christian Existentialism

Existentialists viewed humankind as the residents of a world in which few, if any, permanent guidelines existed. Much existentialist philosophy demonstrated that neither reason, nature, nor human culture were reliable foundations for life. Hence individuals had to decide whether or not they would make their own lives authentic.

Søren Kierkegaard is seen by many as the 'founder' of existentialism, but other philosophers also inspired theologians. Martin Buber, an influential Jewish philosopher, developed an existentialist philosophy in his *I and Thou* (1929). According to Buber, we can choose to relate to the world two ways. In the abstract mode, defined as "I–It," humankind views the world as something human beings control through science and technology. In contrast, in the personal mode, people relate to the world in an "I–Thou" or intimate relationship.

History of religions scholar Rudolf Otto (1869–1937) in his 1917 *The Idea of the Holy* argued that religions reflected humankind's encounter with the Sacred. The Holy was something that was both within and outside our experience, and, hence, drew us to it in "fascinated dread."

Before the Holy, humans had to make a response that involved their whole being.

The most noted advocate of Christian existentialism, however, was Paul Tillich (1886–1965). After Hitler seized power, Tillich, a Christian socialist, fled to America where Reinhold Niebuhr secured a position for him at New York's Union Seminary. Tillich participated in the cosmopolitan intellectual life of New York and was noted for his vast knowledge of art, philosophy, and religion. He presented his theology in various collections of his sermons, such as *Dynamics of Faith* (1956), and in his three-volume *Systematic Theology* (1951, 1957, and 1963).

Tillich's theology assumed that human beings are creatures that both make commitments and are defined by those commitments. Some decisions are more important, some less. In the midst of these competing decisions, Tillich believed many people have a single concern (which Tillich called ultimate) that takes precedence. Whether that focus is wealth, social status, politics, or Christ, our ultimate concern functions as our "God."

Tillich believed that theologians needed to adopt what he called a theological method of correlation in which the existential situation posed the questions, and theologians used their knowledge of Christian symbols to respond. The theological "answer" is not "knowledge" in the usual sense of the term. Like a psychotherapist, the theologian enables us to explore the depths of our own being.

For Tillich, "God" was not an object among the many other objects that people find in the world. Much of his theology was an attempt to speak differently about the ultimate. Like many mystics and idealists, Tillich wanted to describe the "God beyond God." At times, Tillich used the idea of symbol to express the limits and nature of our ultimate knowledge. Because symbols work indirectly, people cannot identify them with what they symbolize; yet, because symbols penetrate our depths, they can integrate our experience. At other times, Tillich preferred to use the more cryptic phrase, "the ground of being."

Tillich offered his own solution to the problem of the historicity of the New Testament accounts of Jesus. Like Barth and Brunner, Tillich welcomed biblical criticism and wanted the critics to do their work thoroughly and accurately. Yet Tillich was profoundly aware of the limitation of all historical enquiry. All studies of the past are subject both to new knowledge and to inevitable reinterpretation. If the theologian were to wait for historians to finish their work, Tillich reasoned, the theologian would never say anything meaningful about the Scripture. The only solution to this problem, Tillich concluded, was to admit that every detail in the New Testament account of Jesus' life might be erroneous, and yet affirm that the overall New Testament picture of Jesus as the Christ, the New Being, was reliable.

Rudolph Bultmann (1884–1976) was among the first scholars to apply form critical analysis to the Gospels. For him, the most serious theological problem was the gap between the first and the twentieth centuries. The worldview of the New Testament, he believed, was thoroughly mythological. The Bible pictured reality as a three-storied universe in which earth was suspended midway between heaven and hell. In this world, God interrupted the course of events from above, and Satan and his angels invaded from below. Further, while ancient people differentiated between ordinary and extraordinary events, they did not have our idea of the continuum of nature.

What Bultmann believed modern Christians needed was a way to interpret mythological thought. Without such a method, he did not believe twentieth-century people could share the meaningful life that the first Christians found in Christ. Bultmann's research indicated that the key to the New Testament was the demand of the *kerygma* (the early Christian preaching) that people make an existential decision for or against Jesus. Therefore, Bultmann proposed that theologians translate the New Testament demand for decision into modern existential language. Bultmann believed that Martin Heidegger's philosophy was particularly useful in this task, since Heidegger had argued that humans had to decide for or against authentic existence.

American Modernism

In the United States, the liberal tradition continued to inform theological discussion. Although Americans read European theologians, most did not share the anxiety and alienation of their European counterparts. Yet American liberalism was influenced by European crisis theology in three ways: a new appreciation of the Church, an awareness of existential psychology, and a renewed sense of human fragility and sin.

William Adams Brown (1865–1943) of New York's Union Seminary spanned liberalism and the period of the theological renaissance. Brown worked closely with the Federal Council of Churches during the First World War. In his later years, he studied theological education and the documents of the various councils of churches. Although he admitted that liberalism needed more of a consciousness of sin, Brown believed that it still was the key to a faith that was intellectually believable.

In the 1920s, Andover-Newton Theological School began to apply clinical psychology to ministry and established a training center at Worchester State Hospital. Although interest in the counseling ministry developed slowly, two Baptist pastors showed its value for large city ministry: Harry Emerson Fosdick (New York) and Theodore F. Adams (Richmond, Virginia). After the Second World War, modern pastoral counseling entered the American mainstream. Popular newspaper columns, such as "Dear Abby," urged people to see their minister when they had personal problems.

A more radical wing of liberalism, often called modernism, also became prominent. The pioneer of this new approach was George Burman Foster (1858–1918), Professor of Theology and, later, of the Philosophy of Religion at the University of Chicago. In the early 1900s, Foster moved toward religious humanism. In his 1906 *The Finality of the Christian Religion*, Foster dismissed metaphysical and theological claims for Christian ultimacy. Douglas C. Macintosh (1877–1948), Foster's student and a professor at Yale, believed that theology should become an empirical science. In *Theology as an Empirical Science* (1919), Macintosh distinguished the variable features of religion (culture, tradition) from its three constant elements: faith in the divine, the need for a right adjustment to the divine, and the value of human life. Religions gave these elements their historical, and, hence, temporary form.

Henry Nelson Wieman (1884–1975) of the University of Chicago argued that modern theology needed to go beyond theism and identify God with the natural order. For Wieman, nature was the center of dynamic processes, such as evolution, that enabled humankind to appreciate the good and to live with moral purpose. Although Wieman's perspective was superficially optimistic, his speculations had their dark side. For Wieman, the observation that God was good did not mean that God was nice or kind. The human experiment might end with nature destroying humankind through a new disease or with humankind destroying itself in war. Wieman's Jesus was only important as the creative founder of a new religion.

The Brothers Niebuhr

Reinhold (1892–1971) and H. Richard (1894–1962) Niebuhr were the most widely read and respected twentieth-century American theologians. Although contemporaries often interpreted them as neo-orthodox theologians, the theology of the Niebuhrs was not Barth or Brunner translated into American English.

H. Richard Niebuhr's key problem was how human beings could know or understand the God of the Bible. In *The Social Sources of Denominationalism* (1929) and *Christ and Culture* (1951), Niebuhr explored theological relativism. All theological thought was to some extent subject to non-theological—and especially social and historical—influences. Theologians had to accept this as part of the givens of the current situation. In his 1941 *Meaning of Revelation*, Niebuhr argued that historical experience can be understood either as outer history or as inner history. Outer history is subject to the natural restraints of all historical existence. Human beings are culture-bound creatures that cannot escape their own space and time. Yet history also has an inner meaning. A person's birthday is an objective historical occurrence that the historian can interpret with the ordinary tools of his craft. Yet we stand in a unique relationship to our birthdays. The analogy of a person joining the church is also useful. We can speak of John Jones joining the church in terms of social class, his need for economic contacts, his marriage to a member, or other such categories. Although these interpretations may be accurate, Jones may understand his decision as the beginning of a new life.

In *Radical Monotheism and Western Culture* (1960), Niebuhr argued that since God is being itself, every moment of human experience is conditioned by our relationship to God. In every moment we must decide whether we will allow being or non-being to shape our values. When we decide for being, we make a monotheistic decision. If we decide for a lesser gods, we are idolaters, and if we decided for many gods, we are polytheists.

Reinhold Niebuhr was primarily an ethicist, and much of his most creative work was a response to concrete historical events. For example, at a time when most American religious leaders were pacifists, Niebuhr realized that only armed power might remove Hitler's government and founded the journal *Christianity and Crisis* to argue this case. After the Second World War Niebuhr joined Americans for Democratic Action (A.D.A.), which advocated the use of ordinary political means, especially organization, to achieve a radical program of social justice.

Niebuhr supported his activism with a sophisticated theology that he called "realism" that combined the social gospel, the Bible, and modern politics. In *Moral Man and Immoral Society* (1932), and *The Nature and Destiny of Man* (1941–1943), Niebuhr argued that human beings, bound by sin and finitude, could never fulfill their highest aspirations. Even if an individual attained a measure of personal rectitude, the collective nature of human life limited that person's capacity to change the system. Part of Niebuhr's "realistic" ethics was his insistence that

Christians accept the ambiguity of human actions and learn to appreciate the give and take of political compromise. Every action has ironic and unintended consequences.

Had Reinhold Niebuhr stopped at this point, he might have been just another cynic in a cynical age. However, Niebuhr went on to insist that, despite everything, Christians must make efforts to achieve relative justice. The fact that humans cannot be perfectly just does not mean that they cannot be more just or that society's standard of justice must remain where it is.

Dietrich Bonhoeffer

Dietrich Bonhoeffer (1906–45) has become a saint for many modern Christians because he resisted Hitler's takeover of the churches. When the dictator came to power in 1933, Bonhoeffer's friends at Union Seminary (N.Y.) found him a position. Nonetheless, Bonhoeffer returned to Germany to share his country's burdens. Bonhoeffer became a leader in the Confessing Church (a group which opposed the policies of the Nazi regime), taught in an underground seminary, and argued that the Church needed to admit that anti-semitism was a heresy. However, confronted with the military draft, Bonhoeffer enlisted in the intelligence service of the German army.

Toward the end of the war, Bonhoeffer joined a conspiracy to assassinate Adolf Hitler. After the conspirators failed, the government arrested them. The Nazis executed the inner circle immediately and imprisoned the others, including Bonhoeffer. As the Allied army moved toward the Flossenberg concentration camp, the commander ordered Bonhoeffer's execution, perhaps on instructions from Berlin.

Bonhoeffer's theological development passed through three important stages. As a graduate student, the doctrine of the church fascinated him. Bonhoeffer outlined his understanding of the Christian community in his dissertation *The Community of Saints* and his subsequent second dissertation *Act and Being*. In these complicated works, Bonhoeffer proved that the church could be analyzed both socially and theologically. In both cases, he concluded that the church was the form in which Christ existed as community.

The theme of Bonhoeffer's second phase was the costly character of grace. In *The Cost of Discipleship*, Bonhoeffer used the Sermon on the Mount as a paradigm for the obedience that Christ demanded of those who received his grace. *Life Together*, the most personal and intimate of all Bonhoeffer's works, dealt with the daily discipline of the members of a Christian community.

Bonhoeffer's last works suggested that his thought has taken yet another direction. What survived of his uncompleted *Ethics* attempted to show what it meant for Christians to participate in their own times. As he thought about this theme, Bonhoeffer's understanding of the world expanded. By the time that Bonhoeffer was imprisoned in 1944, he was calling for a "religionless" Christianity that could encounter secular humanity on its own terms. Aware of the dangers in his proposal, Bonhoeffer demanded that Christians maintain their "arcane discipline" and be loyal to their own theological tradition. In biblical terms, Bonhoeffer wanted to know what it might mean for Christians to be "in but not of the world."

CHAPTER TWENTY-FIVE

THE CHURCH
AND THE DICTATORSHIPS

Between the world wars, authoritarian governments held power in Italy, Germany, Russia, Spain, and Japan that were modeled on the wartime experience of the various states. During this period governments regulated every aspect of life, from the sale of sugar to the hours when entertainment was available. Dictators argued that their nation's present crisis—whether political unrest, the danger of a communist or capitalist takeover, or a Great Depression—demanded a similar surrender of individual rights.

Russia and Communism

Militarily, Russia lost the war sometime in 1916. Yet Czar Nicholas II (1868–1918), who assumed personal command in 1915, wanted to hold out as long as possible. The czar believed that Germany would be unable to defeat France and England and, hence, that he would benefit at the eventual Peace Conference. Further, Nicholas hoped that the United States would join the Allies. But delay only exacerbated the problems of defeat as shortages of food, military supplies, and consumer goods grew. After a series of riots, Nicholas II abdicated in March 1917 and was replaced by a revolutionary government.

Meanwhile, the German high command encouraged Vladimir Lenin (1870–1924) to return to Russia. Lenin quickly assumed control of the workers' and soldiers' Soviets or committees. From this political base Lenin seized power and established a dictatorship in October 1917. Needing time to consolidate his government, Lenin quickly concluded the treaty of Brest-Litovsk with Germany in March 1918. Under this agreement, Russia recognized the independence of Poland, the Balkan states, Georgia, and the Ukraine.

The new communist government was openly hostile to religion. Under Lenin's direction, the party enacted progressively harsher laws against the Orthodox Church. In 1917 the government proclaimed the separation of church and state and secularized education. Punitive measures quickly followed. The clergy lost their civil rights, the party denounced them as servants of the ruling classes, the state nationalized all church lands, religious marriages were ruled invalid, and teaching religion to minors was prohibited.

In addition, the Communists launched propaganda attacks against the Church. The party established a newspaper dedicated to the promotion of atheism that vigorously poked fun at the churches and their leaders. The 1928 Five-Year Plan contained steps designed to weaken the churches and to discourage attendance. As in revolutionary France, the government replaced the seven-day calendar with one without Sundays or religious holidays.

In 1917 the Orthodox reestablished the patriarchate, and elected Basil Ivanovitch Belavin (Tikhon, 1866–1925) to that office. Archbishop Tikhon tried to separate the Church from the counter-revolutionaries by declaring that the Church accepted the new Soviet government. Yet Tikhon's moderation was ineffectual. In 1922 the state demanded that the church surrender its remaining wealth to fight a famine sweeping Russia. When Tikhon and the other bishops refused, the state acted quickly to punish this clerical disobedience. Progovernment clergy and lay people (including many government agents) organized the "Living Church" whose 1923 synod deposed Tikhon and gave the state what it wanted. The "Living Church" then disappeared.

After Tikhon's death, a new patriarch was not elected, and Ivan Nikolaievitch Stragorodski (Sergius, 1867–1944) became administrator. Sergius resolved to placate the government and issued a 1927 statement which thanked the Communist government for its recognition of Russia's spiritual needs. When many bishops, priests, and monks denounced the document, the secret police arrested many and either shot them or sent them to Siberia.

In 1938 the government moderated its stance, partly in recognition of the fact that it had won. Although many people learned the rituals and teachings of the Orthodox faith from their parents or grandparents, old women and children made up the bulk of the congregations. But persecution was not completely discontinued, for the police continued to arrest, exile, and murder religious leaders. The new attitude toward religion was also a response to the political situation. Europe was preparing for another world war, and Lenin's successor, Joseph Dzhugashvili Stalin (1879–1953) believed that a return to tradition was needed to prepare the nation. The dictator reinstated nationalism, reorganized the army along more traditional lines, and liquidated alternative leaders. In 1939 Stalin negotiated a treaty with Hitler that allowed the Soviet leader time to complete his rearmament.

During World War II, Stalin saw religion and nationalism as potential allies. Once the war ended, the Communists allowed the church to reorganize under a new patriarch. This new constitution permitted the state to govern the church by controlling its head. Further, the patriarch's relationships with other eastern churches were useful sources of intelligence. The state used the church as a propaganda source. Whether from conviction or compulsion, Russian Orthodox officials parroted the Communist Party line in the international press.

In 1945 Russia was the sole military power in eastern Europe, and the Soviets established Communist governments throughout the region. While these new client states were often more open to religion than Russia, the new communist states also subjected their churches and ecclesiastical leaders to harassment and persecution. The official position of the new governments was atheism, and the schools were resolutely secular.

Russian Communism frightened many Western church leaders. Pastors often denounced Communism from the pulpit, and the prayers after mass were for its end. Often any non-Communist alternative was acceptable, and the churches often allied themselves with various anti-communist movements, including many fascist parties.

Italy

In 1915, Italy broke its alliance with Germany and entered the First World War, hoping for substantial territorial gains, but these hopes were unfulfilled. After the war, burdened by a large war debt, Italy was near economic collapse. Although the papacy made some substantial concessions to other secular states, its ban on participation in Italian politics continued. The People's Party, similar to the German Center Party, was unable to get support from the hierarchy. Simultaneously, papal opposition to the Socialists denied that party a strong enough majority to govern. In 1921 Benito Mussolini (1883–1945), a former socialist, created the Fascist Party. The Fascists were a party of order that valued military action as a means to national goals. At the movement's core was the belief that national greatness depended on a strong leader. Party regulars wore a paramilitary uniform with a black shirt. In October 1922 Mussolini marched on Rome at the head of a ragtag Fascist army. Fearful, King Victor Emmanuel III asked Mussolini to form a new government. Mussolini devoted his first years to undermining Parliament's remaining authority and in 1928, he became dictator (*Duce*) of Italy.

Since 1814 the Catholic Church had advocated strong governments to check modern liberalism, and Pius XI, alarmed by socialism and the great depression, turned to Mussolini. In 1929, the pope and the dictator signed the Lateran Treaty. From the church's perspective, the concordat was generous. It acknowledged papal sovereignty over Vatican City and that most Italians were Catholics. The pope was to nominate all Italian bishops, and the state agreed to make Catholic instruction available in the public schools under church-approved teachers. Italy also agreed to pay the salaries of Italian Catholic officials and clergy.

Portugal and Spain

In Portugal, Antonio Salazar (1889–1970), a professor of political economics, was Portugal's finance minister. In 1926, he resigned because he was not given sufficient power over Portugal's economy. Recalled by President Antonio de Carmona in 1928, his power expanded until he became dictator in 1928 and established his *Estado Nova*, a semi-Fascist state, in 1933. Like Mussolini, Salazar based his government on the ideal of a corporate state. Also like his Italian mentor, Salazar relied on the church's support of his government and gradually removed the restrictions that earlier governments had imposed on Catholicism. In 1940 Salazar signed a concordat that provided state support for parochial schools and prohibited secular divorce.

The Spanish situation was more bloody. After the king was deposed in 1931, Spain established a republic. When that government turned toward the left, General Francisco Franco (1892–1975), a military commander in Spanish Morocco, invaded Spain at the head of the Falange, a Spanish Fascist party. From 1936 to 1939 the Spanish fought a bloody civil war that was also an international struggle. Mussolini and Hitler aided Franco with warplanes and other armaments, and Stalin supplied the Republic.

Franco had the support of the church, and his opponents, the Popular Front, burned churches and murdered many priests, religious, and bishops. Once the civil war ended, the Franco government struggled to make Spain solidly Catholic again. Spain closed Protestant places of worship and prohibited the circulation of Protestant books. Although Spain officially liberalized its religious policies after World War II, religious persecution continued sporadically through the 1960s.

Catholic leaders quickly became dissatisfied with Fascism. Unlike traditional strong governments, the Fascist parties often reigned through terror. When most of Catholic Europe either became Communist or threatened to become Communist after World War II, the church changed its policy towards democracy which it came to believe provided Christianity with its best protection. The Second Vatican Council (1962–65) forthrightly sought reconciliation with the modern world and blessed religious freedom as a natural human right.

Germany

Fascism and Nazism were superficially similar political movements. Both advocated a cooperative state; both supported dictatorship to maintain order; both were nationalistic; and both advocated the territorial expansion of their nations by military means. Further, both controlled dissent in similar ways: the press and the radio were under a ministry of propaganda, and secret police liquidated political opponents.

Where they differed was race. In Hitler's ideology, the Aryan race should rule, because only Aryans were biologically capable of the finest literature, art, and music. Yet, this noble race was threatened by lesser peoples. Although Nazi racial theory condemned all Africans and Asians, the Nazis reserved their most savage hatred for the Jews. Unlike other "inferior" peoples, the Jews lived among the Aryans and "controlled" important areas of European life, including the professions and banking. Since the Nazis believed that intermarriage was increasing, they felt that they had to act soon to prevent the "bastardization" of the continent.

Although Hitler used religion to help him secure political power, he personally believed that religion had no place in the modern world. Had Germany won the Second World War, he planned to adopt anti-Christian measures similar to Russia's. Curiously, many of Hitler's advisors believed that the party should reintroduce Germany's pre-Christian pagan religion. Although Hitler tolerated the neo-pagans, he planned to eliminate them, along with Christian leaders, after the war.

In the early days of the Weimar Republic, the government easily contained the Nazis. When Hitler attempted a *putsch* at the height of German's postwar economic crisis in 1923, his failure was almost comic.

After forcing a handful of Bavarian authorities to support his dictatorship, Hitler allowed them to escape and rally the armed forces. The would-be leader was arrested, tried, and imprisoned. However, Hitler did learn a lesson, and he resolved to achieve power by constitutional means. While in prison, he wrote *Mein Kampf*, a summary of his program, in order to raise money for regular campaigning.

Germany's economic recovery after 1924 was supported by an expansion of foreign aid and investment. The depression ended both abruptly. After that, German politics disintegrated into street fights between the Communists and the Nazis. President Hindenburg (1847–1934) resorted to coalition after coalition, only to see his cabinets disintegrate. In 1933 Hindenburg—believing that he could control Hitler—appointed the Nazi leader as chancellor.

Although Hitler never achieved a majority in the Reichstag, his 1929–32 political campaigns were propaganda masterpieces. He repeatedly reminded the Germans of their humiliation at Versailles and blamed the current economic crisis on the Jews and their western allies. He also appealed to religion. Under the slogan of "positive Christianity," Hitler promised that his government would restore the churches' place in society. Voters believed that Hitler might halt the proposed replacement of Germany's religious schools with more secular institutions.

Although the papacy viewed Hitler favorably, he did not impress German Catholic leaders. Throughout the late 1920s, the annual conference of Catholic bishops at Fulda condemned aspects of the party's program. A few bishops went further and prohibited Catholics from attending mass in party regalia, and some bishops warned Catholics of excommunication if they joined the party.

Yet Hitler's first diplomatic triumph was the conclusion of a concordat with the papacy. In this treaty, Hitler pledged to protect Catholic religious organizations from nationalization and to provide the church with legal protection. In addition to retaining existing parochial schools, Germany promised to provide Catholic schools wherever a sufficient number of parents requested them. The German states were to continue to pay the subsidies to the church and to protect the church's freedom. In turn, the Church agreed to suppress any Catholic organization with secular goals or objectives. Ironically, these included the Center Party, the Reichstag's second largest political party, and a strong supporter of the Weimar Republic. The church also allowed the government a "political" veto over any nomination to a bishopric. All bishops were required to swear an oath of allegiance to the government when they assumed office, and a prayer for the German Reich and Volk was to replace the traditional prayers for the German ruling houses.

The Catholic Church also agreed to a secret clause to the treaty. Under this agreement, the state agreed to exempt priests and monks (but not theological students) from any future military draft. Most significantly, the church agreed to the appointment of a military bishop to supervise Catholic military chaplains. This provision allowed Hitler to increase the size of his army without alerting the German hierarchy to the size of the buildup.

The church agreed to the terms of the concordat for two reasons. First, the treaty provided Catholicism with more guarantees than even the most optimistic diplomats had hoped to gain. Second, the pope hoped that the treaty might restrain Hitler from another *Kulturkampf.* Hitler agreed to the treaty because he had no intention of abiding by its provisions. After a long record of violations Pius XI issued his 1937 encyclical *Mit brennender Sorge* ("With Burning Sorrow"), which listed Hitler's failures to live up to his treaty obligations.

The encyclical had little impact on Hitler, who began a campaign to discredit the church. The police accused some prominent monks of homosexual activities and tried other religious for violating the currency laws. Despite canon law, Hitler formally extended the anti-Jewish laws to the church and demanded that the church serve Catholics of Jewish descent separately at mass. Further, the state proposed the mutual annulment of Jewish-Catholic marriages.

The 1938–41 euthanasia (mercy killings) campaign shocked Catholic conscience. In this program, the government executed the infirm and mentally challenged by lethal injection. When the church protested, the government promised to end the program. In addition, the German Catholic bishops' 1943 letter, "The Ten Commandments as Laws of Life for Nations," indirectly mentioned the destruction of the Jews in a discussion of the commandment, "you shall not murder." But the bishops did not discuss the Holocaust clearly. Unless one already knew what was happening, one might not suspect that the letter referred to the German government's mass murders of Jews.

Hitler and the Protestant Churches

Hitler, who was reared as a Catholic in Austria, never understood the Protestant churches. His initial plan for the Protestant *Landeskirchen* was to create a single national church that he could control from the top.

However, Hitler miscalculated, and his attempt to intervene in Protestant church life backfired, producing resistance.

From 1932 to 1934 the Nazi's played an active role in German church politics. Protestants sympathetic to Hitler formed the German-Christian Movement (*Glaubensbewegung Deutsch-Christen*) that called for racial purity in the church. They also insisted that churches end the Jewish mission and outlaw marriages between Christians and Jews. The German Christians also had a radical wing that wanted to remove the Jewish elements from Christianity. Theologians were to reinterpret Jesus to make him an Aryan, and the church was to cease to use the Old Testament as Scripture or in services. These radicals believed that every nation had its own preparation for the coming of Christ in its unique national myths, folklore, and legends. To prevent this radical wing from disrupting Hitler's own campaigns, the party appointed Ludwig Müller to lead the German Christians.

The German Christians won the church elections of 1932 and 1933. They assumed control of all the *Landeskirchen* with the exception of Bavaria and Württemberg. The German Christians used their power to effect three changes. First, they took control of the movement for a national church federation and forced the churches to accept their leader, Ludwig Müller, as Reich (national) bishop. Second, they reorganized the churches where they had power under the "Führer" principle, concentrating power in the hands of individual leaders. Third, they adopted the "Aryan paragraph" prohibiting Christians of Jewish descent from holding church office.

Those who resisted the ecclesiastical takeover banned together loosely in the Confessing Church. This movement had two wings. One was composed of the opponents in those churches with Nazi leaders or the "disrupted churches." In contrast, those churches that retained their own bishops were called the "intact churches." The anti-Hitler leaders of the disrupted churches attempted to create a shadow church government, to establish their own seminaries, and to present new pastors to parishes. Ministers and lay people who supported the disrupted churches carried red cards that identified them as members of the Confessing Church. However, they had to cooperate somewhat with the regular authorities to have their pastors paid or to see that they received medical benefits. The intact churches continued their pre-Hitler governments, but they were more conservative than the disrupted churches in dealing with the state, perhaps because they had more to lose.

The Confessing Church was somewhat informal. Its most important early statement was the 1934 Barmen Declaration, largely written by Karl Barth, that sought to draw a line separating the Confessing Churches from the errors of Nazism.

Another response to the takeover was the establishment of the Pastor's Emergency League, led by Martin Niemöller (1892–1984). Niemöller was an unlikely person to lead the resistance. A former submarine commander who had received the Iron Cross, Niemöller was the pastor of the fashionable Dahlem Congregation in the Berlin suburbs. The League grew to 4,000 members pledged to support one another during the Nazi crisis. If the state detained a pastor, the Emergency League agreed to pray for the pastor and for his family. Niemöller himself benefited from this solidarity. The authorities arrested the energetic pastor July 1, 1937. Although a civil court acquitted Niemöller, the Nazis confined him at the Dachau concentration camp.

The struggle in the churches effectively ended in 1935 when Hitler and his government deserted the German Christians, although pressure continued to be put on Confessing Church leaders. Hitler was resolved to go to war, and he did not need a church battle hindering national unity. But the truce was never absolute. Whenever a pastor became politically active, the government either imprisoned him or, after the war began, drafted him into the army.

Although the situation of the Jews deteriorated continually during Hitler's early years, the decision to destroy the Jewish people was apparently not reached until after the war began. While most church leaders did not protest the mass executions, the Confessing Church synod of 1943 took a step in that direction when it urged pastors to lead their congregations to meditate on the Ten Commandments.

Christian leaders in lands occupied by the Germans were often silent about the Jewish fate. Except in Denmark and Norway, citizens of occupied countries helped the Germans round up the Jews for transfer to "resettlement" camps. Denmark had the most notable resistance. The Danes hid their Jewish citizens until they could secretly be moved to neutral Sweden. Aside from such corporate acts, some individual Christians behaved nobly. In Holland, Corrie Ten Boom and her family hid Jews in their attic until the Nazis sent the entire Ten Boom family to a concentration camp. In Rome, the church provided sanctuary for many Jews after the Germans occupied the city following the fall of Mussolini.

Part of the heartbreak of the Holocaust was that those Jews who escaped Hitler had nowhere to go. The United States enforced its strict immigration laws, and other nations did not welcome Jewish immigrants. Once the war ended, Jews—horrified by the number of doors still closed to them—established the independent state of Israel.

When the war ended, some leaders of the Confessing Church, led by Pastor Niemöller, met at Stuttgart in 1946 and passed a declaration confessing Germany's guilt for the death of six million Jews. Few joined them. Once a handful of war criminals were tried and executed, the Allies discovered that West Germany was a needed ally in the cold war. Although a handful of German theologians discussed the issue earlier, the main German discussion of the Holocaust in Germany was postponed to the late 1970s and beyond.

CHAPTER TWENTY-SIX

EVASIVE UNITIES

The twentieth century was the great century for Christian cooperation or ecumenism. The word "ecumenism" comes from a Greek root that means those who inhabit the house and, by extension, the world. Twentieth-century Christians have increasingly worked together in many types of ministry, and some denominations have taken important steps toward institutional unity. Even where formal union has not occurred, most churches have removed barriers to intercommunion. For instance, the German *Landeskirchen* now welcome all baptized believers to their altars.

Historically, Christians worshiped in many "one true" churches. Usually the boundaries between these mutually exclusive bodies were theological. Beginning with the Council of Nicea (325), Christian creeds often pronounced anathemas on those who disagreed. For centuries, Lutheran and Reformed Christians were kept apart by their disagreement over the real presence of Christ in the sacrament of the altar.

Other churches drew sharp lines over polity. Church government was the primary issue that divided Congregationalists, Presbyterians, and Low Church (Evangelical) Anglicans. In 1888, the Anglican churches, meeting at Lambeth, adopted four principles to guide them in their search for unity. One non-negotiable principle was that non-Anglicans had to accept the historic episcopate before discussions began. The Catholic position was similar. In Pius XI's 1928 encyclical *Mortalium animos*, Rome required other Christians to accept papal infallibility as a condition for conversations.

Origins of the Ecumenical Spirit

Revivalism was interdenominational. In England, Wesley boasted that he would cooperate with any one person whose heart was like his.

George Whitefield's ministry illustrates the comprehensiveness of the revival movement. During his seven trips to America, Whitefield preached to audiences that contained members of all the colonial American denominations. Further, almost every denomination had members who read Whitefield's *Journals* and contributed to Whitefield's orphanage and travels.

The Second Great Awakening also brought Christians together. The early voluntary societies enlisted people of different denominations in their membership. The 1801 Plan of Union united the Congregationalists and the Presbyterians in a common campaign to convert the west. Lutheran Samuel Schmucker (1799–1873) believed that no denomination or existing alliance of Christians was numerous enough to influence American national life. In his 1838 *A Fraternal Appeal to the American Churches* Schmucker proposed that the various American churches form a federation to coordinate their various benevolences. Each church in Schmucker's rough draft would retain its own distinctive theology.

Dwight L. Moody was the epitome of the revivalist who stood above denomination. To Moody, the only important question was whether people met Christ. Moody's Chicago enterprises, which included the nation's largest Y.M.C.A., a Sunday school for poor children, and the Moody Church, were non-denominational. In 1886 students at Moody's summer conference formed the Student Volunteer Movement, dedicated to the "evangelization of the world in this generation." John R. Mott (1865–1955) was among those who dedicated their life at that meeting. Until his death in 1955, Mott was a leading architect of cooperation among the world's Christians. Mott spoke to large interdenominational groups on every continent. He raised money for the Young Men's Christian Association and, during World War I, raised the money that provided religious services for the troops.

In the mid-twentieth century, the evangelistic crusades of William "Billy" Graham (1918–) also had a broad ecumenical base. His 1950s meetings brought together Christians from different theological and denominational persuasions. Graham was active in efforts to build ecumenical relationships among evangelicals and helped to create the National Association of Evangelicals.

Missions

Missionary work was the most important source of ecumenical sentiment. Compared to the need, the numbers of missionaries in any country were always small. Once new missionaries arrived they found ways to cooperate with each other, often making informal agreements about who would work in which areas or establishing common enterprises. By 1900 the larger boards had formal comity agreements that assigned different regions to different agencies.

The need to support missionary work frequently contributed to an ecumenical spirit. The Laymen's Missionary Movement, among the most effective financial campaigns in American history, held meetings between 1907 and 1909 throughout the United States to raise money for missions. In the Movement's first three years, average missionary giving increased by almost 200 percent. The long-ranged effects were equally impressive. The amount given to American missions increased from $8,980,000 in 1906 to $45,272,000 in 1924.

Federative Christianity

In a federation, each denomination preserves its own theology and polity, while agreeing to work with others for certain common purposes. Josiah Strong (1847–1916), the energetic leader of the Evangelical Alliance from 1886 to 1898, was an early advocate of such interchurch cooperation. In *Our Country: Its Possible Future and Its Present Crisis* (1885) and *Expansion Under New World Conditions* (1915), Strong argued that American Protestants should join together to influence public policy.

Elias B. Sanford (1843–1932) began his career in the institutional church movement. Institutional churches combined traditional religious services with such social services as youth organizations, sewing clubs, and where financially possible, a gymnasium. The sponsors of these early superchurches organized the Open and Institutional Church League and later the National Federation of Churches and Church Workers. In 1902 this latter organization asked Sanford to organize a conference for those interested in denominational cooperation. In 1905 this Conference met at Carnegie Hall in New York under the chairmanship of William H. Roberts.

The Carnegie Hall Conference's program included sessions on religious education, the needs of theological schools, missionary work, evangelism, Christian Endeavor, and other shared ministries. Toward the end of the sessions the conference adopted a Plan of Federation to enable individual denominations to work together without compromising their doctrinal differences. Three years later, in 1908, thirty-three denominations met together in Philadelphia to form the Federal Council of Churches.

The new Council had five objectives:

1. To deepen the fellowship between all its participants.
2. To unite the churches in common service to humankind.
3. To encourage devotional fellowship.
4. To focus the churches' influence on moral and social issues.
5. To promote cooperation on the state and local level.

The provision for a common social and moral witness was especially important. In 1912 the Federal Council of Churches adopted the "Social Creed of the American Churches," taken from a 1908 Methodist statement. Despite often angry opposition, the Federal Council addressed many controversial issues, including the bitter labor-management conflicts of the 1920s and 1930s. In World War I the Council supervised the provision of military chaplains for the armed forces. This task was not as easy as it may seem. Protestantism was too divided for each church to provide its own chaplain corps, and chaplains served under a generic "Protestant" label. Federal Council leaders helped the government establish criteria for the appointment of military chaplains, one of the most successful ecumenical ministries.

The war work of the Federal Council had important indirect effects. The experience of formulating common standards for appointment to the military chaplaincy convinced American theological educators that they needed to establish common standards for the theological seminaries. As the first step in this direction, they commissioned William Adams Brown and Mark May to do a thorough survey of the graduate institutions that trained ministers. The results of the study were bleak. While the nation had some seminaries that provided quality theological education, most schools for ministers were small, poorly staffed, and even more poorly taught. In response, theological educators began a program of reform that ended in the establishment of the American Association of Theological Schools, now the Association of Theological Schools in the United States and Canada.

In 1950, the Federal Council of Churches joined twelve other interdenominational agencies to form the National Council of Churches. The Council hoped to consolidate many different ministries in such areas as education, communication, and stewardship under one central organization. The first two decades of the National Council's history sparkled with successes, and new denominations, including some Eastern Orthodox, Holiness, and Pentecostal churches, joined the Council. Further, the Council and many of its members actively participated in the civil rights movement.

In the late 1970s, the National Council began to lose influence. Contributions from member denominations decreased sharply, in part because the mainstream churches that provided the Council's primary support experienced some financial difficulties. Fiscal restraints forced the Council to curtail programs. Much of the National Council's current income comes from its ownership of the copyrights on the New Revised Standard Version of the Bible and the Uniform Lesson Plan.

The National Association of Evangelicals represented another approach to federative Protestantism. In 1943 one thousand delegates met in Chicago to form the National Association, which was committed to "cooperation without compromise" in doctrinal matters. Like the National Council, the National Association of Evangelicals maintains a world service—World Relief—and works with the government on issues concerning the preparation of military chaplains. The Association played an important role in the development of religious broadcasting. Evangelicals formed National Association of Religious Broadcasters, an agency of the National Association of Evangelicals, to defend freedom of access to the airwaves. The policy of the radio networks was to allocate public service time (free-time that the government required broadcasters to provide) through the National Council of Churches. As the National Association of Religious Broadcasters matured, the organization developed an important Code of Ethics for religious broadcasting. Although most self-financed radio and television evangelists were devoted, upright people, a small number of religious frauds and charlatans harmed the reputation of the whole vocation. Presently, religious broadcasting, which is predominantly non-denominational, reaches at least as many people weekly as the largest denominations. For some Americans, these ministries are their church.

Church Unions: Post-Protestant Christianity

Despite the interest and commitment to ecumenical Christianity, formal unions between different Christian denominations were unusual. The most successful unions were within the same confessional family.

Lutherans formed many small denominations when they came to America that represented different ethnic groups or theological emphases. As ethnic identity weakened, many of these churches united. In 1962 the Lutheran Church in America was formed by the merger of the United Lutheran Church, the American Evangelical Lutheran Church, the Finnish Evangelical Lutheran Church (Suomi Synod) and the Augustana Synod. In 1960 the American Lutheran Church was formed by the merger of the American Lutheran Church (itself the result of the earlier Union of the Ohio, Buffalo, Iowa, and Texas synods) with the

United Evangelical Lutheran Church and the Evangelical Lutheran Church. The Lutheran Free Church (a Norwegian body) joined the American Lutheran Church in 1963. In 1988, Lutherans formed the Evangelical Lutheran Church in America through the union of the Lutheran Church in America, the American Lutheran Church, and the Association of Evangelical Lutheran Churches. While some smaller Lutheran bodies still exist, the vast majority of American Lutherans are either members of the Evangelical Lutheran Church of America or the strongly confessional Lutheran Church— Missouri Synod.

Methodists have also largely overcome the centrifugal effects of their American past. In 1939, the Methodist Episcopal Church merged with the Methodist Episcopal Church, South, and the Methodist Protestant Church, to form The Methodist Church, thus healing the breach caused by the Civil War. In 1968 this united church merged with the Evangelical United Brethren Church (itself the result of the 1946 union between the Church of the United Brethren in Christ and the Evangelical Church) to form The United Methodist Church.

In 1931 the Congregational Churches of New England merged with the Christian Churches, a branch of the Disciples founded by Barton Stone. At about the same time (1934) the General Synod of the Reformed Church and the Evangelical Synod of North America merged to form the Evangelical and Reformed Church. These two streams united in 1957 to form the United Church of Christ.

American Presbyterians have long had problems finding unity among themselves. During both the First and Second Great Awakenings, the church experienced schism and, later, reunion. Besides theology, the most divisive issue was the conflict between North and South. In 1983 the Northern church, the United Presbyterian Church in the United States of America, and the Southern church, the Presbyterian Church in the United States, merged to form the new Presbyterian Church (USA).

The Consultation on Church Union (COCU) was the most comprehensive proposal for church union. Although the consultation began with four denominations, it quickly grew to encompass nine separate churches: the African Methodist Episcopal, the African Methodist Episcopal Church, Zion, Christian Methodist Episcopal Church, the Christian Church (Disciples of Christ), the Episcopal Church, the United Church of Christ, the Presbyterian Church (USA), and The United Methodist Church. During the 1960s the participating churches made progress toward finding common ground. After long discussions, the churches discovered that they shared many common ideas on ministry, theology, and Christian faith. These theological agreements led to the adoption of the 1970 *A Plan of Union for the Church of Christ Uniting*. Unfortunately, the Plan called for an elaborate, bureaucratic system of church government that proved too cumbersome to put into operation. In 1988 the participating churches agreed to try a different system of church union "covenanting." The new proposals shifted COCU's emphases from the development of a formal plan of church union to the development of a system of shared practice in which common participation in the Eucharist, the mutual recognition of baptism, and acts of fellowship gradually became an awareness of common faith.

An important church union was the United Church of Canada created on June 10, 1925. The pathway to this union was long and arduous. In 1893 the Presbyterian Church of Canada declared itself willing to consider union with other Christian churches and appointed a committee for that purpose. The Methodists expressed a similar interest in 1902. In that same year, the Congregational Union asked to join any proposed merger. A joint committee to work toward union began to meet in 1904 and that body reached consensus in 1908. Next, the churches presented the Plan to their members. The Methodists overwhelmingly approved the proposals, but a third of the Presbyterians did not. As the churches moved toward union, animosity grew between those Presbyterians favoring the new church and opposing it. After a hot debate, Parliament passed legislation needed to affect the union in 1924. The new law protected the rights of those who wanted to retain their denominational identity. Besides their own parochial property, the act awarded the dissenters a share of the foreign missions investment and two theological colleges: Knox in Toronto and the Presbyterian College in Montreal.

India has a special place in the history of modern Anglo-American missionary work. All of the principal British societies sent missionaries to India, and Christianity grew steadily there. Unfortunately, the missionaries imported many historic divisions between the British churches, divisions which made little sense in that country. In 1947 the largest churches in South India—The Church of India, Pakistan, Burma, and Ceylon (Anglican); the Methodist Church of India; The South India United Church (whose antecedent bodies were Presbyterian, Congregationalist, and Reformed)—united to form the Church of South India. Although the Church of South India has an historic episcopate, the government of the church is democratic. While its liturgy reflects ancient church worship, the United Church took special care to include Indian customs and culture. For example, since poverty in India is widespread, a bowl is placed at the door of every church for the collection of food.

The Council of Baptist Churches in North India, the Church of India (northern dioceses), The Church of the Brethren, the Disciples of Christ, the Methodist Church, and the United Church of North India (Presbyterian and Reformed) united to form the Church of North India. While only half as large as its neighbor to the South, the Church of North India represents an even broader theological consensus.

Both of the Indian Churches accept the historic episcopate, and they face many common problems; both draw their membership primarily from among the poor and the lower castes. Although the Indian constitution prohibits discrimination based on the Hindu caste system, such discrimination still exists at every level of Indian government and society. In that context, the Indian churches have to struggle constantly with issues of justice and equal opportunity. The other problem comes from the missionary past of these churches. The various missionary societies invested considerable amounts in various social ministries in India, and the united churches have inherited this property. However, given the poverty of much of their membership, these churches have difficulty financially supporting these ministries.

The World Council of Churches

In 1900 few Christians thought about their faith in global terms. Since then, Western Christians have become aware of the full extent and variety of the Christian movement. Some Christian leaders, such as John R. Mott, the energetic Y.M.C.A. college secretary, were world leaders. Mott spoke in most of the major cites in Europe, Africa, Asia, and the Americas, and Protestants everywhere knew his name.

One aspect of this new global consciousness was the formation of world federations among members of the same confessional family. To cite only two examples, the Baptist World Alliance was formed in 1905 and the World Alliance of Reformed Churches holding the Presbyterian System of Church Government in 1877. While these world federations had small budgets and staffs, their meetings brought together Christians from many different countries and eased discussions across national boundaries. These world bodies sped the development of indigenous churches and provided indigenous leaders with needed prestige.

The most important of the various world organizations was the World Council of Churches, whose history is interwoven with the story of the missionary movement. As early as 1857 world missionary leaders felt the need to meet together to discuss common problems and plan common strategies. The world missionary conference that met in Edinburgh in 1910 was particularly significant. Many missionary leaders believed that it was possible for Christianity to reach the whole world. When the conference opened, more than twelve hundred delegates representing one hundred sixty missionary societies gathered to plan the coming century.

Two Y.M.C.A. leaders, John R. Mott and Joseph H. Oldham (1874–1969), worked for four years on the Edinburgh program together with Sherwood Eddy (1871–1963), the Y.M.C.A. secretary for Asia. Participants discussed every aspect of missionary work thoroughly. Missionary weaknesses, including the poor preparation that many missionaries received, were gently, but firmly, exposed.

An immediate result of the Edinburgh meeting was the establishment of the International Missionary Council, a federation of national bodies and conferences. The Council hoped to coordinate missionary research and discussion. In 1928, 1947, and 1952 it held conferences attended by missiologists from many lands. In 1961 the Council merged with the World Council of Churches and became the Council's Commission on World Missions and Evangelism.

Two other unitive movements were inspired by Edinburgh 1910: the World Conference on Faith and Order, and the Universal Christian Council for Life and Work. While the two movements were technically separate, they flowed in parallel streams with the same leaders often active in both. The Universal Christian Council for Life and Work was primarily concerned with the practical aspects of church life. Among the Council's professed goals were better communication among the world's churches, common devotion to a deeper spiritual life, and the application of the Gospel to the world's social and political situation. Nathan Söderblom (1866–1931), the Archbishop of Upsala, Sweden, helped to plan the first conference, held in Upsala in 1927. The Upsala Conference established a committee to plan for a continuation of the conference. In 1937 the Council met at Oxford, England, and coined the phrase "Let the Church be the Church." The leaders directed the slogan against continental dictators and asserted the independence of the churches from all secular ideologies.

The Faith and Order Conference held its first meeting in Lausanne, Switzerland, in 1927. The conference wanted to confront frankly and openly the theological differences between the different Christian churches. While participants often held heated discussions, the Conference noted that more than 85 percent of all Christian affirmations were common to the whole church. The Conference appointed a continuation committee, and a second Faith and Order Conference was held at Edinburgh in 1937.

The conjunction of the two conferences in Great Britain during the same year gave church leaders the opportunity to consider a single world body. In pursuit of that goal the two conferences appointed a joint committee which met in 1938 under the leadership of Bishop William Temple in Utrecht. The committee adopted a plan of cooperation that stressed the consultative and voluntary character of the new World Council.

Wisely, considering the international situation at the time, the Council appointed an interim committee under W. A. Visser 't Hooft. The committee was to provide leadership until the new body's general assembly could meet. The "World Council of Churches in Process of Formation" provided contacts between churches located on both sides of the war and was an important conduit for humanitarian aid. In 1948 the new organization met at Amsterdam to formalize its work.

The World Council's membership has gradually expanded since its founding. In 1948 the Council had 144 members; in 1970, 244 members, and in 1980, more than 300 members. The Orthodox Churches of the East, including the Russian Orthodox Church, entered the Council when they were assured that the doctrinal requirement of faith in Jesus Christ as Lord and God included a confession of faith in the doctrine of the Trinity. As Christians organized new churches in the Third World, the World Council admitted them as full members.

When the Council was first proposed, most of the world's Christians were white and residents of the Northern Hemisphere. By the year 2000, it is possible that most of the world's Christians will be darker skinned and will live in the Southern Hemisphere. The Council brings both together. At the Council, the missionary dynamic of these younger churches may transfer to the more jaded traditional churches. *Vice versa,* the Council may provide a non-imperialistic way for the older churches to transmit some of their theological and organizational sophistication.

The World Council has made important contributions to our theological understanding of the church. In part, the changes were in perspective. Western churches historically began their ecclesiology by considering the structure of the church. In contrast, the World Council encouraged theologians to begin with more dynamic, historical ideas, such as the people of God and mission.

The Fifth Assembly of the World Council of Churches held at Nairobi, Kenya, in 1975 was particularly rich in theology. The meeting featured the theologies of liberation that had become more common in the Third World. While theologians were familiar with these perspectives, the Nairobi meeting made them well known everywhere. Although the Council's willingness to invest some of its funds in radical movements, particularly in South Africa, caused considerable controversy, the Council became an important voice for oppressed people. For example, Council support was crucial to the church leaders battling apartheid and did much to show the Christian foundations of much of that struggle.

The Council has not influenced the course of international affairs as much as some early ecumenical leaders had hoped. Nonetheless, it has done much to make Christians aware of the problems faced by Third World countries and to make tentative proposals about the resolution of those issues.

CHAPTER TWENTY-SEVEN

TOWARD OUR PRESENT

After World War II, the European empires collapsed, and their former colonies requested and received independence. Most of these new governments restricted missionary activity, often only allowing missionaries to provide essential social or medical services. Many passed laws that required Christian organizations to be under the control of nationals. National independence meant ecclesiastical independence.

Although the newly independent churches began with Western theologies and liturgies, their belief and worship have increasingly incorporated indigenous elements. Simultaneously, Western Christians have learned some Two-Thirds World hymns and worship forms. Many Western theologians, inspired in part by liberation theology, studied in Latin America or Africa.

Many Two-Thirds World churches are not part of any major Western confessional tradition. These churches include the African *aladura* churches, which exist only for prayer and healing. Similarly, "radio" churches enable isolated Christian believers to unite in worship. Other churches are composed of individuals who communicate with other believers primarily through correspondence.

The indigenous African churches blend Christian and African motifs and often stress the manifestations of the Holy Spirit mentioned in Acts. Their services include healings, exorcisms, prayers for protection from evil spirits, and speaking in tongues. Although some indigenous African churches will accept members who practice polygamy, these new denominations demand a radical renunciation of the outward signs of African religion, especially fetishes. Almost all African churches require their members to renounce alcohol, tobacco, and gambling.

South Africa has the largest number of independent African denominations. The numerous South African Zionist churches believe that their leader is a special prophet who holds the keys to heaven. A similar situation existed until recently in Zaire, where the government took an officially anti-Christian stand in the 1970s. Experts believe more than 500 indigenous churches exist in that country.

Some African churches developed directly from African roots. In 1913–15 William Wade Harris, a Liberian and a Methodist, felt a deep burden for the people of the Ivory Coast. Harris entered the then-French colony and began to preach that the people should abandon their fetishes. Harris's style was unique. The prophet wandered through the colony wearing a white robe and turban and carrying a Bible and a bamboo cross. More than 100,000 people accepted Christ under Harris' ministry, and he organized them into independent chapels. Fearing that Harris might foment a revolution, French colonial officials deported him to Liberia and made every effort to stamp out the congregations that he had established. Although many Harrists joined the Wesleyan Methodist Church, the majority went underground. Despite numerous schisms, the Harrists remain active today.

Simon Kimbangu, a Baptist catechist, began preaching in the Belgian Congo in 1921. Kimbangu believed that God anointed him as a prophet, much as God appointed prophets in biblical times. The Belgian authorities suspected that Kimbangu was stirring up political rebellion. They sentenced him to death, although the sentence was later changed to life imprisonment. Although Kimbangu died in exile in 1951, his church grew rapidly. In the 1950s Kimbangu's sons reorganized the church, and in 1959 the Belgian authorities recognized the Church of Jesus Christ on Earth through the Prophet Kimbangu. The World Council of Churches has since admitted the Kimbangists to membership.

The Western Churches Adjust

The 1947 Whitby (Canada) meeting of the International Missionary Council warned Western churches that the age of the classical missionary was about to end. Nonetheless, Western missionary organizations were unprepared for the changes that came in the 1950s and 1960s. In the 1960s the mainstream American denominations began to withdraw from missionary activity and to transfer their property to the newly created national churches. Mainstream American boards believed that they could help the newer churches by providing consultation and indirect support. Unfortunately, once Americans renounced control, they also often ceased to fund the expensive enterprises—colleges, seminaries, hospitals, and agricultural stations—that they had so generously given away.

Much missionary idealism secularized into a concern for international aid or service. The Peace Corps and other volunteer agencies attracted many young people who might have enlisted as missionaries in an earlier time. Church-sponsored humanitarian aid, largely through the Church World Service, retained its popularity.

The change in missionary strategy had some benefits, but it also had some indirectly negative consequences. Previously, foreign missions program spearheaded denominational fund-raising efforts. When those programs declined, mainstream church budgets diminished. The Southern Baptist Convention was the largest denomination to continue a traditional missionary strategy. In their Bold Missions Thrust (1979), Southern Baptists committed themselves to establishing missions in every country that would allow them entry. Southern Baptists, perhaps because of their tradition of lay participation in the church, were particularly successful with agricultural, medical, and music missions.

The more conservative boards, especially the faith missions, have also increased their commitment to evangelism. While the figures for these independent boards are not always current, these societies support half the American missionaries serving abroad.

A Nuclear Age

The Second World War ended with a major change in the world distribution of power. The two nations on the fringe of traditional European settlement, the United States and the Soviet Union, became so strong militarily that they dominated world politics. The peace between the two superpowers was often maintained by a nuclear balance of terror: war was avoided because armed conflict was as dangerous to win as to lose. Traditional morality eroded during the era of the Cold War, as often happens in times of soocial stress, and divorce, promiscuous sexual activity, and drug and alcohol abuse increased. Every post-war decade was preoccupied with the self.

The churches had difficulty addressing these anxious concerns. For some Christians, the present implied the need for change in traditional ecclesiastical standards of personal morality. Joseph Fletcher's *Situation Ethics* (1966) was a revealing examination of the moral situation. Traditional Christian ethics assumed that we understood moral principles in terms of the most usual cases. Fletcher reversed this procedure. By examining such questions as the decision faced by a woman who had a chance to trade her personal chastity for her husband's life, Fletcher argued that the moral act was one motivated by love.

Fletcher's study appeared coincidentally with the widely touted sexual revolution. Divorce laws were liberalized, while divorces themselves appear to have become more unjust; in 1990 divorced women and their children were the nation's poorest minority. Colleges removed almost all restrictions on students' personal behavior. Advice columnists frankly discussed how parents should respond when their children brought a "friend" home for a weekend.

Following a 1968 police riot at the Stonewall, a gay bar in Manhattan, gay and lesbian persons began to move out of the "closet" and to demand their civil rights. The American psychological community reclassified homosexuality and noted that, like heterosexuality, it was part of the core of a person's personality that was unlikely to change. Further, some psychologists noted that many gay and lesbian persons lived fulfilling lives. Popular response to the gay rights movements varied. The average person became more aware of homosexual persons and, especially among the young, homosexual behavior lost some of its stigma. More gay and lesbian couples began to contemplate a permanent relationship analogous to marriage, and some churches developed same-sex covenant services. Many Christian ethicists also changed their understanding of both homosexuals and homosexual behavior, but not all Christians have accepted these arguments. In the 1980s and 1990s many Christian denominations debated the ordination of admitted homosexuals. With few exceptions, they voted to maintain (or establish) a prohibition of ordination or to require homosexuals to agree to a celibate life.

The most dramatic debate over sexual ethics was the continuing battle over the legality and morality of abortion. Many states liberalized their laws on abortion in the late 1950s and 1960s, and in a 1973 decision, *Roe versus Wade*, the Supreme Court struck down existing state laws restricting abortion as a violation of a woman's right to privacy. The abortion issue polarized American politics during the 1980s and 1990s. Some have argued that the *Roe versus Wade* decision protects a woman's right to choose; others have maintained that the unborn child has rights which the courts cannot abridge.

The Waning of the Age of Good Will

At the end of the 1950s, American religion seemed to be entering a period of good will. Ecumenical organizations and dialogues were breaking down ancient barriers. The Roman Catholic Church of Pope John XXIII (1881–1963) was ready to join with other Christians in cooperative ventures. Yet at century's end, theology deeply divided American Christian churches. While many people held carefully nuanced positions, the same fault ran through many American denominations. Churches tended to have one party that wanted to return to a more traditional viewpoint and another that wanted further theological and social change.

Whether the late twentieth century is in truth any less stable than other periods is less important than people's belief that it is so. Television and radio brought changes and crises into the home. From 1960 to 1990 Americans watched the Vietnam War, the rapid deterioration of the cities, the Civil Rights movement, the new feminism, the gay rights movement, Woodstock, the population explosion, changes in sexual behavior, the end of the *pax Americana,* the drug problem, heavy metal rock and roll music, the expansion of mass communications, ecological crises, the massive use of migrant labor, changes in the Eastern bloc system of power, an unstable Middle East, and revolutions in Latin America.

During the late 1950s churches had experienced a major revival. New churches were built, new converts won, and new national and state employees hired. Further, the churches regained some of their national moral influence. Despite this new strength, mainstream churches went into decline in the late 1960s. American religion experienced a realignment as basic as when Baptists and Methodists replaced Congregationalists and Presbyterians as the most numerous denominations in the late eighteenth and early nineteenth centuries. The conservative or evangelical churches became an increasingly larger percentage of the total number of American Christians. "Conservative" seminaries, such as Gordon-Conwell, Fuller, and Trinity, witnessed a general steady increase in their enrollments and endowment. In contrast, more "liberal" seminaries had more difficulty recruiting students and donors. Some of Protestantism's most prestigious seminaries, including Oberlin and Hartford, closed, merged with other schools, or redefined their mission. The mainline denominations steadily declined in Western countries, and the National Council of Churches reduced its staff. Many once flourishing campus ministries are in disarray.

One sign of the depth of this realignment was the large number of church debates and schisms. The merger of the Presbyterian Church, U.S.A. (Southern Presbyterian Church), with the Presbyterian Church, U.S. (Northern Presbyterian Church) led to the 1983 formation of the Presbyterian Church in America. The Lutheran Church–Missouri Synod experienced a small but significant schism in 1974, when the 90 percent of the faculty of Concordia Seminary resigned under pressure from the national denomination.

The Southern Baptists had the most large scale controversy. Beginning in 1979, conservatives in that denomination gradually established control over all of the denomination's boards and agencies. Although the denomination had always been conservative, the various boards and agencies moved much further to the right. Many moderates and liberals either left the denomination or became less active supporters.

A Roman Revolution

Pope John XXIII's 1958 election began a period of excitement and reform in the Roman Catholic Church. John called the Second Vatican Council (1962–65) to reconcile the ancient church with the modern world. Centuries of tradition were modified when, for example, the council emphasized the role of the laity in the church's work and declared religious liberty to be a natural human right. Catholics recognized Protestants as separated brothers and sisters and took the first steps toward reconciliation with the Jews.

The Catholic Revolution deeply affected the practices of the ordinary Catholic. The church ended the old prohibition against eating meat on Friday and translated the mass into vernacular. Language was not the only change in the service. Local congregations moved the altar from the wall and placed it in the midst of the congregation. Priests added hymns to the mass, and the sermon became more important. Penance, perhaps the most personal Catholic act, continued, but it was no longer emphasized or required. The hierarchy revised the calendar of saints, and prayers through them were discouraged. The Vatican publicly stated that St. Christopher, one of the most popular saints, was not a historical figure. Historical criticism became a featured part of seminary education.

Whether or not as a consequence, attendance at Sunday mass has progressively declined since Vatican II, and Catholic divorce rates have climbed. Most Western Catholic couples now routinely practice birth control. More seriously, the clerical and religious life seems to have lost much of its attraction. Many priests left the ministry, often to marry, and the number of young Catholics entering seminary radically declined. Few religious orders were able to retain their membership at pre-Vatican II levels, and many historic ministries, particularly in education, have been abandoned.

In Eastern Europe Vatican II signaled a rebirth of popular Catholic devotion. The council encouraged the various national Catholic churches to work out their own accommodation with the Communist governments. These informal agreements often bound the church to join in Communist-sponsored peace movements and other approved activities. At the same time the church provided a place where dissent could be heard. By the mid-1980s, the Roman Catholic Church in Eastern Europe provided much of the leadership that created new, noncommunist governments in the region.

Pope Paul VI (1897–1978), John XXIII's successor, had both progressive instincts and a desire to preserve church authority. In 1968 he issued *Humanae Vitae*, reaffirming the church's ban on contraception. John Paul II (1920–), the first non-Italian elected pope since Hadrian VI (1522), has similar loyalties. John Paul II took an active role in the struggle to create democracy in Eastern Europe. But on internal matters the pope supported a more hard line. For example in 1980 John Paul II affirmed the church's teaching on clerical celibacy, women priests, and homosexuality. Since then the Vatican has consistently supported the more conservative interpretation of the Vatican II documents and urged Catholic theologians to teach the church's official positions.

Theological Developments

Theologians began searching for a new consensus in the late 1960s when the older neo-liberal theologies went out of vogue. Consensus proved elusive, however, since like everyone else Christians theologians had to cope with problems in both church and society to which they had no definite answers. One theologian's "yes" was met by another theologian's "no."

In Alfred North Whitehead's 1925 *Science and the Modern World* and 1926 *Religion in the Making*, the philosopher argued that the world was not understandable in the static categories of traditional philosophy. Instead, science had shown that everything participated in a continually changing process. Whitehead's arguments were developed theologically by Charles Hartshorne (1891–) who argued that both of the traditional understandings of God, theism and pantheism, were philosophically unthinkable. In his 1948 *Divine Relativity: A Social Conception of God*, Hartshorne maintained that humans can only conceive God in terms of God's dynamic relationship to the whole world. While God is not the substrata of being, as in traditional pantheism, God does not stand apart from the world as in traditional theism either. God's being is enhanced by God's experience of the world and by the experience of other intelligent beings.

Daniel Day Williams's (1910–73) *The Spirit and the Forms of Love* (1968) gave one of the clearest explanations of the value of process philosophy for Christian theology. The biblical God, Williams argued, was a God that decided to be God for the human race. Hence, God took risks similar to those we take when we dare to love another. Just as humans cannot love without altering their very being, so God's love alters God's being as well. John Cobb, in *A Christian Natural Theology: Based on the Thought of Alfred North Whitehead* (1965), also argued for an affinity between process thought and biblical categories. Cobb's own version of process theology stressed God's interaction with humankind in the person of Christ.

In retrospect, African American theologian Martin Luther King, Jr. (1929–68) may have been the most important theologian in the last decades of the twentieth century. King, the most visible spokesperson for the American Civil Rights movement, combined the teachings of the Indian revolutionary Gandhi (1869–1948) with the language of the African American pulpit to create a doctrine of non-violent resistance. His use of biblical images and metaphors translated African Americans' hopes for freedom into a powerful theology.

In 1969 James Cone published *Black Theology and Black Power*, setting forth many new presuppositions which would inform other late twentieth-century theology. According to Cone, the historical experience of black people in a white world has created a black interpretation of the gospel. Although sometimes obscured by the various ways in which black people dealt with their situation, this black theology aimed at the liberation of black people from bondage. Cone argued that the historical religious experience of African Americans was a useful guide to the interpretation of the Bible that might enrich all believers.

Cone's discussions of the black use of the image of Moses was an important contribution to hermeneutics. Traditional Christian theology interpreted Moses almost exclusively as the giver of the law. But Cone argued that African Americans better understood his work when they saw him as the founder and liberator of his people.

A similar model informed both liberation and feminist theology. Such liberation theologians as Gustavo Gutiérrez, José Míguez Bonino, Leonard Boff, and Rubem Alves found their primary inspiration in the experience of the Two-Thirds World, especially Latin America. In these countries poverty is so widespread and so systemic that traditional Western philosophy is unable to interpret, much less change, the situation. Since the prosperity of the developed world rests on the oppression of others, the greatest present need is a new international socioeconomic order. The liberation theologians believe that the church should stand with the poor and oppressed in this struggle.

Latin American liberation theologians' interpretations of Jesus have particular value for the whole church. Traditional theology was interested in the vertical relationship of Christ with the Father, and liberal theology was primarily interested in Jesus as a historical figure. In contrast, liberation theologians interpret Jesus as a model for Christian *praxis*. Jesus, they believe, stood with the poor and the oppressed; his words enabled the poor to hope for a new life in this world.

Since the 1950s, women have increasingly taken leadership positions in Western societies. Almost all Western governments have sought to outlaw, or at least discourage, discrimination against women in the workplace. While women were historically more than 60 percent of the membership of Protestant churches, the churches were slower to enroll women in their leadership than the rest of society. However, the bars to women's service have gradually fallen with the major Christian churches ordaining women in increasing numbers.

Feminist theology attempts to find the theological and religious foundations of discrimination against women and provide theological resources for change. The patriarchical nature of Christian Scripture and symbolism was one place for theological criticism. But the church's tradition also provided some guidance for women in their struggles. In her *Human Liberation in a Feminist Perspective* (1974), Letty Russell argued that such traditional biblical ideas as the exodus, prophecy, and the parental character of God could inform women in their struggle. Rosemary Ruether took a similar position in her *Religion and Sexism: Images of Women in the Jewish and Catholic Communities* (1974).

When feminists studied the history of women's religious understanding, they found new resources for the present. In *Beyond God the Father* (1973) and *Pure Lust* (1984), Mary Daly argued that feminist theology must increasingly look outside Christianity for models. Other women theologians, such as Carol Christ, have argued for a return of the "goddess" as one of the needed changes in contemporary religion.

The European theology of hope has many similarities with liberation theologies. In his *The Theology of Hope* (1964), Jürgen Moltmann proposed that Christian theologians return eschatology to the central place that it held in the New Testament. As Moltmann understood the Scriptures, the resurrection of Jesus was the only event in human history that was absolutely new. In his 1974 *The Crucified God*, Moltmann struggled with the centrality of the cross for the Christian understanding of God. The same work dealt with the implications of belief that God entered human suffering and pain. In so taking suffering upon God's own self, God creates the possibility of a new history for us.

Wolfgang Pannenberg wrote some of the most difficult theology of the twentieth century. Pannenberg's early study of the resurrection, *Revelation as History*, sought to show that theologians could study revelation using the same rational and scientific categories as other areas of reality. His test case was the resurrection of Jesus which theologians had long interpreted as standing "outside" the ordinary course of human events. In his *Jesus Christ, Man and God*, Pannenberg argued that Christianity began with the historically verifiable facts about Jesus of Nazareth. This naturally included Christ's resurrection which, Pannenberg argued, scholars can document within history. However, Pannenberg's program went beyond Christology. Pannenberg wanted to show the possibility of a total view of the world where God's creative power acted at every moment. Two later studies, *Theology and the Philosophy of Science* (1969) and *Anthropology in a Christian Perspective* (1985), carried Pannenberg's discussion with modern methods of knowing further.

Christ and the World Religions

The rise of modern transportation and communication raised anew the ancient problem of how Christians, their churches, or their theology ought to relate to the major world religions. Some non-Christian religions, especially Islam, have renewed their own missionary endeavors. The great religions of the East have migrated into Western countries, and these ancient faiths have begun to win converts. In many American colleges and universities the standard introduction to the study of religion is a course on world religions.

American theologians have wrestled with this question since the World's Parliament of Religions met in Chicago in 1893. While the Parliament did not want to eliminate the differences between the different faiths of the world, its organizers hoped that the meeting might increase mutual religious understanding and toleration.

John Hick, a contemporary English philosopher, advocates something like this earlier position. According to Hick, the world's great religions represent diverse responses to the Real that reveals itself to humankind. If Christians move beyond their preoccupation with Christ, they will see that other religions also have a saving experience of the Divine. On this basis Christians can share their best insights with people of other faiths while learning from them. The present goal ought to be an expanded discussion among the world's faiths.

In *Christ in a Pluralistic World* (1976), John Cobb argued that Christian faith in the incarnation made religious accommodation possible. For Cobb, the principle of creative transformation (the *logos*) was truly incarnate in Jesus Christ, but it was not *only* incarnate in him. This principle exists in all of the world's faiths and, therefore, the world's religions point to Christ and Christ to the world's diverse religions.

BIBLIOGRAPHY

Some Suggestions for Further Reading

Collinson, Patrick. *The Birthpangs of Protestant England: Religion and Cultural Change in the Sixteenth and Seventeenth Centuries.* New York: St. Martin's, 1988.

Dickens, A. G. *The English Reformation.* London: Bateford, 1989.

Dolan, Jay. *The American Catholic Experience: A History from Colonial Times to the Present.* Garden City: Doubleday, 1985.

Dussel, Enrique. *History of the Church in Latin America: Colonialism to Liberation.* Translated by Alan Neely. Grand Rapids: Eerdmans, 1981.

———, editor. *The Church in Latin America, 1492–1992.* Maryknoll: Orbis, 1992.

Fedotov, G. P. *The Russian Religious Mind.* New York: Harper, 1965.

Feige, Franz. *The Varieties of Protestantism in Nazi Germany: Five Theological Positions.* New York: Edwin Mellen, 1990.

Gabler, Ulrich. *Huldrych Zwingli: His Life and Work.* Translated by Ruth Gritsch. Philadelphia: Fortress, 1986.

Handy, Robert T. *A History of the Churches in the United States and Canada.* New York: Oxford University Press, 1977.

———. *A Christian America: Protestant Hopes and Historical Realities.* New York: Oxford University Press, 1984.

Hastings, Adrian. *A History of English Christianity, 1920–1985.* London: Collins, 1986.

Helmreich, Ernst Christian. *The German Churches Under Hitler: Background, Struggle, and Epilogue.* Detroit: Wayne State Press, 1979.

Holl, Karl. *What Did Luther Mean by Religion?* Translated by Fred W. Meuser and Walter Wietzke. Philadelphia: Fortress, 1977.

Isichei, Elizabeth. *A History of Christianity in Africa*. Grand Rapids: Eerdmans; and Lawrenceville, New Jersey: Africa World Press, 1995.

Latourette, Kenneth Scott. *Christianity in a Revolutionary Age*. 5 volumes. New York: Harper, 1958–62.

Moffett, Samuel Hugh. *A History of Christianity in Asia*. Volume 1: *Beginnings to 1500*. San Fransciso: HarperSanFrancisco, 1992.

Neill, Stephen. *A History of Missions*. Harmondsworth: Penguin Books, 1965.

———. *Anglicanism*. Harmondsworth: Penguin Books, 1958.

Noll, Mark A. *A History of Christianity in the United States and Canada*. Grand Rapids: Eerdmans, 1992.

Oberman, Heiko. *Luther: Man Between God and the Devil*. Translated by Eileen Walliser-Schwarzbart. New Haven: Yale University Press, 1989.

Ozment, Steven E. *The Reformation in the Cities: The Appeal of Protestantism to Sixteenth Century Germany and Switzerland*. New Haven: Yale University Press, 1975.

Pinson, Koppel S. *Pietism as a Factor in the Rise of German Nationalism*. New York: Octagon Books, 1968 (reprint of 1934 edition).

Rix, Richard. *Henry VIII and the English Reformation*. Houndsmulls, Basington: Macmillan, 1993.

Rupp, Gordon. *Religion in England, 1688–1781*. Oxford: The Clarendon Press, 1986.

Vidler, Alex R. *The Church in an Age of Revolution: 1789 to the Present Day*. Grand Rapids: Eerdmans, 1961.

Wallace, Ronald S. *Calvin, Geneva, and the Reformation: A Study of Calvin as Social Reformer, Churchman, Pastor, and Theologian*. Edinburgh: Scottish Academic Press, 1988.

Wendel, François. *Calvin: The Origin And Development of His Religious Thought*. Translated by Philip Mainet. New York: Harper, 1963.

INDEX